Investing in Youth: Norway

OECD
BETTER POLICIES FOR BETTER LIVES

This work is published under the responsibility of the Secretary-General of the OECD. The opinions expressed and arguments employed herein do not necessarily reflect the official views of OECD member countries.

This document, as well as any data and any map included herein, are without prejudice to the status of or sovereignty over any territory, to the delimitation of international frontiers and boundaries and to the name of any territory, city or area.

Please cite this publication as:
OECD (2018), *Investing in Youth: Norway*, OECD Publishing, Paris.
http://dx.doi.org/10.1787/9789264283671-en

ISBN 978-92-64-28362-6 (print)
ISBN 978-92-64-28367-1 (PDF)

Series: Investing in Youth
ISSN 2412-6330 (print)
ISSN 2412-6357 (online)

Photo credits: Cover © Paul Oakley

Corrigenda to OECD publications may be found on line at: *www.oecd.org/about/publishing/corrigenda.htm*.

Foreword

As highlighted in the OECD Action Plan for Youth, successful engagement of young people in the labour market is crucial not only for their own personal economic prospects and well-being, but also for overall economic growth and social cohesion. Therefore, investing in youth is a policy priority in all countries, including Norway, requiring concerted action to develop education systems and labour market arrangements that work well together.

Following the launch of the OECD Action Plan for Youth in May 2013, the OECD is working closely with countries to implement the plan's comprehensive measures in their national and local contexts and to provide peer-learning opportunities for countries to share their experience of policy measures to improve youth employment outcomes.

This work builds on the extensive country reviews that the OECD has carried out previously on the youth labour market and vocational education and training (*Jobs for Youth*, *Learning for Jobs* and *Skills beyond School*), as well as on the OECD Skills Strategy.

The present report on Norway is the eighth of a new series, "Investing in Youth", which builds on the expertise of the OECD on youth employment, social support and skills. This series covers both OECD countries and countries in the process of accession to the OECD, as well as some key emerging economies. The report presents new results from a comprehensive analysis of the situation of disadvantaged young people in Norway exploiting various sources of survey-based and administrative data. It provides a detailed diagnosis of the youth labour market and education system in Norway from an international comparative perspective, and offers tailored recommendations to help improve the school-to-work transition. It also provides an opportunity for other countries to learn from the innovative measures that Norway has taken to strengthen the skills of youth and their employment outcomes. Additional information related to this review can be found on the OECD website (http://oe.cd/youth-norway).

The work on this report was mainly carried out within the Social Policy Division of the Directorate for Employment, Labour and Social Affairs (ELS). The report was prepared by Raphaela Hyee and Sebastian Königs under the supervision of Stéphane Carcillo (Head of the Jobs and Income Division) and Monika Queisser (Head of the Social Policy Division). Kari Vea Salvanes (Nordic Institute for Studies in Innovation, Research and Education) contributed to the review as consultant, Liv Gudmundson and Lucy Hulett provided editorial support. The report benefited from many useful comments provided by Stefano Scarpetta (Director for Employment, Labour and Social Affairs) as well as by staff in the OECD Economics Department and the Directorate for Education and Skills.

Acknowledgements

The OECD Secretariat would like to thank the Norwegian Ministry of Labour and Social Affairs for their support in carrying out this project and for organising the initial fact-finding mission in October 2014. Thuy Nguyen, Tor Morten Normann and Anne Cecilie Bentsen deserve special thanks for their considerable contributions to ensuring a successful completion of this project. The OECD Secretariat is also very grateful to Tonje Haugberg from the Directorate for Education and Training for her input for Chapter 4, and to the experts at Statistics Norway for their advice and for carrying out the analysis of the administrative data.

This report is dedicated to the memory of Heidi Lohrmann in recognition of her contributions and dedication to the project.

Table of contents

Tables

Figures

Acronyms and abbreviations

CWS	Child welfare services
DB	Disability Benefits
EU	European Union
EUR	Euros
IP	Introduction Programme
NAV	Norwegian Labour and Welfare Administration
NOK	Norwegian Kroner
NRR	Net replacement rate
PES	Public employment service
PPT	Pedagogical and Psychological Service
QP	Qualification Programme
SA	Social Assistance
SSB	Statistics Norway
TA	Transitional Allowance
UB	Unemployment Benefits
VET	Vocational education and training
WAA	Work Assessment Allowance

In figures, "OECD" refers to the unweighted average of OECD countries for which data are available.

The signs (↘) and (↗) in the legend relate to the variable by which countries are ranked from left to right in decreasing and increasing order, respectively.

Executive summary

Labour market conditions of 15-29 year-olds in Norway are among the most favourable across OECD countries, but the trend over the last decade has not been as positive:

- The youth employment rate is high, at 59% in 2016 (OECD average of 52%), but it substantially declined in recent years and is now seven percentage points below its pre-crisis peak. This decline does not so much reflect the effects of the economic crisis, but rather a rapidly growing youth population, mainly because of strong positive net migration from Central and Eastern Europe.
- The share of young people who are not in employment, education or training (the "NEETs") stood at 9% in 2016, which corresponds to 86 000 young people. This is substantially below the OECD average of 14%, but two percentage points higher than in 2008 and above the rates in the best-performing OECD countries.

To further reduce its NEET rate, Norway will have to focus its efforts primarily on those young people who are currently not engaged in active job search, i.e. the *inactive* NEETs. They account for 70% of all NEETs.

Because of the low NEET rate, NEETs in Norway tend to be more disadvantaged than in other OECD countries:

- More than half (56%) of all NEETs have not completed upper-secondary education, making low education the primary risk factor for NEET status. This is particularly concerning as Norwegian early school leaving rates are high in OECD comparison.
- Young people born abroad are more than twice as likely to be NEET as their Norwegian-born peers. One reason is that young migrants tend to have lower education levels than their native-born peers. Those who arrived in the country as children and still went to school in Norway for a few years do significantly better than those who arrived in late adolescence or early adulthood.
- Health problems are widespread: NEETs are nearly six times as likely to feel depressed as other young people in Norway, and more than nine times as likely to report poor health. These risk ratios are much higher than the EU or OECD averages.

Norway is one of the few OECD countries without a significant gap in NEET rates between young women and men, thanks, in particular, to the widespread availability and acceptance of institutionalised childcare.

Combatting early school leaving has been a policy priority in Norway for decades, but the challenge remains. While almost all compulsory-school graduates enrol in upper-secondary school, completion rates are low: almost one-in-five (19%) 25-34 year-olds do not have an upper-secondary qualification, well above the OECD average of 16%, and nearly twice as high as in Finland. Students with poor grades in compulsory school, those whose parents only have at-most a compulsory education and young migrants are particularly likely to drop out.

Early school leaving is especially prevalent among students in vocational education and training (VET), and the relatively academic nature of VET contributes to these low completion rates. The first two years of VET are mostly school-based, and many students then struggle to find an apprenticeship place with a company for the following two years. Students who do not succeed at securing an apprenticeship have the option to switch to a school-based pathway, but one-in-five drop out. Employers' reluctance to take on apprentices relates to the fact that VET provision is largely driven by student choice rather than labour market demand. As most students only settle on a specific occupation during their apprenticeship, they initially only have limited job-specific skills. Meanwhile, collectively agreed apprentice remuneration is comparatively generous.

Norway has an effective system in place to reach out to NEETs and provide them with comprehensive support. "Follow-Up Services", run by the county educational authorities, track all 16-21 year-olds who have not completed and are currently not attending upper-secondary education, and attempt to bring them back to school. They have proven very successful at getting in touch with their target group and connecting them with a suitable activity. The Norwegian Labour and Welfare Administration (NAV) acts as a "one-stop shop" for employment and social support, and collaborates closely with schools and county-level Follow-Up Services. NAV offices are generally well-equipped to serve young users, usually employing special youth teams or having specific contact persons for young people. Caseload numbers of youth specialists tend to be moderate, at below 70 on average. The Norwegian Youth Guarantee, which dates back to the early 1980s, entitled young jobseekers to additional, targeted employment support. After a series of studies raised doubts about its effectiveness, Norway replaced it by the "New Youth Effort" in 2017, entitling all registered employable jobseekers below the age of 30 to personalised employment support within eight weeks of registration.

Overall spending on active labour market programmes is lower than in the other Nordic countries, but NAV strongly targets programme participation to the most disadvantaged users whom it identifies in a careful profiling process. For users who face mild or more severe barriers to employment, NAV heavily relies on public- or private-sector work experience measures. A series of evaluations have however cast doubt on the effectiveness of these work experience measures. Users with permanently reduced work capacity primarily benefit from subsidised employment in sheltered workplaces or the regular labour market. NAV generally does not offer longer training programmes for most users.

Young jobseekers access income support more easily than in many other OECD countries. Unemployment benefits are conditional on having the required minimum earnings record of around one-quarter of the annual average wage in the previous year. Benefits are paid for 24 months and replace about 67% of previous net earnings for a person who gained half of average annual earnings, a little below the OECD average. Low-income youth above the age of 18 are entitled to means-tested Social Assistance benefits irrespective of their parents' income. Payment levels vary locally, but are much lower than in the other Nordic countries, and generally far from sufficient to lift recipients out of poverty.

In spite of recent reforms, Norway has the highest receipt rate of incapacity-related benefits across all OECD countries. Mental disorders have become a primary cause of benefit receipt for young people, but a countercyclical benefit receipt pattern also indicates that incapacity benefits have served as a source of income support for difficult-to-employ jobseekers in times of labour market slack. Young people with reduced work capacity often remain registered for very long periods, making up the majority of young NAV users. Users remain "locked" in incapacity benefits as caseworkers lack the necessary guidance to carry out rigorous work capacity assessments for those who have undergone medical treatment or rehabilitation and as there are too few effective support options for those with more complex health issues and a lack of work experience.

Key policy recommendations

- Align VET provision more closely with labour market demand by bringing forward specialisation in the school-based part of VET and combining school- and work-based training from day one.
- Encourage the social partners to reconsider apprentice remuneration to better align apprentice wages with productivity.
- Continue expanding lower-level VET tracks to enable academically weak or practically minded young people to attain a qualification.
- Create awareness of the New Youth Effort and its contents among NAV caseworkers and systematically monitor its implementation. Ensure that NAV's resources match the increased follow-up requirements.
- Ensure rigorous work capacity assessments and better gatekeeping for Disability Benefits through clearer guidelines to NAV staff and general practitioners and better compliance monitoring.
- Devote additional resources to supporting young Social Assistance recipients with (mental) health problems and little work experience.
- Re-assess the strong reliance on work experience measures, possibly with a view to restricting it to private-sector employers and by strengthening and formalising the training component.
- Expand the use of training programmes for jobseekers to include vocational training for low-skilled jobseekers and Norwegian-language classes for migrant jobseekers.
- Intensify reporting on local-level implementation of employment and social support to national authorities to promote the identification and sharing of best practices.
- Facilitate data exchange between the educational authorities and NAV to permit NAV caseworkers to better follow up on their users and observe their transitions into education and training.
- Make rigorous impact evaluations a pre-requisite for national funding for educational, employment and social-support programmes for NEETs.

Assessment and recommendations

How do young people fare in the Norwegian labour market?

Labour market conditions for young people (15-29 years) in Norway are among the most favourable across OECD countries, but the trend over the last decade has not been as positive. While the youth employment rate is high, at 59% in 2016 (compared to 52% in the OECD on average), it declined substantially in recent years and is now seven percentage points below its pre-crisis peak.

This decline does not so much reflect the effects of the economic crisis – as in other OECD countries – but rather a rapidly growing youth population. Indeed, the number of employed young people has *risen* in absolute terms since the start of the crisis. This positive net job growth was outpaced by even faster population growth resulting mainly from strongly positive net migration from Central and Eastern Europe. And while a higher number of (non-working) students account for more than half of this differential, the other half is reflected in a higher number of young people who are not in employment, education or training (NEET).

In spite of its recent rise, the NEET rate remains low in Norway by international standards – at 9% of the youth population in 2016, or 86 000 young people. This is substantially below the OECD average of 14%, but two percentage points higher than in 2008 and above the rates in Iceland (5%), the Netherlands (6%) or Luxembourg (8%). To further reduce its NEET rate, Norway will have to focus its efforts primarily on those who are currently not engaged in active job search, i.e. the *inactive* NEETs, who account for 70% of all NEETs. Re-engaging them in education or employment is particularly challenging, however: *inactive* NEETs are – by definition – further away from the labour market than *unemployed* NEETs, and they are often not in regular contact with the public services.

Who are the NEETs and what are risk factors?

Spells of NEET status are generally not an unusual feature of a young person's transition from school into the labour market, and more than two-thirds of all young people in Norway spend at least some time out of school or work between the ages of 16 and 24. But while short NEET spells do not necessarily indicate problems with labour market integration, longer stretches out of education and employment can prevent young people from building up skills, work experience and professional networks and cause lasting "scarring" effects on future employment opportunities and earnings.

The low incidence of NEETs in Norway is associated with a higher concentration among those who are educationally disadvantaged, who come from low socio-economic backgrounds and who suffer from (mental) health problems than in other OECD countries. Many were not born in Norway, and a high share of them is detached from the labour market:

- *Low education is the most important risk factor*: 56% of NEETs in Norway have not completed upper-secondary education, compared to 36% across the OECD on average. Those without an upper-secondary qualification are seven times more likely to be NEET than university graduates, the largest gap across the OECD. This is concerning in particular as a much greater share of young people in Norway leave school without an upper-secondary degree than in the OECD on average.
- *There is no significant gender NEET gap*: Norway is one of the few OECD countries where young women are not more likely to be out of education or work than young men. Thanks to the widespread availability and acceptance of institutionalised childcare, only 17% of all mothers below the age of 30 are NEET, compared to nearly half across the OECD on average;
- *Immigrants face a much greater risk:* Young people born outside of Norway are more than twice as likely to be NEET as their Norwegian-born peers (16 vs. 7.5%). One reason is that young migrants have lower education levels than their native-born peers. Young migrants' age of arrival however makes an important difference: those who have come to Norway as children do significantly better than those who arrived in late adolescence or early adulthood. In particular, completing at least some education in Norway seems to somewhat protect young immigrants from becoming NEETs later on: young people who arrived in Norway before turning 16 are only 30% more likely to be NEET than those born in Norway.
- *(Mental) Health problems are widespread:* Norwegian NEETs are nearly six times as likely to feel depressed, and more than four times as likely to feel nervous, than other young people. These risk ratios are much higher than in the EU, where frequent feelings of depression and nervousness are only twice as prevalent among NEETs as among the general youth population. Also the ratio of NEETs to other young people who report poor self-assessed health is much higher in Norway than in the OECD on average (9 to 1 and 5 to 1, respectively).

NEET status moreover tends to be much more *persistent* for disadvantaged young people:

- While upper-secondary graduates typically only experience short bouts of unemployment or inactivity upon labour market entry, many upper-secondary drop-outs become NEETs in their teens and remain NEET for longer. Young people who have not graduated from upper-secondary school by age 24 are more than three times as likely to be long-term NEETs: 70% of drop-outs vs. 22% of upper-secondary graduates are NEET for over a year.
- Young people born abroad are 50% more likely to be long-term NEETs than their Norwegian-born peers. More than half of this difference is caused by higher rates of upper-secondary drop-out – the remainder can likely be attributed to the fact that recently arrived young migrants tend to start upper-secondary school at a later age.

Raising upper-secondary school completion is hence essential for lowering the NEET rate in Norway.

Income support and youth poverty

While the main goal of public policies for disadvantaged young people must be to help them on the path to self-sufficiency, those on low incomes – including the NEETs – may require support to avoid poverty. Income support schemes such as unemployment benefits, social assistance, housing benefits or family benefits play an important role in ensuring decent incomes of young people and their families. They also act as automatic macroeconomic stabilisers, alleviating income shocks for households affected by joblessness or a decline in earnings and hence bolster aggregate demand.

The Norwegian income support system for jobseekers has a two-tiered structure:

- Earnings-related Unemployment Benefits are available for young jobseekers with an earnings record of at least around one-quarter of the annual average wage in the last calendar year, or half the annual average wage of the last three years. While benefits are paid for relatively long (generally 24 months), the payment level is comparatively low: the share of previous net earnings replaced through benefits lies at 67% for a person with earnings of half of the average wage, a little below the OECD average.
- Young persons in low-income households, including those without Unemployment Benefit entitlements, can apply for time-unlimited, means-tested Social Assistance and a Housing Allowance. Payment levels are determined by caseworkers and vary locally, but are generally not high enough to lift recipient households out of poverty: a single person receiving Social Assistance and a Housing Allowance reaches only 35% of the median equivalised household income, much less than in the other Nordic countries.

The overall share of young people who receive these benefits is close to the OECD average, and benefit spell durations tend to be short.

Meanwhile, Norway has the highest receipt rate across the OECD for incapacity-related benefits, i.e. the Work Assessment Allowance for persons in vocational rehabilitation or medical treatment and Disability Benefits for those permanently unable to work full-time because of a disability. A countercyclical benefit receipt pattern during the economic downturn suggests that incapacity benefits serve as income support for difficult-to-employ young people in times of labour market slack. A concern is moreover that within the branch of incapacity benefits, there has been a gradual shift away from the temporary Work Assessment Allowance towards the more permanent Disability Benefit. This is problematic, because Disability Benefit durations are very long. Mental disorders have become a primary cause of Disability Benefit receipt among young people.

The youth poverty rate in Norway is very high by OECD standards, but these numbers are probably not a sign of widespread economic vulnerability. The high share of low-income youth rather reflects the fact that young people tend to move out of their parents' home for studies at a relatively young age; many of them finance their studies through loans provided by the Norwegian State Educational Loan Fund, which are not considered part of income. However, also the poverty rate for NEETs is somewhat higher than in the OECD on average, which reflects the low generosity of Social Assistance.

Promoting school completion and providing high-quality vocational training

The Norwegian education system is highly decentralised. Primary and lower-secondary schools are run by municipalities, while upper-secondary schools are run by counties, who are also responsible for apprenticeship training. Compulsory education is inclusive in that there is no tracking, no grade repetition and limited scope for school choice. All graduates have the right to upper-secondary education in one of their three preferred programmes, regardless of their compulsory-school grades.

Combatting early school leaving has been a policy priority in Norway for decades, but the challenge remains. While Norway is very successful in attracting young people into upper-secondary school – almost all compulsory-school graduates enrol – completion rates are below expectations. Almost one-in-five (19%) 25-34 year-olds have not completed upper-secondary education, well above the OECD average of 16%, and far above best-performers such as Korea (2%), but also peer countries such as Finland (10%).

Early school leaving is especially prevalent among VET students: only 63% graduate within two years of the end of the regular programme duration, compared to 72% in Sweden or 80% in Austria. Students who were weak-performers in compulsory school, those whose parents have at-most compulsory education and those who were born abroad are particularly likely to drop out.

The relatively academic nature of VET in Norway contributes to these low completion rates. The first two years of VET are mostly school-based; students spend the next two years as apprentices with companies. As an offer to school-tired young people, Norway introduced a shorter VET track featuring work-placed training from day one in 2016. Such a programme can be a good alternative for practically minded young people, and a stepping-stone to higher qualifications.

The most difficult transition for VET students is moving from the second year of school-based VET training to an apprenticeship – about 30% of all applicants did not find a training place in 2016. Those who are not able to secure an apprenticeship have the option to switch to a school-based pathway, but one-in-five drop out of school. Employers' reluctance to take on apprentices is connected to the fact that VET provision is largely driven by student choice and not by labour market demand – the apprenticeship only starts in year three, long after students have chosen their programme. School-based VET training is also relatively broad, with most students only settling on a specific occupation in the course of their apprenticeship. As a consequence, the level of job-specific skills new apprentices bring to employers is limited. Collectively agreed apprentice remuneration is also relatively generous, both compared to that in other countries and to average salaries.

School attendance is tightly monitored. Counties track all 16-21 year-olds who have not completed and are currently not attending upper-secondary education and offer them guidance and interventions with a view to bringing them back to school. These "Follow-up Services" established contact with 94% of all young NEETs in their target group in 2017, up from 88% in 2012. They engaged nearly half of them in an activity, such as an active labour market or training programme – of the other half, many were waiting for a suitable activity, ill or institutionalised, in informal education or had refused contact.

Norway could further promote school completion and expand good-quality vocational training along the following dimensions:

Strengthen the labour market ties of the VET system

- *Align VET provision more closely with labour market demand:* Combining school- and work-based training from day one is one way to ensure that young people acquire skills that are valuable on the local labour market.
- *Bring forward specialisation in the school-based part of VET*: School-based VET training is relatively broad, with students only settling on a specific occupation during the apprenticeship. Favouring depth instead of breadth earlier in the programme curriculum could make aspiring apprentices more attractive for employers.

Make hiring apprentices more affordable for employers

- *Encourage the social partners to reconsider apprentice remuneration:* A flatter wage increase in the second year would better align apprentice wages with their productivity.

Make the VET system more inclusive for the weakest students

- *Continue expanding lower-level tracks in VET:* Academically weak or practically minded young people can lack motivation to complete the two-year school-based component of VET training. Norway recently rolled out nationally a lower-level VET track. Norway should continue to promote alternative pathways in VET that enable those young people who otherwise would have dropped out to attain a qualification.

Consistently evaluate efforts against school drop-out

- *Make rigorous evaluations a pre-requisite for national funding of programmes:* Counties and municipalities have made considerable efforts to support drop-outs and at-risk students locally through a variety of measures – additional instruction, individualised follow-up, counselling – and these efforts are often supported by national funds. Without rigorous evaluations, it is hard to know which measures are effective, deliver value for public money, and deserve a broader roll-out. Conditioning funds on rigorous programme evaluations would help ensure that disadvantaged young people receive the best interventions.

Guaranteeing employment and training options for NEETs

Norway provides comprehensive support to NEETs through the Norwegian Labour and Welfare Administration (NAV), which acts as a "one-stop shop" for social and employment support and often a range of other municipal services. To reach out to young people out of education or work, NAV closely collaborates with the county-level Follow-up Services.

NAV offices are generally well equipped to serve young users: larger offices usually employ special youth teams, most smaller offices have specific contact persons for young people. Caseload numbers of youth specialists tend to be moderate, at below 70 on average. Non-governmental providers play an important role in delivering employment services, but provider compensation does not account for performance. Social services are largely publicly provided.

As one of the pioneers of so-called youth guarantees, Norway has had comprehensive provisions in place for over three decades that entitle young jobseekers to additional, targeted employment support. After a number of studies raised doubts about the Youth Guarantee's effectiveness, Norway carried out a substantial reform in 2017 replacing its Youth Guarantee by the "New Youth Effort". Under the new framework, all registered employable jobseekers below the age of 30 are entitled to personalised employment support within eight weeks of registration. It is still too early, however, to assess the impact of this reform on the quality of support for young people.

Overall spending on active labour market programmes in Norway is lower than in the other Nordic countries, but Norway strongly targets programme participation to the most disadvantaged users. All new users undergo a careful profiling process upon registration – NAV then classifies them into four support categories, which determine the support intensity. Users with no obvious barriers to employment initially receive little support. For those with mild or more severe barriers, NAV heavily relies on work experience in the public or private sector. A series of evaluations have cast doubt on the effectiveness of this type of measures, however; for public-sector work experience programmes, this finding is supported by evidence from other countries. Most users generally do not have access to longer training programmes via NAV – this may change in the future, however, after a recent legislative change opened the upper-secondary education system to jobseekers in their early twenties. NAV users with permanently reduced work capacity primarily benefit from subsidised employment in sheltered workplaces or the regular labour market.

Norway devotes considerable funding to evaluating its employment-related policies and programmes – often drawing on its excellent administrative microdata for empirical analyses – and authorities systematically rely on such studies for policy design.

Young people with reduced work capacity make up the majority of registered young NAV users, as many of them remain registered for very long periods. Caseworkers seem to lack the necessary guidance to carry out rigorous work capacity assessments for users who have undergone medical treatment or rehabilitation, and there are few effective support options for users with more complex health issues and a lack of recent work experience. As a result, these users often remain "locked into" the Work Assessment Allowance unless if they find work or are moved to Disability Benefits. In an effort to promote employment of those highly disadvantaged jobseekers, Norway tightened access to the Work Assessment Allowance in early 2018 and strengthened work incentives and support for benefit recipients.

Norway could further strengthen the support for NEETs along the following dimensions:

Further promote labour market integration of young people with reduced work capacity

- *Ensure rigorous work capacity assessments:* Receipt rates of incapacity benefits remain very high in spite of significant reform efforts. Norway should monitor the effects of the recent Work Assessment Allowance reform on the receipt of incapacity benefits, and ensure notably that NAV caseworkers receive clear guidance on how to carry out work capacity assessments. Gatekeeping for Disability Benefits should be improved by providing clearer guidelines to general practitioners who carry out disability assessments and by better monitoring their compliance with these guidelines.

- *Strengthen support for young Social Assistance recipients:* As a result of the tightened access to the Work Assessment Allowance, Social Assistance receipt will likely surge, in particular for jobseekers with (mental) health problems and little work experience. Norway should devote additional resources to supporting these users. This may include expanding the Qualification Programme, which has proven effective for highly disadvantaged jobseekers. The currently low Social Assistance benefit levels could be raised to tackle youth poverty.

Improve the effectiveness of labour market measures

- *Permit tendering of social services and strengthen pay-for-performance for service providers:* Labour market measures for jobseekers are largely delivered by non-governmental providers, who are compensated per hour or per user irrespective of their performance. The tendering of social support services remains rare. Norway should grant NAV offices greater freedom in contracting out social service delivery, and strengthen the link between the compensation of employment and social service providers and the results they achieve.
- *Re-assess the strong reliance on work experience measures:* Work practice in the public or private sector is the most widely used labour market measure for young people, but a series of studies have suggested that it is ineffective at moving young people into stable employment. Norway should re-consider the widespread use of this measure, possibly with a view to restricting it to private-sector employers and strengthening and formalising its training component.
- *Expand the use of training programmes:* NAV currently provides training to jobseekers mostly through very short programmes in basic skills. After the recent opening of the public upper-secondary education system to young people in their early 20s, NAV and educational authorities should consider jointly expanding vocational training programmes for low-skilled jobseekers. NAV should moreover introduce Norwegian-language classes for the growing share of young migrants.
- *Increase the use of rigorous impact evaluations:* The Ministry of Labour and Social Affairs and NAV regularly commission evaluations of their policies and programmes to support NEETs. Most of these studies are qualitative in nature, however, providing little insights on programmes' actual impacts. To ensure an efficient use of resources, Norway should expand the use of randomised controlled trials and quasi-experimental techniques for evaluating employment and social support programmes for young people, and implement new programmes in ways that facilitate rigorous impact evaluations.

Ensure a systematic application of the New Youth Effort

- *Create awareness of the New Youth Effort and systematically report on its implementation:* The discontinued Youth Guarantee failed to effectively shape youth employment support because NAV caseworkers were often insufficiently aware of – and bound by – its contents. For the New Youth Effort to bring substantial improvements, Norway should clearly communicate to NAV specialists the entitlements that the New Youth Effort grants to young people. It should also establish an effective monitoring system that permits comparing jobseeker outcomes across NAV offices against clear benchmarks.

- *Make sure that resources match the increased requirements:* NAV caseworkers have pointed to the importance of low caseload numbers and intensive follow-up as perceived success factors for an effective support of NEETs. In light of the higher follow-up entitlements under the New Youth Effort, Norway should commit additional resources to strengthening NAV's youth teams and permit raising participation in labour market measures, which is lower than in other Nordic countries.

Expand data collection and exchange

- *Intensify reporting on local-level implementation of employment and social support:* NAV offices enjoy considerable discretion in implementing employment support and developing their own social support policies. To promote the identification and sharing of best practices and facilitate cross-regional learning, Norway should require local offices to collect data on the implementation of labour market measures and social service delivery and transmit these to national authorities.
- *Facilitate data exchange between the educational authorities and NAV*: In the context of relatively high early school leaving rates, NAV rightly focuses primarily on moving young jobseekers back into education or training. NAV caseworkers currently do not have access to administrative information on the educational attainment of their users, however, and they have no reliable way of telling whether and when their users move into education or training. Norway should improve data exchange between the educational authorities and NAV to facilitate a better follow-up of users through their caseworkers, and to permit NAV to observe and analyse movements into education and training.

Chapter 1. Youth labour market outcomes in Norway

This chapter presents a brief overview of labour market outcomes of young people in Norway. It sets off by summarising the demographic situation in Norway. It then describes the situation of young people in the labour market, looking at trends in employment, educational enrolment, unemployment and inactivity. The chapter concludes by outlining the challenge posed by young people who are not in employment, education or training (NEET).

The statistical data for Israel are supplied by and under the responsibility of the relevant Israeli authorities. The use of such data by the OECD is without prejudice to the status of the Golan Heights, East Jerusalem and Israeli settlements in the West Bank under the terms of international law.

Introduction

Norway has experienced dynamic growth in its youth population over the past decade as a result of high fertility and immigration. Job growth has not kept pace with demographics, however. While Norway has weathered the Great Recession relatively unscathed, an increasing number of young people are unemployed or inactive.

This chapter presents a brief overview of the labour market situation of young people and outlines the most recent trends. It sets off by summarising the demographic situation in Norway (Section 1.1), and then looks at labour market outcomes of young people over the past decade in terms of employment, unemployment and inactivity (Section 1.2). It concludes by describing the challenge of young people who are not in employment, education or training, the "NEETs" (Section 1.3).

1.1. The demographic context

Unlike in many other OECD countries, the number of young people aged 15 to 29 has been rising in Norway in recent years – by 18% between 2007 and 2016 (+157 000 young people). Immigration accounted for over four-fifths of this increase (Figure 1.1, Panel A).

The past decade saw net migration well above the OECD average (Figure 1.1, Panel B). While in the 1980s and 90s, refugees and family reunification made up the bulk of total immigration to Norway, the 2004 European Union enlargement led to increased labour immigration from Central and Eastern Europe (Bratsberg, Raaum and Røed, 2014[1]). Norway was especially attractive to labour migrants because of high wages and low unemployment. In 2011, Norway received nearly as many inflows from Central and Eastern Europe as Iceland, Finland, Sweden and Denmark combined (Tronstad and Joona, 2013[2]).

Following the 2008/09 economic downturn, however, the number of people settling in Norway for work, particularly those from Eastern Europe and Sweden, started falling (Figure 1.1, Panel C). Rising unemployment and a weak Norwegian *Krone* made Norway less attractive for labour migrants, and non-Norwegian citizens started leaving the country – indeed, 2016 set a modern-day record for the number of emigrants from Norway (SSB, 2017[3]; SSB, 2017[4]). This explains the clear drop in the net migration rate from a peak of 9.5 per 1 000 inhabitants in 2011 to 5.0 in 2015, despite a growing number of recognised humanitarian refugees and those joining their families in Norway (Figure 1.1, Panel C). Relative net migration now is only slightly above the OECD average (Figure 1.1, Panel B).

The remainder of the rise in the youth population is due to above-average fertility in the 1980s, following a dip in the birth rate throughout the 1970s. This led to a moderate uptick in the number of 15-29 year-olds from 2005 onwards, and explains around one-fifth of the overall increase (Figure 1.1, Panel C and D). Fertility has largely remained stable since; and while it is above the OECD average, at 1.8 it is clearly below the replacement level needed to keep the population constant (around 2.1 in developed countries). Hence, in the absence of immigration, the youth population would slowly decline over the coming decades.

Figure 1.1. Immigration drives the growth in the youth population

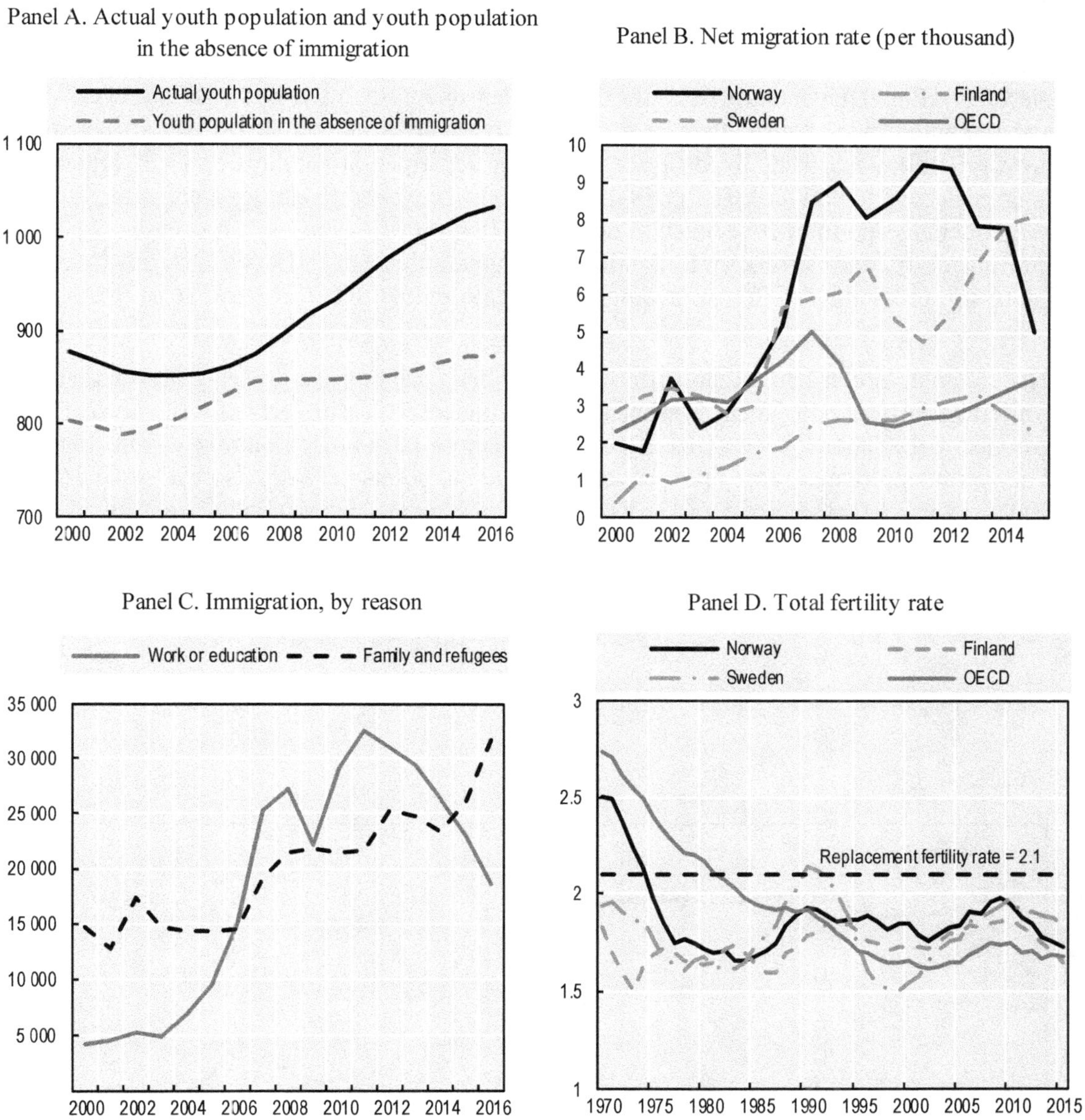

Note: Immigration counts include foreigners with a non-Nordic citizenship, who hold a residence permit and intend to stay for at least six months. Asylum seekers are only counted as immigrants once they have been granted a residence permit.

The net migration rate takes account of immigration and emigration of foreigners and nationals. The OECD average excludes Canada and Denmark from 2012- 2013, Greece from 2009-2013, Japan from 2012-2015, the Netherlands from 2011-2013, Slovenia, Turkey and the United Kingdom before 2014 and the United States from 2011.

The total fertility rate gives the number of children a woman would on average bear during her lifetime given the prevailing age-specific fertility rates.

The youth population in the absence of immigration is calculated by adjusting the birth-cohorts 15-29 years before each year by their age- and year-specific survival probabilities, averaged over five years. That is, the expected size of the group of 15-20 year-olds in 2015 is calculated as the size of the 1995-2000 birth cohort, adjusted by the proportion that survived until age 17.5 in 2015. Averaging over five years is necessary as the observed population numbers are only available for five-year age groups. This exercise assumes no emigration from Norway.

Source: Youth population: (Statistics Norway, 2017[5]), Norwegian population statistics: Table: 05531: Live births, by month, 2017, Table: 07902: Life tables, by sex and age, 2017, Table: 07459: Population, by sex and one-year age groups. 1 January (M). Net migration rates: 2000-2013: (OECD, 2017[6]), 2014-2015: (OECD, 2017[7]). Immigrations by reason of immigration: (SSB, 2017[8]). Total fertility rates: (OECD, 2018[9]).

1.2. The labour market situation of young people

While the Norwegian labour market weathered the Great Recession comparatively well, the recovery has been more tentative than across the OECD on average. In the wake of the 2007 Global Financial Crisis, the Norwegian unemployment rate rose more slowly, and remained much lower, than in the OECD on average. Unemployment did increase, however, following the 2014 oil price shock and remained at an elevated level, although it is projected to fall in 2018 (OECD, 2017[10]). The overall employment rate fell by 3.7 percentage points between 2008 and 2016 (Figure 1.2, Panel A), translating mainly into inactivity, and is forecast to continue to stagnate through 2018 (OECD, 2017[11]). In contrast, across the OECD on average, aggregate employment is back at its pre-crisis level.

The sluggish labour market situation has partly been driven by a growing labour force – while aggregate employment has been growing since 2011, this growth fell short of the growth of the labour force. This effect is even more pronounced among young people. The youth employment rate fell by over 7 percentage points between its peak of 66.5% in 2008 and its 2016 value of 59%, and continues to stagnate. In contrast, across the OECD on average, the youth employment rate fell by 5 percentage points to its lowest value in 2013 and has been slowly increasing since (Figure 1.2, Panel B)

Figure 1.2. Employment rates in Norway have been stagnating

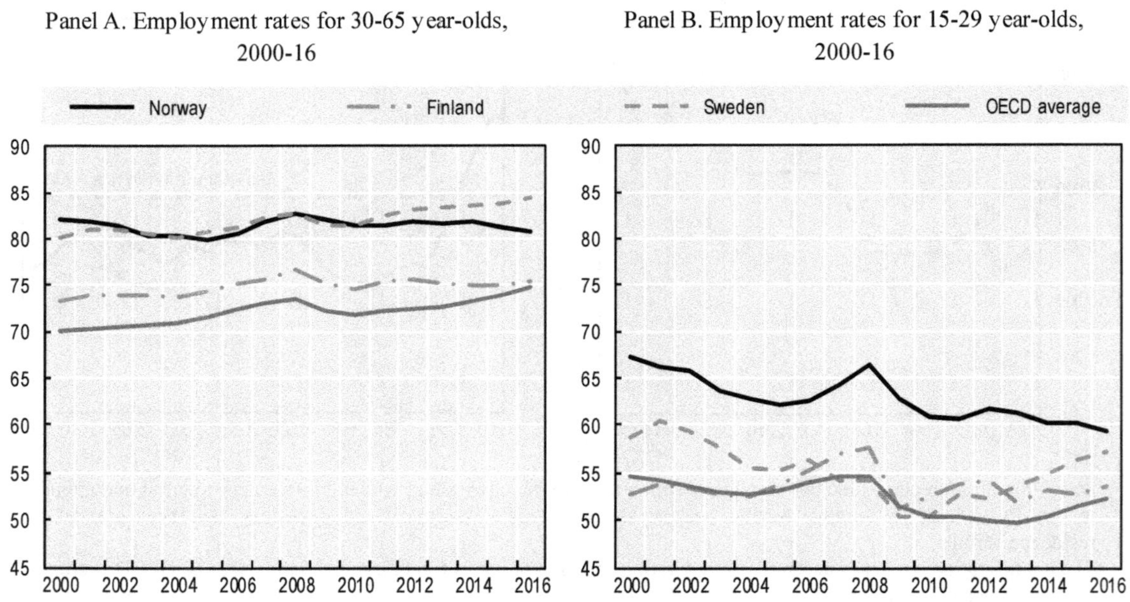

Source: OECD Employment Database.

This sharp and, to date, persistent decline in the youth employment rate was not so much due to a decrease in *the number of employed young people* (the nominator) but rather an increase in the *youth population* (the denominator). Between 2008 and 2010, 28 000 jobs held by 15-29 year-olds were lost (5%). In 2011, however, youth employment started to pick up again, surpassing its 2008 value in 2012. While this development began to falter following the 2014 oil price shock, the number of employed young people still grew by

8% between 2007 and 2016. This employment growth, however, fell well short of the substantial growth in the youth population over this same time period (+15%).

In the absence of this population growth, and holding the pace of job creation constant, the youth employment rate would only have fallen by 3 percentage points (rather than 7), and it would have regained its pre-crisis value in 2012. Indeed, it would have surpassed its 2008 peak by 2016 (Figure 1.3, Panel A).

The bulk of the increase in the youth population is attributable to immigration (Figure 1.3, Panel B). Also the increase in the fertility rate in the mid-1980s plays a role, a trend that is gaining relevance as the smaller cohorts born in the late 1970s and early 1980s age out of the youth population. This effect will become even more important in the future because the birth rate remained stable throughout the 1990s.

Figure 1.3. Growth in the youth population outpaced employment growth

Panel A. Observed youth employment rate, (notional) youth employment rate if the youth population had remained at its 2007 level, decomposition in fertility and migration effect, 15-29 year-olds, as percentages, 2007-16

Panel B. *Change* in the absolute number of young people by activity status, 2008-15 (left axis), and percentage-point change in the share of young people by activity status (right axis), 2008-15

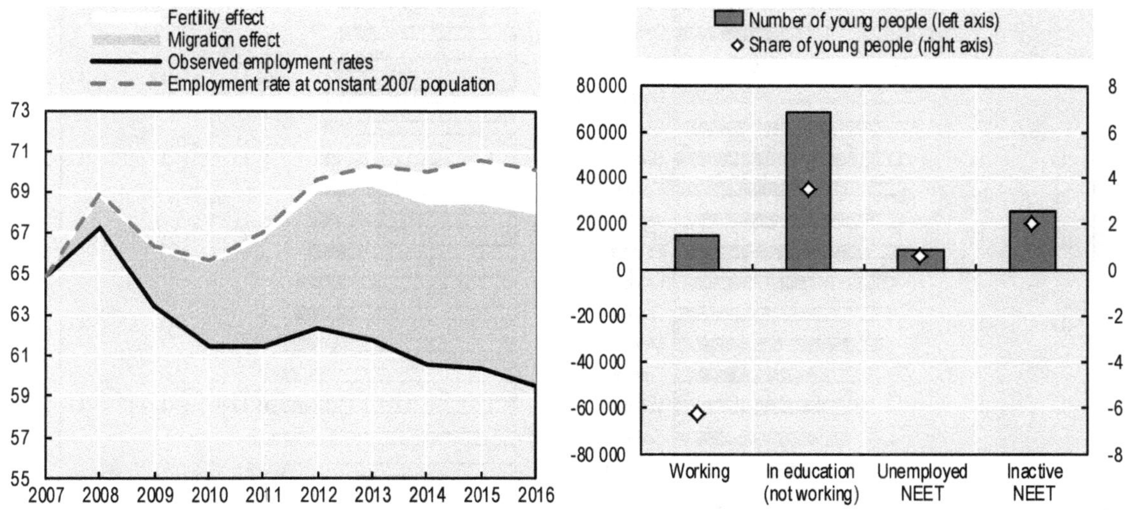

Note: The fertility effect is calculated by adding the absolute annual increase in the youth population implied by the birth rate 15-29 years earlier (see note to Figure 1.1) to the youth population in 2007. The observed number of working young people aged 15-29 is then used to calculate a hypothetical employment rate in the absence of migration. The fertility effect is the difference between the (hypothetical) employment rate at a constant 2007 youth population and the employment rate that allows for birth-rate-driven population growth. The migration effect, in turn, is the difference between this hypothetical, and the observed, employment rate.
Source: Panel A: OECD Employment Database. (Statistics Norway, $2017_{[5]}$), Norwegian population statistics: Table: 05531: Live births, by month, 2017, Table: 07902: Life tables, by sex and age, 2017, Table: 07459: Population, by sex and one-year age groups. 1 January (M). Panel B: OECD calculations based on the EU-LFS.

However, actual youth population growth outpaced net job creation by about 6% of the youth population between 2008 and 2015.[1] The rise in the number of non-working students accounts for more than half of this differential. The rise in *inactive* NEETs – that is, not working or studying, but neither looking for work – accounts for one-third, and the remaining sixth became *unemployed* NEETs (Figure 1.3, Panel B).

The Norwegian youth employment rate however remains above the OECD average, at 59% (52%, Figure 1.2, Panel B), though lagging behind best-performers Iceland (81%), Switzerland (71%) or the Netherlands (68%). The high employment rate partly reflects that a large number of young people combine work and studies: 22%, nearly half of all 15-29 year-olds who are in education, are also working (Figure 1.4). This share is significantly higher than the OECD average (13%) and even above that of countries with established apprenticeship systems that combine school and work-based training, such as Germany (20%) and Austria (18%).

Figure 1.4. Nearly half of all Norwegian students also work

Labour market and educational status of young people as a percentage of all 15-29 year-olds, 2015

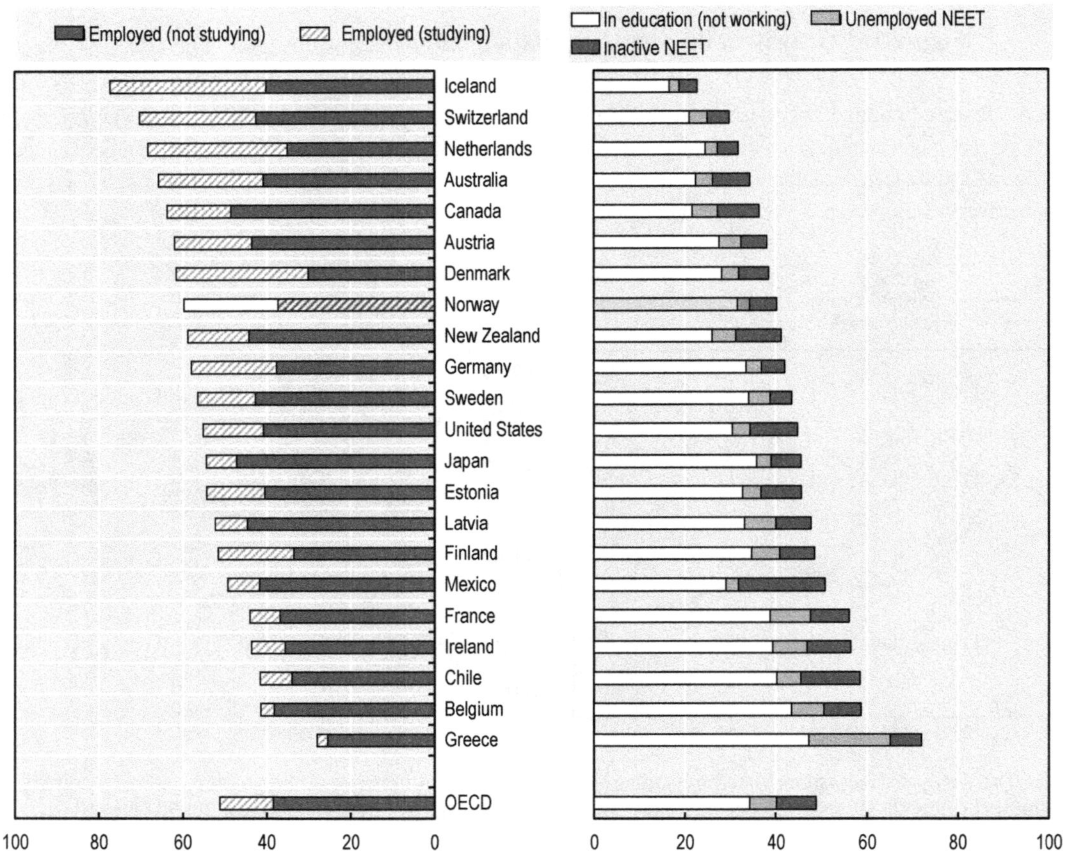

Note: NEET refers to young people not in employment, education or training. Countries are sorted by the employment rate in descending order. Data are for 2013 for Korea and New Zealand, for 2014 for Japan and for 2016 for Mexico.

Source: OECD calculations based on the EU-LFS, national labour force surveys and OECD (2016) "Transition from School to Work", http://stats.oecd.org/Index.aspx?DataSetCode=EAG_TRANS (for Australia, Germany and Korea).

Working a moderate number of hours (below 15 a week) has been shown to lower the risk of early school leaving, possibly because it helps develop important life skills such as conscientiousness and motivation, and can steer students towards a career path. There are also benefits for university students, especially if they work moderate hours (less than half-time) in a job related to their field of study (Quintini and Martin, 2014[12]).

1.3. The NEET challenge

The unemployment rate is easily misinterpreted as an indicator for the labour market situation of young people for two reasons. First, it does not capture young people who are out of work but not actively looking for work. Second, it is calculated as the share of active jobseekers among all those *who participate in the labour market* (i.e. the employed and the unemployed), but participation rates among young people vary widely across countries – from 42% in Italy to 83% in Iceland (OECD, 2016[13]). These variations do not only result from differences in economic climates, but reflect different national education systems – labour force participation of young people tends to be higher in countries with apprenticeship systems and lower in those where many young people continue on to tertiary education. Consequently, the youth unemployment rate will be lower in countries with higher labour force participation, even if the share of young people who are unemployed is similar.

Box 1.1. Measuring the size of the NEET population - a note on data quality

The statistical analysis presented in this review relies on a range of different data sources, including register-based data managed by Statistics Norway, labour force surveys (notably the EU-LFS) and household surveys (notably the EU-SILC). In spite of all efforts made to harmonise the statistics produced using these different sources, there remain some discrepancies because of differences in data quality and coverage.

One such example is unfortunately the size of the NEET population, where the results produced diverge for register-based and survey data, in particular for migrants. In 2014, the last year for which administrative data are available, 9% of all 15-29 year-olds born in Norway were NEET according to administrative data compared to only 7.5% according to the EU-LFS. For youth born outside of Norway, administrative data give a NEET rate of 27%, compared to 17% in the EU-LFS.

These high discrepancies for the migrant population result mainly from a high non-response rate among migrants in the EU-LFS, which moreover correlates with employment status (Villund, 2012[14]). It leads to an *underestimation* of the number of migrants in the general population (the number of young people born outside of Norway is about one-third higher in the administrative data than in the EU-LFS), and an *overestimation* of the employment rate of migrants as non-working migrants are particularly prone to non-response in the EU-LFS.

While the administrative data are generally more reliable, this review presents data from the EU-LFS for cross-country comparisons.

A more complete measure of the labour market situation of young people – and one that is easier to interpret – is the share of young people who are NEET, the "NEET rate".[2] The Norwegian NEET rate is low by international standards – 9% of all 15-29 year-olds were NEET in 2016, 86 000 young people, compared to 14% across the OECD on average (Figure 1.5, Panel A – see Box 1.1 for a note on data quality). It is above that in peer countries such as Iceland (5%), however, as well as that of the Netherlands (6%) and Luxembourg (8%). A breakdown of NEETs into those who *do* and *do not* actively seek work illustrates the importance of looking beyond unemployment rates when discussing the labour market situation of young people: Seven out of ten NEETs in Norway are *inactive* (i.e. not looking for work), compared to just over half across the OECD on average – only the remaining three-out-of-ten are engaged in job search (the *unemployed* NEETs).

Norway will hence have to look primarily towards ways of engaging inactive NEETs into education or work to further reduce its NEET rate. This is particularly challenging, however: across OECD countries, inactivity rates have been relatively stable over the crisis and the recovery as the number of inactive youth primarily reflects structural factors – meanwhile, the number of unemployed NEETs responded very strongly to the business cycle (Carcillo et al., 2015[15]; OECD, 2016[16]). A similar pattern can be observed for Norway: while the economic boom of the turn of the millennium made a real dent in NEET inactivity rates, they have been relatively stable since, though creeping upwards slowly over the last decade (Figure 1.5, Panel B). The share of unemployed NEETs has fluctuated more strongly, but the unemployed account for a much smaller proportion today than two decades ago.

Re-engaging inactive NEETs into education or employment is particularly challenging because they are – by definition – further from the labour market and often not in touch with public services and hence more difficult to reach out to. In a country like Norway, where the NEET rate is comparatively low overall, NEETs moreover tend to be particularly disadvantaged (see Chapter 2 for an in-depth profile).

Figure 1.5. A stable proportion of about two-thirds of all NEETs in Norway are inactive

Inactive and unemployed NEETs, as a percentage of all 15-29 year-olds

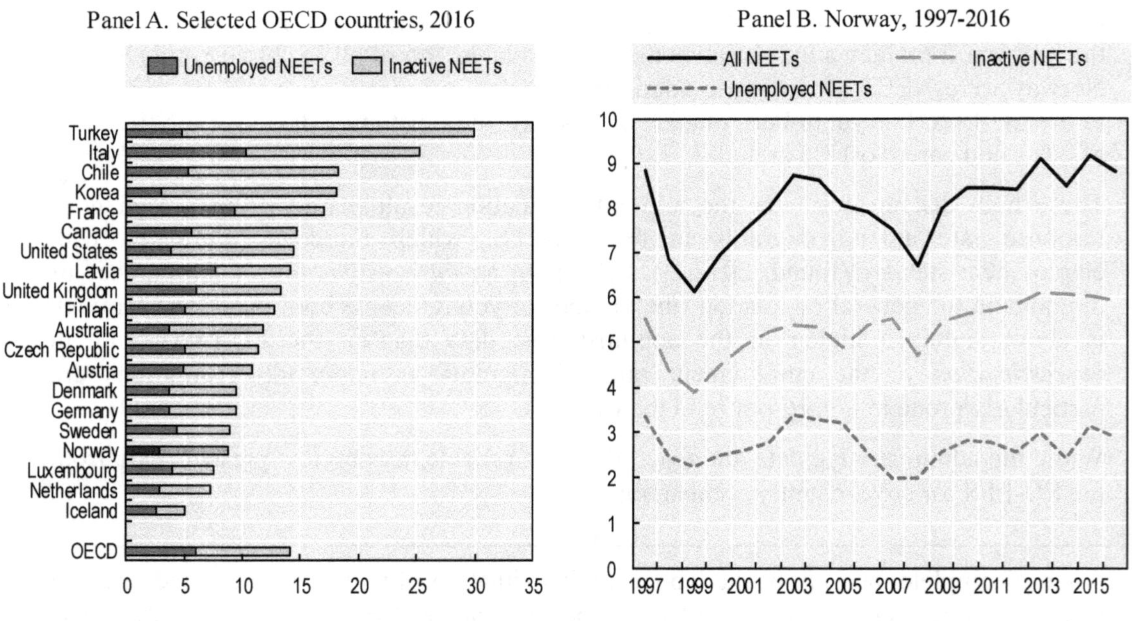

Note: 2016 Statistics for European countries are preliminary. Data are for 2015 for Australia, Canada, Chile, Israel, Korea, New Zealand and the United States,

Source: Norway 1997-16, Australia, Israel, Korea and New Zealand: OECD (2016), *Education at a Glance*. All other countries and Norway 2016: OECD estimates based on the EU-LFS and national labour force surveys.

Regional differences in NEET rates across Norway are comparatively modest and reflect wider regional disparities. NEET rates are highest in South-Eastern Norway – in the counties of Telemark, Østfold and Vestfold (Figure 1.6) – where GDP per capita is lowest

(OECD, 2016[17]). They are lowest in Western Norway – in the counties of Sogn og Fjordane, Hordalandand Rogaland – which are among the richer regions in Norway behind Oslo and Akershus.[3] Meanwhile, the disparities correspond only partly to the overall labour market situation – working-age unemployment, for example, is lower than the national average for most counties in Northern Norway, which exhibits NEET rates close to the national average (OECD, 2017[18]). The cross-county differences in regional NEET rates are however not particularly striking in international comparison: the rate in the best-performing county, Sogn og Fjordane, is about half as high than in the poorest-performing county, Telemark – in Japan, for instance, local NEET rates vary by over 300% (OECD, 2017[19]).

Figure 1.6. NEET rates are highest in South-Eastern Norway

NEETs as a percentage of 15-29 year-olds, by county, 2014

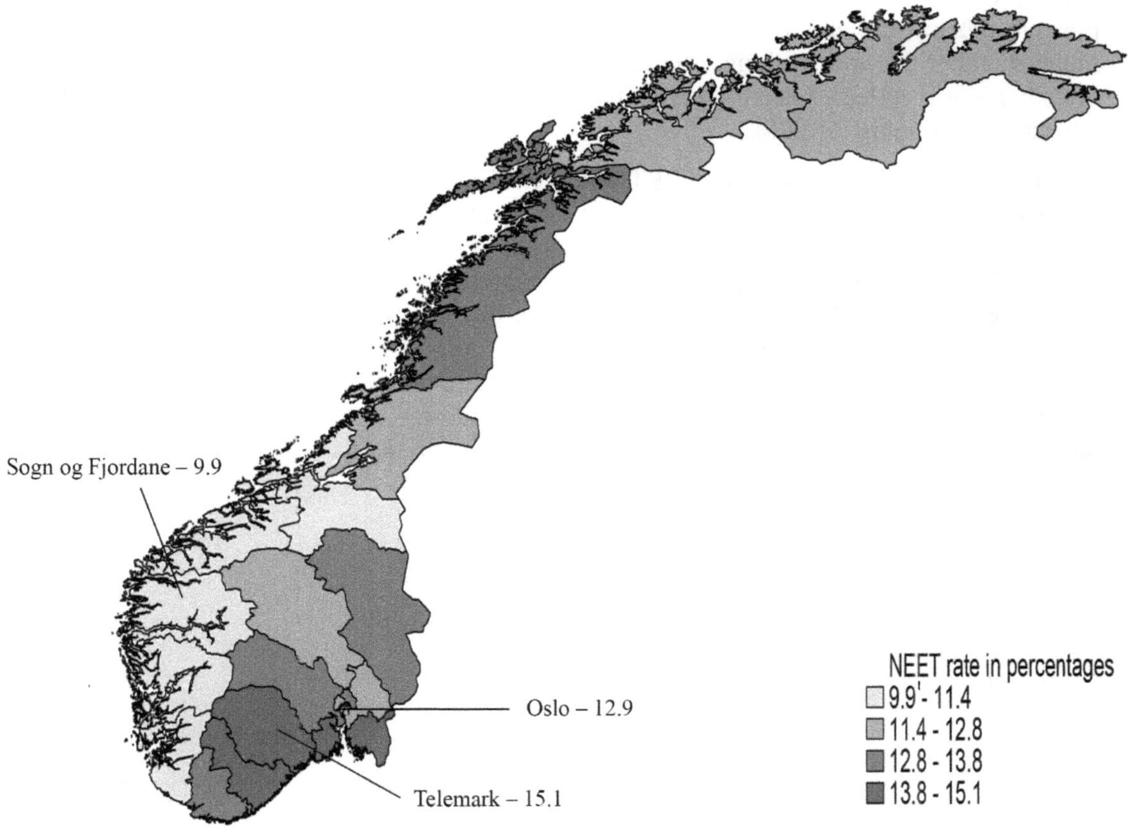

Source: Statistics Norway calculations based on administrative data.

Round-up

The number of 15-29 year-olds is growing quickly in Norway – by 18% between 2007 and 2016 alone (+157 000 young people) – while it is on the decline in many other OECD countries. Immigration, mainly from Central and Eastern Europe, accounted for over four-fifths of this increase.

Labour market conditions for young people are among the most favourable across OECD countries, but the trend over the last decade has not been as positive. While the youth employment rate is high, at 59% in 2016 (compared to 52% in the OECD on average), it declined substantially in recent years and is now seven percentage points below its pre-crisis peak.

This decline does not so much reflect the effects of the economic crisis – as in other OECD countries – but rather a rapidly growing youth population. Indeed, the number of employed young people has *risen* in absolute terms since the start of the crisis. This positive net job growth was outpaced by even faster population growth. And while a higher number of (non-working) students account for more than half of this differential, the other half is reflected in a higher number of young people who are not in employment, education or training (NEET).

In spite of its recent rise, the NEET rate remains low in Norway by international standards – at 9% of the youth population in 2016, or 86 000 young people. This is substantially below the OECD average of 14%, but two percentage points higher than in 2008 and above the rates in Iceland (5%), the Netherlands (6%) or Luxembourg (8%). To further reduce its NEET rate, Norway will have to focus its efforts primarily on those who are currently not engaged in active job search, i.e. the *inactive* NEETs, who account for 70% of all NEETs. Re-engaging them in education or employment is particularly challenging, however: *inactive* NEETs are – by definition – further away from the labour market than *unemployed* NEETs, and they are often not in regular contact with the public services.

Notes

1. At the time of writing, detailed activity status data from the LFS are not available for 2016.

2. This review defines NEETs as 15-29 year-olds who are "not in employment" (unemployed or not in the labour force according to the ILO definition, identified by the EU-LFS variable ILOSTAT) and "not in education or training" (young people who are not enrolled in a course of formal education or training, such as school, university, or an apprenticeship programme). That is, students must be enrolled in a programme of study leading to a recognised qualification in the education system, including as identified by the variable EDUCSTAT in the EU-LFS. Young people who are in informal education only are not counted as being in education or training according to this definition. For Norway, young people who attend a folk high school (folkehøgskole) are treated as being in formal education and thus not as NEETs, because they cannot be separately identified in the LFS or administrative data.

Eurostat does define young people who are in informal education (identified by the EU-LFS variable COURRAT) as non-NEETs, which leads to significantly lower NEET rates for some countries. This review disregards informal education because the labour market relevance of informal education is not clear as these could be hobby courses. Information on informal education is moreover not available for all non-European countries, which would distort cross-OECD comparisons.

3. Over the economic crisis, South–Eastern Norway experienced somewhat stronger increases in NEET rates, with the notable exception of Oslo: in the capital, the NEET rate remained almost constant between 2008 and 2014, while it rose everywhere else, including the best-performing counties of South-Western Norway.

References

Bratsberg, B., O. Raaum and K. Røed (2014), "Labour migrant adjustments in the aftermath of the financial crisis", *Discussion Paper Series*, No. 19, Centre for Research and Analysis of Migration Department of Economics, University College London, http://www.cream-migration.org. [1]

Carcillo, S. et al. (2015), "NEET Youth in the Aftermath of the Crisis: Challenges and Policies", *OECD Social, Employment and Migration Working Papers*, No. 164, OECD Publishing, Paris, http://dx.doi.org/10.1787/5js6363503f6-en. [15]

OECD (2016), *Society at a Glance 2016*, OECD Publishing, Paris, http://dx.doi.org/10.1787/9789264261488-en. [13]

OECD (2016), "Norway", in *OECD Regional Outlook 2016: Productive Regions for Inclusive Societies*, OECD Publishing, Paris, http://dx.doi.org/10.1787/9789264260245-38-en. [17]

OECD (2016), *Society at a Glance 2016: OECD Social Indicators*, OECD Publishing, Paris, http://dx.doi.org/10.1787/9789264261488-en. [16]

OECD (2017), *International Migration Outlook*, OECD Publishing, Paris, http://dx.doi.org/10.1787/migr_outlook-2017-en. [7]

OECD (2017), *Population and vital statistics*, http://stats.oecd.org/Index.aspx?DataSetCode=ALFS_POP_VITAL (accessed on 26 May 2017). [6]

OECD (2017), *OECD Employment Outlook 2017*, OECD Publishing, Paris, http://dx.doi.org/10.1787/empl_outlook-2017-en. [11]

OECD (2017), *Investing in Youth: Japan*, OECD Publishing, Paris, http://dx.doi.org/10.1787/9789264275898-en. [19]

OECD (2017), *OECD Regional Labour*, OECD regional statistics (database), http://stats.oecd.org/Index.aspx?DataSetCode=REGION_DEMOGR. [18]

OECD (2017), *OECD Economic Surveys: Norway 2017*, OECD Publishing, Paris, http://dx.doi.org/10.1787/eco_surveys-nor-2018-en. [10]

OECD (2018), *OECD Family Database - SF2.1 Fertility rates*, http://www.oecd.org/els/soc/SF_2_1_Fertility_rates.xlsx (accessed on 16 March 2018). [9]

Quintini, G. and S. Martin (2014), *Same Same but Different: School-to-work Transitions in Emerging and Advanced Economies*, http://dx.doi.org/10.1787/5jzbb2t1rcwc-en. [12]

SSB (2017), *Table: 06313: Immigrations, by reason for immigration, sex and age*, Statbank, https://www.ssb.no/statistikkbanken/selectvarval/Define.asp?subjectcode=&ProductId=&MainTable=InnvBef04&nvl=&PLanguage=1&nyTmpVar=true&CMSSubjectArea=befolkning&KortNavnWeb=innvgrunn&StatVariant=&checked=true (accessed on 22 June 2017). [8]

SSB (2017), *Lowest net immigration in ten years*, https://www.ssb.no/en/befolkning/artikler-og-publikasjoner/record-high-emigration-lowest-net-immigration-since-2007 (accessed on 21 September 2017). [3]

SSB (2017), *Economic Survey 1/2017*, SSB, Oslo, https://www.ssb.no/en/nasjonalregnskap-og-konjunkturer/artikler-og-publikasjoner/_attachment/301231?_ts=15af12fef98 (accessed on 21 September 2017). [4]

Statistics Norway (2017), *Statistikkbanken*, https://www.ssb.no/statbank/. [5]

Tronstad, K. and P. Joona (2013), "New Patterns of migration from Central and Eastern Europe to the Nordic countries", in Jon Horgen Friberg and Line Eldring (ed.), *Labour migrants from Central and Eastern Europe in the Nordic countries Patterns of migration, working conditions and recruitment practices Labour migrants from Central and Eastern Europe in the Nordic countries*, Council of Nordic Ministers, Copenhagen K, http://www.norden.org. [2]

Villund, O. (2012), "Arbeidsmarkedsstatistikk for innvandrere, basert på Arbeidskraftundersøkelsen (AKU). Utvikling av et nytt beregningsopplegg [Immigrant Labour Market Statistics from the Norwegian Labour Force Survey. Documentation of estimation procedures]", *SSB Rapporter*, Vol. 33, https://www.ssb.no/a/publikasjoner/pdf/rapp_201233/rapp_201233.pdf. [14]

Chapter 2. A profile of young people not in employment, education or training (NEET) in Norway

This chapter describes the characteristics of young people who are not in employment, education or training (NEETs) in Norway. It identifies risk factors of NEET status, and presents evidence on the life satisfaction, and the attitudes of NEETs. It then presents an analysis of the dynamics of NEET status, looking at the incidence, duration and timing of NEET spells among young people, examining which young people are at risk of becoming long-term NEETs.

The statistical data for Israel are supplied by and under the responsibility of the relevant Israeli authorities. The use of such data by the OECD is without prejudice to the status of the Golan Heights, East Jerusalem and Israeli settlements in the West Bank under the terms of international law.

Introduction

While the Norwegian labour market weathered the 2009/10 economic downturn comparatively well, the youth labour market developed significantly less favourably, and the recovery has been more tentative than across the OECD on average. The employment rate of 15-29 year-olds fell by over seven percentage points and continues to stagnate, while showing signs of recovery across the OECD on average.

The share of young people who are Not in Employment, Education or Training (NEET) is low compared to the OECD average (9 vs. 14%), but seven-out-of-ten NEETs are inactive – that is, they are not even looking for a job – compared to just half across the OECD on average (see Chapter 1). Inactive NEETs pose a particular challenge to policy makers because they are – by definition – further from the labour market and less likely to be registered with the public employment services.

This chapter presents a profile of NEETs in Norway. It identifies the principal risk factors for becoming NEET (Section 2.1) before examining the persistence of NEET status over time and characterising young people who are at risk of remaining NEET for long periods (Section 2.2).

2.1. Who are the young people not in employment, education or training (NEET)?

NEETs are a diverse group facing various hurdles to participation in education or employment. Interventions and programmes therefore have to be adapted to the individual if they are to be effective. Some young people are closer to the labour market and require only minimal assistance; others, such as those who lack basic skills or have a disability, need more intensive support.

This section seeks to provide a detailed portrait of young people out of employment, education or training in Norway. It looks at the relationship between personal characteristics such as educational attainment or migration background and the risk of being NEET and explores the views and values of young NEETs.

2.1.1. NEET status and educational attainment

In a labour market that increasingly demands skilled workers, young people with low educational attainment, particularly those lacking foundation skills (such as basic reading, writing and mathematics), often find it hard to establish themselves on the labour market. Across the OECD on average, 41% of all 25-29 year-olds without an upper-secondary degree were NEET in 2015, compared to just 13% of their peers with tertiary education (Figure 2.1, Panel A). In Norway, this difference is even more pronounced: 25-29 year-olds without an upper-secondary degree are more than seven times as likely to be NEET as university graduates (35 vs. 5%) – the largest difference across the OECD.

This can also be seen when looking at skills instead of diploma. Results from the OECD Programme for the International Assessment of Adult Competencies (PIAAC) show that in the OECD on average, young people with low literacy and numeracy skills are more than twice as likely to be NEET as those with medium skills. In Norway, young people with low literacy skills are nearly three times as likely to be NEET as those with medium literacy skills; young people with low numeracy skills are 74% more likely to be NEET than those with medium numeracy skills (OECD, 2016[1]).

Figure 2.1. NEET rates are substantially higher for those with low education

Panel A: NEET rates of 25-29 year-olds by level of educational attainment, as percentages, 2015

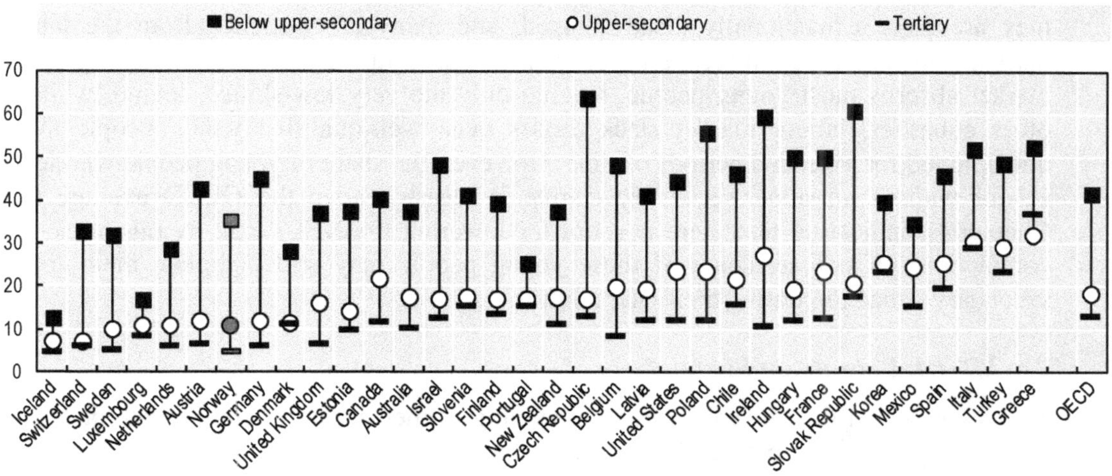

Panel B: Breakdown of NEETs (15 to 29 years) by educational attainment and activity status, as percentages, 2015

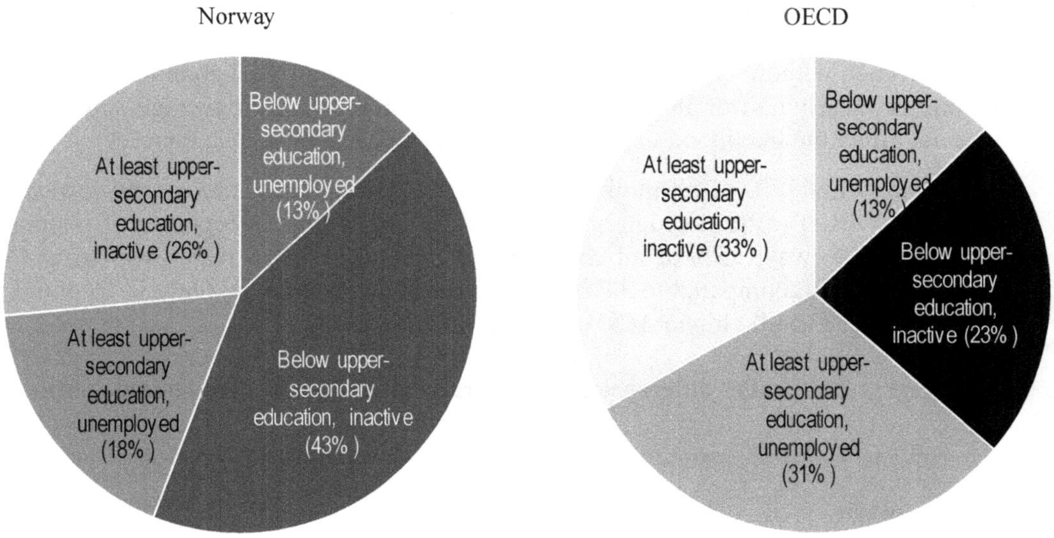

Note: Data are for 2015 except for Japan (2014) and Australia, Germany, Israel, Korea, Mexico, and New Zealand (all 2013). Countries in Panel A are sorted by the overall NEET rate in ascending order. In Panel B, the OECD average does not include Australia, Germany, Israel, Korea and Mexico.

Countries in Panel A are ranked by the NEET rate of 25-29 year-olds in ascending order.

Source: OECD calculations based on the EU-LFS, national labour force surveys and the OECD Education Database (for Australia, Germany, Israel, Korea and Mexico, https://stats.oecd.org/Index.aspx?datasetcode=EAG_TRANS).

Overall, young people without upper-secondary education account for 56% of all NEETs in Norway compared to only 36% of all NEETs across the OECD on average (Figure 2.1, Panel B). The vast majority of young NEETs without an upper-secondary diploma are inactive – over three-quarters – compared to two-thirds across the OECD. Also upper-secondary graduates are much more likely to be inactive in Norway than in the OECD on average, but four-out-of-ten are looking for work (Figure 2.1, Panel B). The fact that those without upper-secondary education are so much more likely to have withdrawn from the labour market indicates that whatever obstacles are keeping them from looking for work may also have kept them from completing upper-secondary education.

Thus, while the group of NEETs in Norway is small compared to other OECD countries, they are more educationally disadvantaged, and many are detached from the labour market. This could be a direct result of the low NEET rate – in Norway, a strong labour market absorbs most young people, leaving only the very low-skilled behind, while in other countries, labour market slack causes even well-qualified young people to be unemployed for extended periods of time. However, the share of young people who leave school without an upper-secondary degree is clearly above the OECD average (see Chapter 4), indicating that there is room for lowering the NEET rate by raising school completion. Of course, some of these young people may still complete their upper-secondary education during their later adult life.

2.1.2. NEET status and gender

Norway is one of the few countries where young women are not more likely to be NEET than young men.[1] Across the OECD on average, the NEET rate among young women was five percentage points higher than among young men in 2015 – that is, women are 40% more likely to be NEET.

Care responsibilities are the driver of these gender differences. Across the OECD on average, NEET rates for young people without children do not differ by gender (indeed, young women without children are slightly *less* likely to be NEET than their male peers). In contrast, nearly half of all young mothers are NEET, while on average, having a child does not affect the likelihood of young men to be NEET (Figure 2.2, Panel A).

In Norway, only 17% of all mothers aged 15 to 29 are NEET, the second-lowest share across the OECD (after Sweden at 9%). This reflects a high acceptance of institutional childcare in Norway: 55% of all children under the age of two were enrolled in formal childcare in 2014, compared to 33% across the OECD on average. Only in Denmark was enrolment significantly higher (65%, (OECD, 2017[2])).

Figure 2.2. Gender differences in NEET rates are driven by care responsibilities

Panel A. NEET rates of 15-29 year-olds by gender and presence of own child in the household, as percentages, 2015

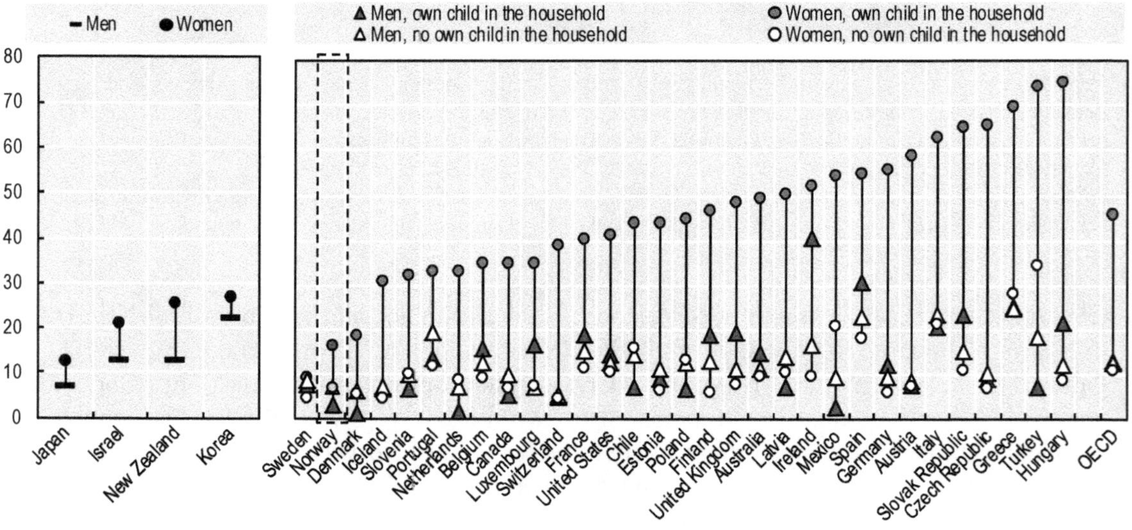

Panel B. Breakdown of 15-29 year-old NEETs by activity status, Norway and OECD average, 2015

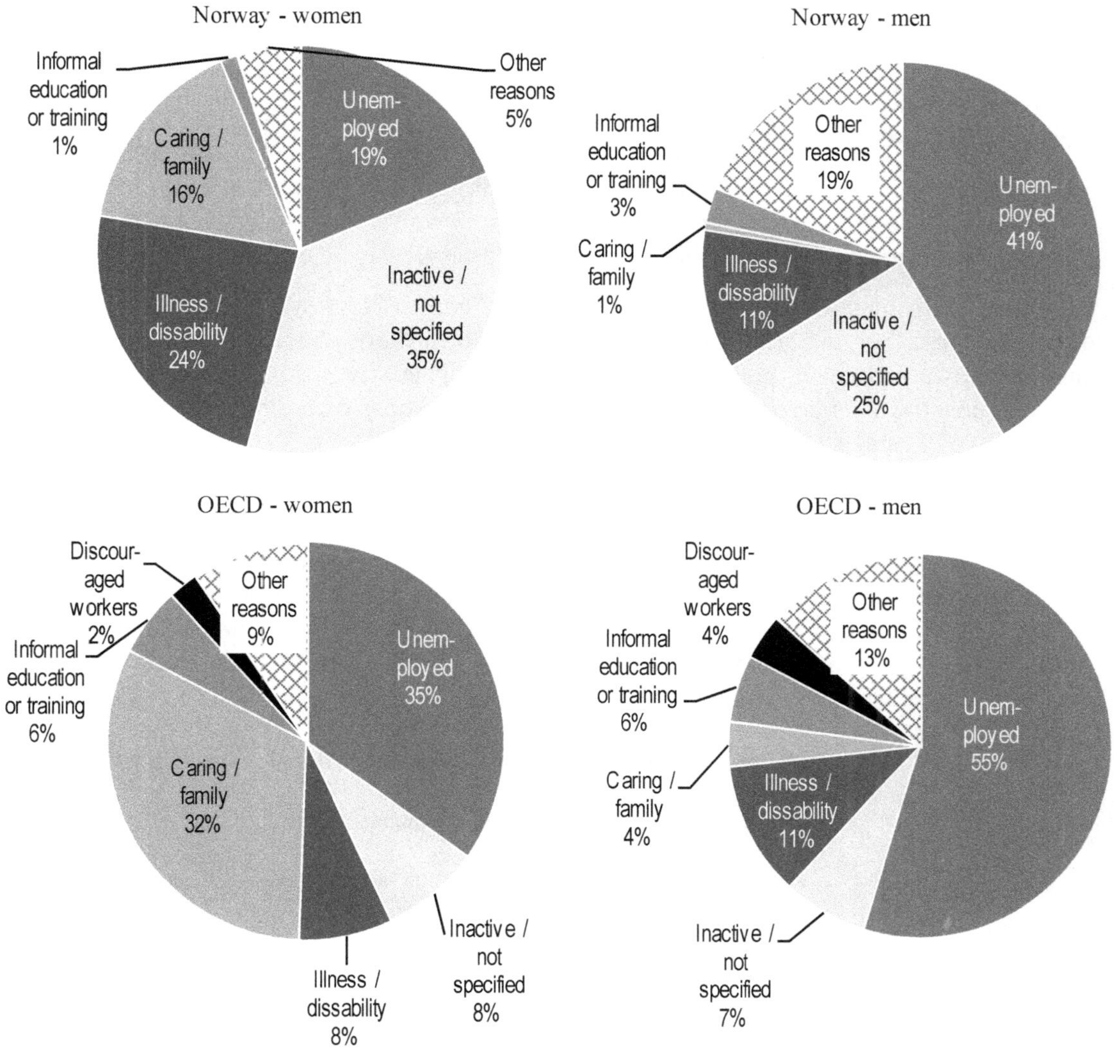

Note: No data on the presence of own child in the household are available for Israel, Japan, Korea and New Zealand. Data on Canada are for 2011 and for Australia, Germany, Korea, Mexico and Switzerland for 2014. On the left-hand side of Panel A, countries are ordered by the NEET rate of young women in ascending order, on the right-hand side of Panel A, countries are ordered by the NEET rate of women with at least one own child in the household in ascending order. In Panel B, the OECD average excludes Australia, Germany, Israel, Japan, Korea, Mexico and New Zealand.

Source: Panel A: OECD Education Database 2016 (Australia, Israel, Japan, Korea, and New Zealand https://stats.oecd.org/Index.aspx?datasetcode=EAG_TRANS), OECD calculations based on national household surveys; Panel B: OECD calculations based on national labour force surveys.

Young men with children are *less* likely to be NEET in Norway than their childless peers (7 vs. 3%), presumably because they help to support their family through employment, and because young men with health or other difficulties that impede their education or employment are also less likely to have a family.

While overall young men and women are equally likely to be NEET in Norway, women are substantially less likely to be *unemployed* than men – only one-in-five NEET women in 2015, compared to one-in-three men (Figure 2.2, Panel B). This is partly because of care responsibilities – 16% of all NEET women state that they are neither working nor looking for a job because of caring or family responsibilities, compared to below 1% for men (Figure 2.2, Panel B) – but mainly because they are more likely to report health problems. Nearly a quarter of all NEET women report an illness or disability as the reason for their inactivity, compared to 11% among Norwegian NEET men and just 8% of all women in the OECD on average. The share of young people who receive incapacity-related benefits is among the highest in the OECD, see Chapter 3.

NEET men are substantially less likely to be unemployed than their peers in other OECD countries, and the share of discouraged workers – who would like to work but have given up their search for employment – is negligible in Norway.

It is also worth mentioning that the NEET gender gap in Norway closed over the last decade because the young men's NEET rate adjusted upwards to that of young women: among Norwegian men, both unemployment and inactivity rose since 2007, while women's inactivity only rose somewhat (against the backdrop of falling inactivity across the OECD on average, see Figure 2.A1.1).

2.1.3. NEET status and migration

Young people born outside of Norway are more than twice as likely to be NEET as their Norwegian-born peers (16 vs 7.5%, Figure 2.3). Across the OECD on average, young people born abroad are 1.5 times as likely to be NEET as native-born youth (Figure 2.3) – a smaller cleavage than in Norway, which however must be seen in the context of very low overall NEET rates, especially among women.

Figure 2.3. Young people born outside of Norway are more likely to be NEET

NEETs as a percentage of all 15-29 year-olds, by migrant status, 2015

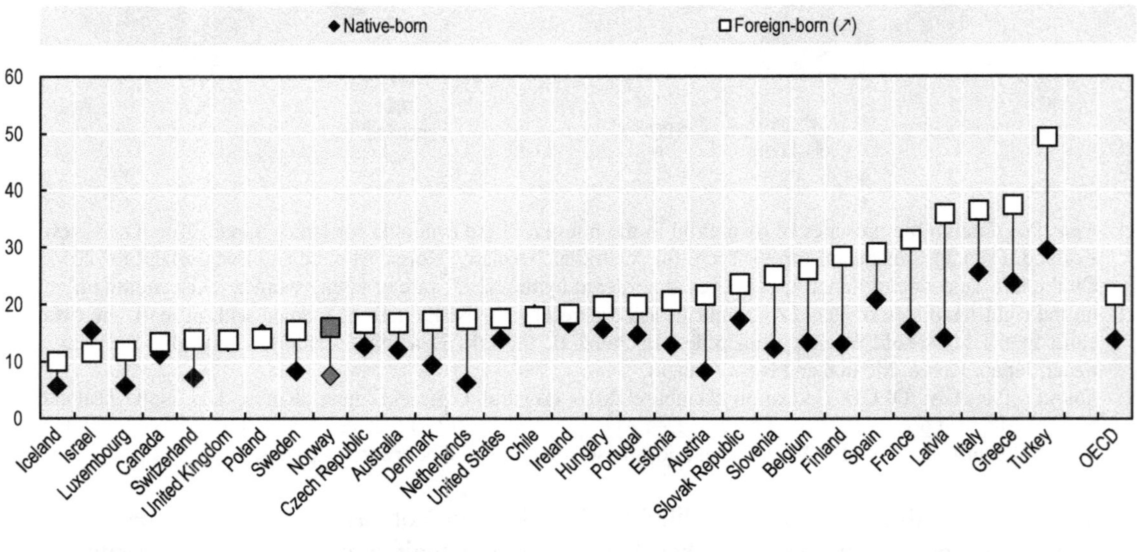

Note: "Foreign-born" includes young people born outside of Norway to Norwegian parents. No data are available on Germany, Japan, Korea and Mexico and New Zealand. Data for Canada refer to 2011.
Source: OECD calculations based on national labour force surveys.

Young migrants can face a variety of obstacles to education and employment – recent arrivals need time to settle in, a lack of language skills makes taking up employment and education more difficult, while foreign qualifications are often not readily recognised. They often have to accept temporary or atypical contracts (Friberg, 2017[3]), which make them more prone to experience bouts of unemployment; and especially those from low-income countries are over-represented in firms that go through mass-layoffs or shut down (Bratsberg, Raaum and Røed, 2017[4]). Young migrants also have lower levels of education than their native-born peers (OECD, 2015[5]), which is a key cause of NEET status (see above). Section 2.2 discusses the role of education in the foreign- / native-born NEET gap in more detail.

Foreign workers are also more vulnerable during recessions. As newcomers to the local labour market, they have lower average tenure, exposing them to "last-in-first-out" layoff policies. They are also more likely to work in industries that are especially exposed to economic fluctuations, such as construction, shipbuilding and fishing, as well as hospitality and transport (Friberg, 2017[3]). Even at the industry level, they are overrepresented in firms that failed during 2009/10 economic downturn (Bratsberg, Raaum and Røed, 2017[4]). During the 2009/10 economic downturn, male immigrants in Norway were nearly twice as likely to lose their job or experience a significant drop in earnings as natives in the same industry, with the same tenure and the same wage level (Bratsberg, Raaum and Røed, 2014[6]).

Young immigrants are particularly at risk, as they are labour market outsiders both because of their migration status and their youth. In Norway, the NEET rate of foreign-born youth increased by three percentage points between 2008 and 2014, compared to just one percentage point for young people born in Norway (Figure 2.4, Panel A).[2]

This increase was entirely driven by young refugees – their NEET rate increased from 24% in 2008, before the onset of the crisis, to 37% in 2014. The NEET rate among young immigrants who are not refugees remained stable during this period (Figure 2.4, Panel A).[3] One reason for this could be that young immigrants who came to Norway to work and lost their jobs during the 2009/10 economic downturn left instead of remaining unemployed, while refugees do not have this option. Refugees have indeed been shown to be less likely to leave Norway than labour migrants (Kornstad, Skjerpen and Stambøl, 2017[7]); however, the size of this effect seems too small to explain this stark divergence in NEET rates.

Instead, it is more plausible that young refugees were particularly vulnerable in a difficult labour market situation. Indeed, Bratsberg et al. (2017[4]) show that not only were immigrants from low-income countries laid off at greater rates during the recession, they were also less successful at finding new work. The authors estimate that between one-third and one-half of the native-migrant employment gap is explained by the unequal effects of involuntary job loss and labour market reintegration.

Young people who came to Norway as children do significantly better than those who came in late adolescence and young adulthood. Those who arrived in Norway under the age of 16 are only 30% more likely to be NEET compared to all young people – especially young women have NEET rates that are hardly distinguishable from the national average. The high NEET risk of young people born abroad is mainly driven by those who arrived over the age of 16 – over two-thirds of all young people born abroad. This result is probably not caused by a higher share of refugees in this group.[4] Young women who arrived as young adults are also significantly more likely to be NEET than men, which drives the aggregate gender gap in NEET rates among the foreign-born (Figure 2.4, Panel B).

Those who immigrated at younger ages are much more likely to undertake some education in Norway, which lowers their probability to become NEET directly while strongly increasing labour market attachment: holding age at migration and local labour market characteristics constant, male refugees who completed their upper-secondary degree in Norway have a 14 percentage-point higher employment rate than those who hold a similar degree from abroad; for women, this difference is a staggering 27 percentage points (Bratsberg, Raaum and Røed, 2017[8]). While this effect is weaker for migrants who came to Norway to join their family, or for those from the new EU member states, completing an upper-secondary degree in Norway still adds around six to 15 percentage points to their average employment rates.

Figure 2.4. Young people who came to Norway as refugees are especially at-risk

Panel A. NEET rates of 15-29 year-olds, by country of origin/reason for immigration, as a percentage, 2008-14

Panel B. NEET rates of 15-29 year-olds born outside of Norway, by age at migration and gender, as a percentage, 2014

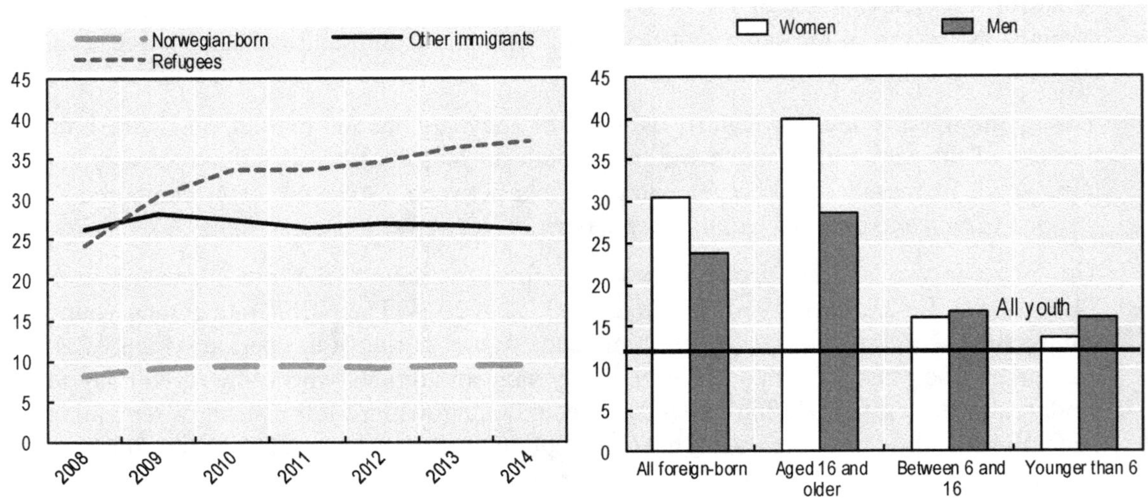

Note: "Foreign-born" includes young people born outside of Norway to Norwegian parents.
Source: Norwegian administrative data prepared for the OECD by SSB.

Refugees, and women who come to Norway to be reunited with family, also significantly benefit from completing an educational degree in Norway that is *below* their highest educational attainment (earned abroad). Bratsberg et al (2017[8]) also find that arriving young (aged 18 to 24 compared to aged 25 to 30) has a direct positive effect on the likelihood of being employed (holding the level and country of education, gender and local characteristics constant), although it is less consistent across reason for migration and gender. They only look at migrants who came to Norway as adults, however.

Looking at NEET rates by country of origin further supports the notion that particularly those who come to Norway as refugees, or to be reunited with family members, struggle to gain a foothold on the labour market. Nearly half of all young people born in Africa are NEET, compared to only about one-fifth of those born in Europe (Figure 2.5). In 2016, over 90% of all new African immigrants to Norway came as refugees, or to join their families, whereas European immigrants mostly came to Norway to work or study (SSB, 2017[9]).

The gender gap in NEET rates among young people born abroad seems to be mainly driven by those born in Asia – over one-third of Asian-born young women are NEET, compared to just 20% of young men. This is likely caused by a traditional gendered division of labour, as, depending on the precise country of origin, women born in Asia are both less likely to work and *less* likely to receive government benefits than other comparable women (Bratsberg, Raaum and Røed, 2017[8]). In addition, immigrant women generally are more likely to not participate to the labour force when they have kids under the age of six (OECD, 2015[10]). Also, women born in Europe have a somewhat higher NEET rate, as do women who come from countries in the residual "rest of the world" category, but they only account for 6% of young people born abroad.

Figure 2.5. Also the children of migrants are more likely to be NEET

NEET rates of young people aged 15-29 who were born abroad or have at least one parent who was born abroad, by gender and country of (parental) origin, in percent, 2014.

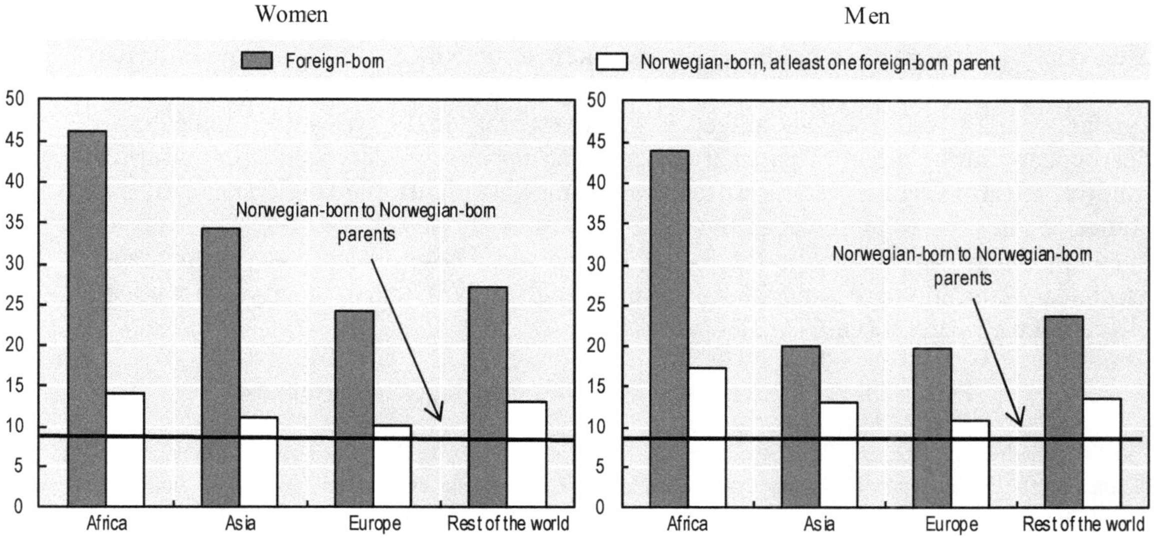

Note: "Foreign-born" includes young people born outside of Norway to Norwegian parents.
Source: Norwegian administrative data prepared for the OECD by SSB.

Young people with a migrant background – who were born in Norway, but have at least one parent who was born abroad – are on average over 30% more likely to be NEET than their peers with two Norwegian parents. These gaps depend on their parents' country of origin: Those whose parent(s) was (were) from Europe are only 16% more likely to be NEET than those with two Norwegian-born parents. This is connected to the fact that three-quarters of young people born to mixed couples have a European parent, while only one-fifth of those with two foreign-born parents do.[5] Mixed households are much more likely to speak Norwegian at home, which means that their children are not at the same disadvantage as children of two foreign-born parents (OECD, 2015[5]).

Young women with migrant background have somewhat better outcomes than young men, particularly those with at least one parent from Africa or Asia. Young men, especially those whose parent(s) come from African or Asian countries, struggle a bit more – those with an African background are 88% and those with an Asian background about 44% more likely to be NEET than their peers with Norwegian-born parents. (Figure 2.5)

Given that these differences are so gender-specific, it seems unlikely that they are due to immigrants clustering in locations with weak local labour markets, or that there are cultural factors at work. Instead, boys from migrant – or socio-economically disadvantaged backgrounds more generally – might struggle more in the Norwegian education system than girls. See Chapter 4 for a detailed discussion of early school leaving in Norway.[6]

2.1.4. NEET status and socio-economic background

Disadvantage is often transferred from parents to children. This intergenerational link has been examined extensively regarding educational attainment and poverty as well as a wide range as other factors, such as divorce (Diekman and Schidheiny, 2013[11]) or values (Min, Silverstein and Lendon, 2012[12]). Parents' socio-economic status is a strong predictor of their children's, see e.g. Clark (2014[13]).

Also in Norway, children born into low socio-economic backgrounds face a higher risk of becoming NEET in their youth. Young people whose mother did not have an upper-secondary education are more than twice as likely to be NEET as the children of tertiary educated mothers (Figure 2.6, Panel A; looking at fathers' instead of mothers' education yields similar results). This effect is strongest for 15-19 year-olds, indicating a particularly strong effect of parental education on upper-secondary school drop-out (not shown, see also Chapter 4). This difference is somewhat higher than in Germany, the only other country for which comparative data are available. Across the OECD on average, young people who still live in the parental home and whose parents have below upper-secondary education are around 80% more likely to be NEET than other youth who still live with their parents (OECD, 2016[1]).

Figure 2.6. NEETs often come from disadvantaged backgrounds

Panel A: Relative risk of being NEET, by educational attainment of the mother when the young person was 16, 16-29 year-olds, Germany and Norway, 2014

Panel B: Relative risk of being NEET, by labour market status of the father when the young person was 16, 16-29 year-olds, Germany and Norway, 2014

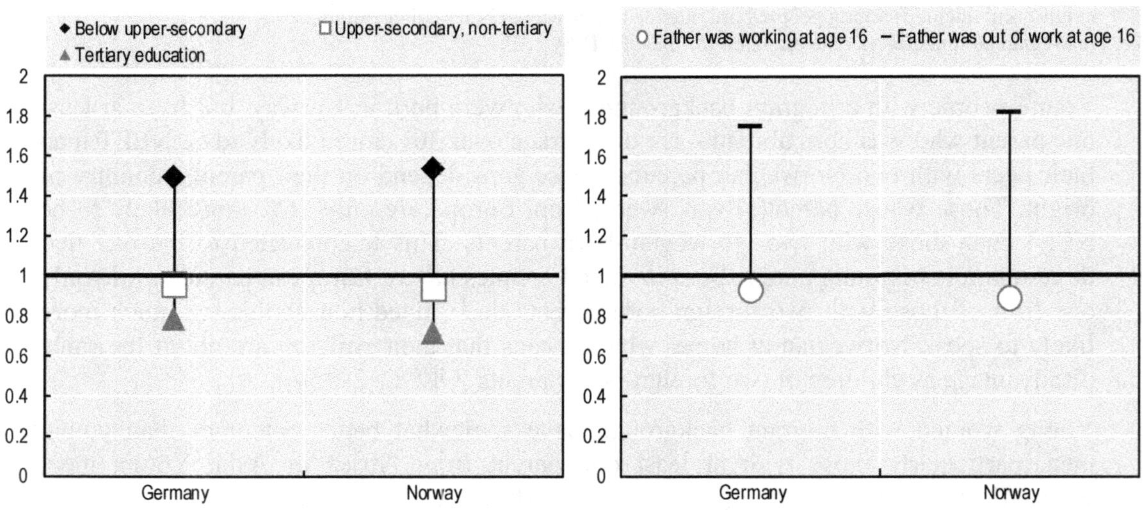

Note: The NEET rate of all 16-29 year-olds is normalised to one. Young people without information on parental education and labour market status are dropped from the analysis (around 15% of the population in Norway, and 14% of the sample in Germany).
Source: Norwegian administrative data prepared for the OECD by SSB and OECD calculations based on the German SOEP.

Similarly, having grown-up in a household with parents who were not gainfully employed puts young people at a disadvantage – those whose father was not working when they were 16 years old are twice as likely to be NEET as those whose father was working, a somewhat bigger cleavage than in Germany (Figure 2.6, Panel B).

Coming from a disadvantaged background can increase the chances of becoming NEET directly – e.g. low-educated parents might struggle to help their children with schoolwork, poverty or overcrowding can impede effective learning, non-working parents lack professional networks to help their children into jobs. Children from disadvantaged backgrounds may also lack desirable social skills that are essential in the modern workplace. International experience shows that intensive interventions in early childhood can be effective in overcoming this advantage – see, e.g. Lee (2008[14]) and Heckman (2008[15]) for the United States. While intervening early on is preferable, also specialised interventions for adolescents from underprivileged backgrounds can improve social skills and economic outcomes, see e.g. Kautz et al. (2014[16]).

2.1.5. Well-being and NEETs' attitudes

Instead of profiling NEETs according to their observable characteristics, this section looks directly at how NEETs are doing – whether they are satisfied with the lives they lead, and how connected they feel to the society and political system that surrounds them. Low life satisfaction and a sense of weariness and disconnection add additional urgency to the NEET phenomenon as a policy problem, while mistrust in others and political institutions can hamper the success of policy interventions for young NEETs.[7]

NEETs in Norway report significantly lower life satisfaction than other young people, and are much more likely to suffer from poor mental health indicated by self-reported anxiety and depression. Four-out-of-ten NEETs reported low life satisfaction, a share that is four times higher than among young people who study or work – a much bigger gap than in the EU on average, where NEETs are only twice as likely to be unsatisfied with their lives as other young people (Figure 2.7, Panel A). This gap emerges because overall, life satisfaction among young people in Norway is higher than across the EU on average, while it is lower than average among NEETs.

Norwegian NEETs are nearly six times more likely to feel depressed, and more than four times more likely to feel nervous than other young people. In contrast, across the EU on average, frequent feelings of depression and nervousness are only twice as prevalent among NEETs as among the general youth population (Figure 2.7, Panel B). Also the shares of NEETs relative to other youth who report suffering from poor health more generally and health limitations in their daily lives is high in Norway (OECD, 2016[1]).

The data do not allow to infer causality – whether young people with poor mental health become NEET, or whether their mental health suffers because they are inactive or unemployed. But the fact that these risks are so much higher than across the EU on average indicates that mental health problems are the cause, rather than the consequence of NEET status in Norway: given the obstacle that mental health issues pose to education and employment, those who suffer from them make up a larger share of a comparatively small NEET population. Indeed, the gap in unemployment between those who do and those who do not suffer from mental disorders is highest in Norway, and a high share of the jobless receive sickness or disability supports, indicating that those with mental health problems are largely excluded from a well-performing labour market (OECD, 2013[17]). Chapter 3 discusses receipt on incapacity-related benefit among young people in Norway in depth.

Figure 2.7. NEETs are particularly unhappy in Norway

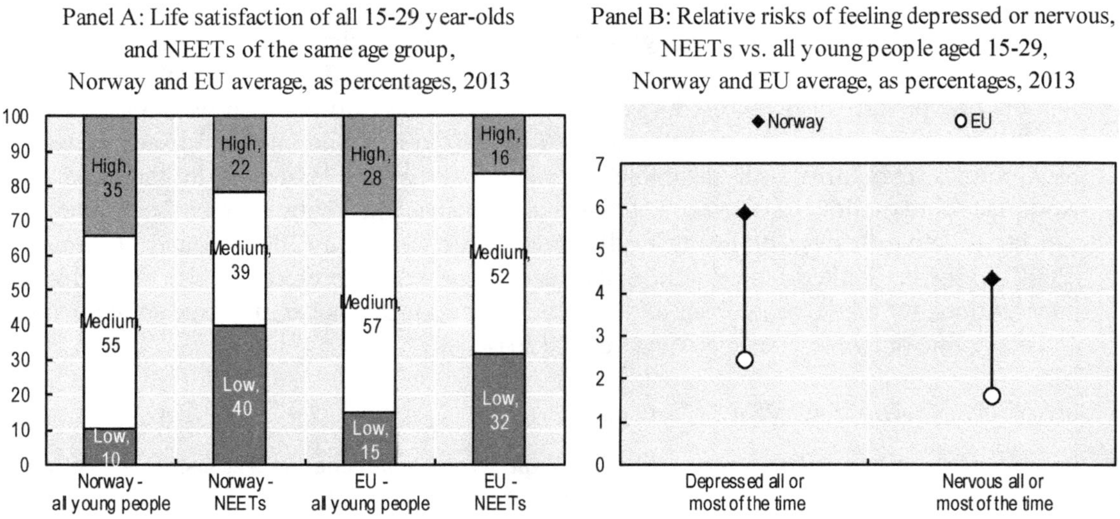

Note: The question about life satisfaction elicits a response from 0 (not at all satisfied) to 10 (completely satisfied). "Low satisfaction" combines answers from 0-5, medium from 6-8 and high satisfaction 9-10. The question on depression is "Have you been feeling downhearted or depressed in the last four weeks?" – the risk ratio is the share of NEETs who answered "all or most of the time" relative to the share of all young people. The question on nervousness is "have you been feeling very nervous in the last for weeks", and the risk ratio is constructed in the same way. The EU average excludes Germany.
Source: OECD calculations based on the 2013 ad-hoc module of the EU-SILC.

NEETs have less confidence in the political system than other young people, especially in Norway, where trust in public institutions is generally high (Figure 2.8). NEETs are nearly twice as likely to have little or no trust in the political system as the general youth population – 74% of NEETs compared to just 39% of all young people. Low trust in political institutions can make young NEETs reluctant to engage with public agencies and participate in support programmes; especially those who are furthest from the labour market and in the most need for interventions.

This "trust gap" is highest in Norway, Denmark and Sweden, because trust in the political system in these countries is generally high among young people – about half of the youth population has at least some trust in the political system. In countries such as Spain, Slovenia or Portugal, where over 90% of all young people report having little to no trust in the political system, there is no room for differences between NEETs and other young people.

Figure 2.8. Mistrust in the political system is widespread among NEETs

Percentage of NEETs and all 15-29 year-olds who have little or no trust in the political system, 2013

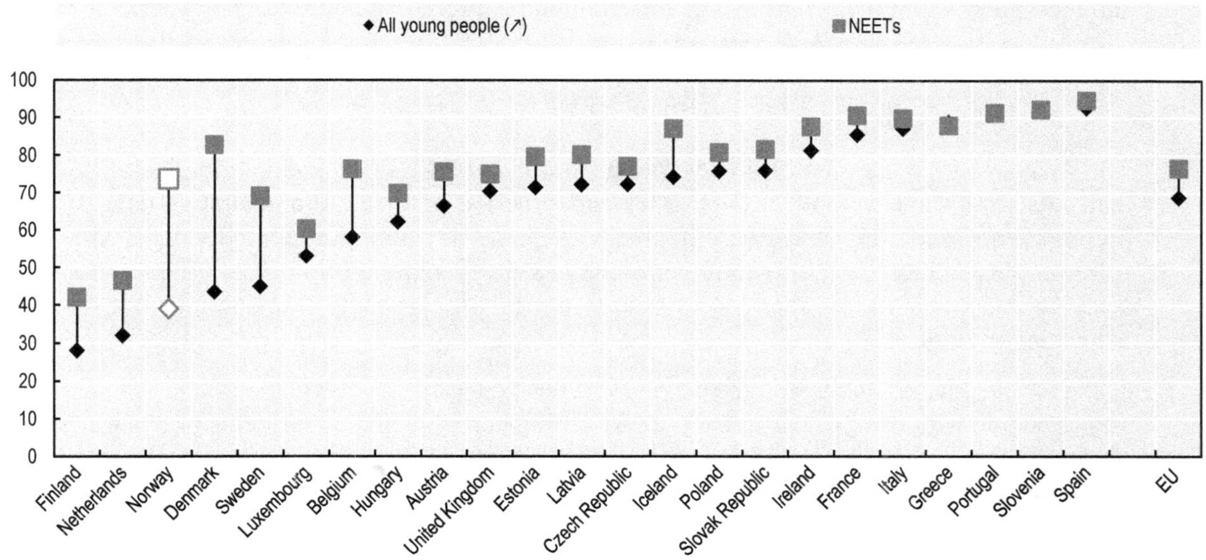

Note: The question elicits a response from 0 ("no trust at all") to 10 ("complete trust"). Little to no trust in the political system encompasses answers from 0 to 5. Countries are ordered by the share of young people who report little to no trust in the political system in ascending order. The EU average excludes Germany.
Source: OECD calculations based on the 2013 ad-hoc module of the EU-SILC.

2.2. Time patterns of NEET status

So far, this chapter has profiled young people who were NEETs *at a particular point* in time without considering *how long* they remain so. Being NEET for a short time period does not necessarily indicate problems with labour market integration – young people can go through short bouts of inactivity or unemployment after completing their education, as it can take time to find employment, and the careers of many start out unstable. Longer stretches out of education and employment are much more problematic, however: long-term NEETs do not build up skills, work experience and professional networks in the same way as their peers do, and they may suffer long-lasting "scarring" effects that negatively affect their future employment opportunities (Schmillen and Umkehrer, 2013[18]; Möller and Umkehrer, 2015[19]) and earnings (Umkehrer, 2015[20]).

This section extends and complements the earlier *cross-sectional* analysis – which gave a snapshot picture of NEETs in Norway at one point in time – by presenting evidence on time patterns of NEET status. It provides insights on the share of young people in Norway who are NEET *at some point* during their transition from school to work, and characterises those who remain NEET for longer. It also provides insights into the timing of NEET periods – that is, at which points in their school-to-work transition young people are most likely to become NEET.

The analysis is based on administrative data on *all* 15-year-olds who were residents of Norway on 31 December 2005 – including those who were born in Norway in 1990 and those born elsewhere who immigrated to Norway before the age of 16. The analysis follows this cohort until 31 December 2013 when they are 23 years old, assigning each month a status of NEET or non-NEET. The NEET status is defined as a residual category of young people who are neither in education nor have a job in a given month, or income from self-employment in a given year (see Box 2.1 for a detailed description of this dataset). Students are defined as being in education (that is, non-NEET) during the summer months if they are enrolled in education in the preceding and following year.[8]

Box 2.1. Time patterns of NEET status – methodology

The analysis of the duration of time young people spend NEET requires longitudinal data that tracks the same individual over an extended period of time. Administrative data is preferable for such an analysis as it precludes panel attrition (i.e. all individuals are followed throughout the observation period, unless they emigrate or die) and offers more accurate data, as survey respondents often do not report especially short periods out of education or work.

This section is based on data on the entire 1990 birth cohort in Norway, specifically on all young people who were *i)* 15 years old on 31 December 2005 and *ii)* residents of Norway on *both* 1 January 2006 and 31 December 2013. That is, young people who emigrated before the age of 16 are part of the analysis, but those who emigrated after the age of 16, as well as those who emigrated or died before the age of 24 are not.

This cohort is followed from the age of 16 until the age of 24. Information on educational enrolment is linked from the National Education Database (NUDB); students are considered to be in education over the summer holiday if they are in education the year before and the year after, foreign study periods are covered if they are supported by the Norwegian State Educational Loan Fund (*Lånekassen*).[1] Monthly data on employment is linked from the Social Security Database (*FD-Trygd*), which contains all registered employment episodes in Norway. A person is considered employed – that is non-NEET – in any entire month where they have at least one job, even if the job is of a shorter duration. Data on self-employment is linked from annual tax return data, which cannot be broken down per month, so any individual who has income from self-employment in a given calendar year is defined as non-NEET for that year. This is a very small share of the youth population, however, increasing from 0.1% at the beginning of the observation period to 1.4% in late 2013 when the observed cohort is 23 years old. Also information on educational attainment is linked from the NUDB and measured once in October 2013, i.e. towards the end of the observation period; it is missing for under 1% of this cohort.

Source: Arve Hetland (2016): "Cohort Analysis. Documentation for the cohort analysis component of the OECD data table delivery", Statistics Norway, Oslo.

1. The National Education database only records non-compulsory schooling (i.e. it starts at the Upper-secondary level). All individuals are assumed to remain in education until the end of their compulsory schooling, that is, are set to be non-NEET for the first six months of the year 2006.

More than two-thirds of this cohort spent at least some time as NEETs between leaving compulsory school and turning 24. Half of them – 35% of all youth – were NEETs for under a year in total, and a further 35 % were NEETs for at least 13 months (Figure 2.9).

Young men are much more likely to be long-term NEETs than young women – 40% are NEET for at least 13 months taken together over the eight-year period the data follows them, compared to just 30% of women. More than one-third of women were never NEET between the ages of 16 and 24, compared to just 28% of young men (Figure 2.9).

Figure 2.9. The majority of young people spend some time as NEETs, and men are much more likely to be long-term NEETs

Young people's total time spent as NEETs between the ages of 16 and 24 (1990 birth cohort, 2006-13)

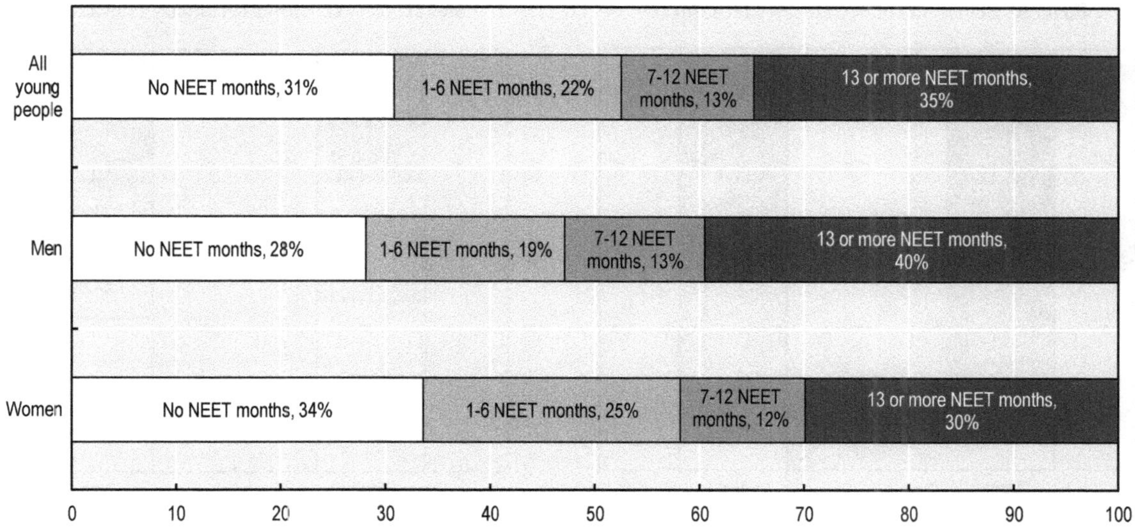

Source: OECD calculations based on register data delivered by SSB.

Gender differences in long term-NEET status are mainly driven by the educational pathways of young people: those who have not graduated from upper-secondary school at the age of 23 – four years after the typical age of upper-secondary graduation – spend much more time as NEETs, *and* are more likely to be male. One-quarter of the 1990 birth cohort did not graduate from upper-secondary school by the age of 23, 28% of 23-year-old men compared to 21% of women; a high share in international comparison (see Chapter 4).

Those who do not graduate from upper-secondary school throughout the observation period are over three times as likely to be long-term NEETs: over 70% spend more than 13 months NEET, compared to only one-fifth of upper-secondary graduates. Reversely, only 8% of early school leavers were never NEET between the ages of 16 and 23, compared to more than a third of upper-secondary graduates (Figure 2.10).

For early school leavers, these shares are virtually identical for men and women (Figure 2.10, Panel A). Among upper-secondary graduates, some gender differences emerge: men are somewhat more likely to spend some time as NEETs, and to remain NEET for longer (Figure 2.10, Panel B). The timing of NEET periods indicates that young men take longer to find a job after upper-secondary school, and/or that they take more time off before starting further education, see below.

These substantial periods out of employment and education are not the result of a build-up of short bouts of inactivity or unemployment at the transition from school to work, or between (temporary) jobs. Only 5% of this cohort had multiple short NEET spells (below three months). In contrast, nearly half of all young men, and over a third of all young women, had at least one NEET stretch of seven months or longer before reaching the age of 24, and a further 10% were NEET for four to six months at least once (Figure 2.A2.1).

Figure 2.10. The majority of early school leavers become long-term NEETs

Cohort of 16 year-olds in 2006, by educational attainment at 23, gender and total time spent as NEETs before reaching the age of 24, in percentages

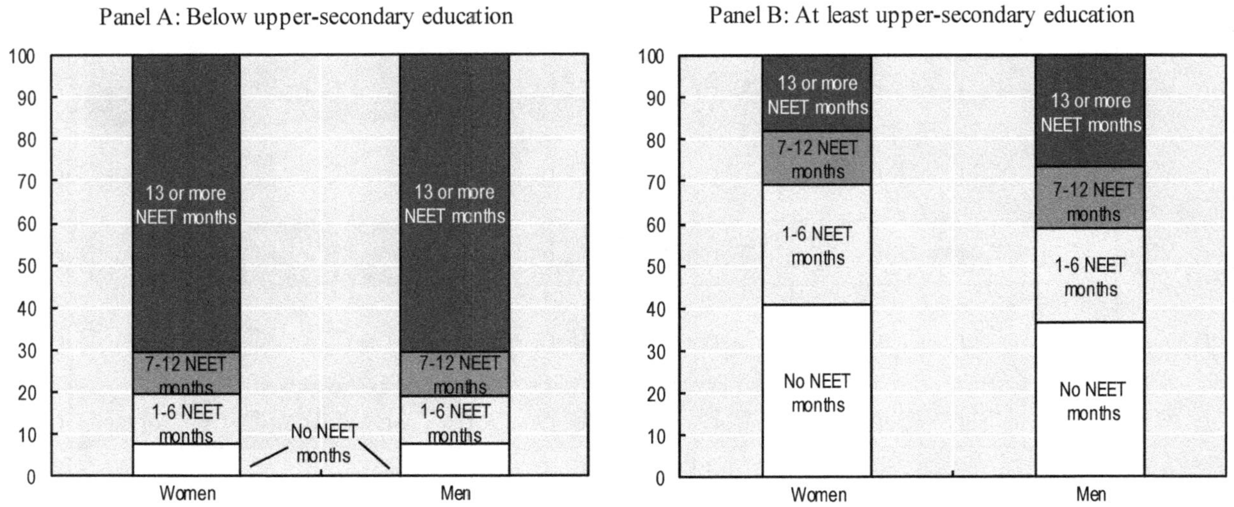

Source: OECD calculations based on register data delivered by SSB.

The timing of NEET periods between the age of 16 and 23 is strongly determined by upper-secondary school graduation. All young people are assumed to be in education for the first six months of 2006, until the end of compulsory school. Among those young people who have not graduated from upper-secondary school by age 23, the share of youth who are not NEET at any time during the year already starts falling at age 16 (Figure 2.11, Panel A). A significant share of young people with short and medium-length NEET spells indicates young people dropping out of school during the year. However, for many of them, unemployment or inactivity becomes persistent: the share of short and medium term spells gives way to longer NEET spells after the age of 19. At age 21, when most of these young people have left upper-secondary school, only about 40% are non-NEET for the entire year, and the same share are NEETs for seven months or more.

Towards the end of the observation period, this trend tails off, and the share of young people who are not NEET over the entire year shows an upward trend. The share of long-term NEETs remains stable, however. NEET patterns for men and women are almost identical until age twenty, when the share of men who are non-NEET grows more quickly than among young women. This could be driven by the fact that well-paying jobs that do not require upper-secondary education, such as construction, are more likely to be typically male (Annex Figure 2.A3.2, Panel A).

The pattern differs greatly for young people who are upper-secondary graduates at age 23. Most of them are in school until they are 19 years old, at which point about one-fifth experience a NEET spell of short or medium duration. These are most likely periods of job search upon labour market entry. At age 20, about one-in-ten graduates experience a long NEET spell; however, these seem to be transitional, and by the end of the observation period, only 6% of upper-secondary graduates are long-term NEETs.

Figure 2.11 Timing of NEET spells is determined by upper-secondary school graduation

Timing of NEET spells by age, in percentages of the cohort of 16-year-olds in 2006, by educational attainment at 23

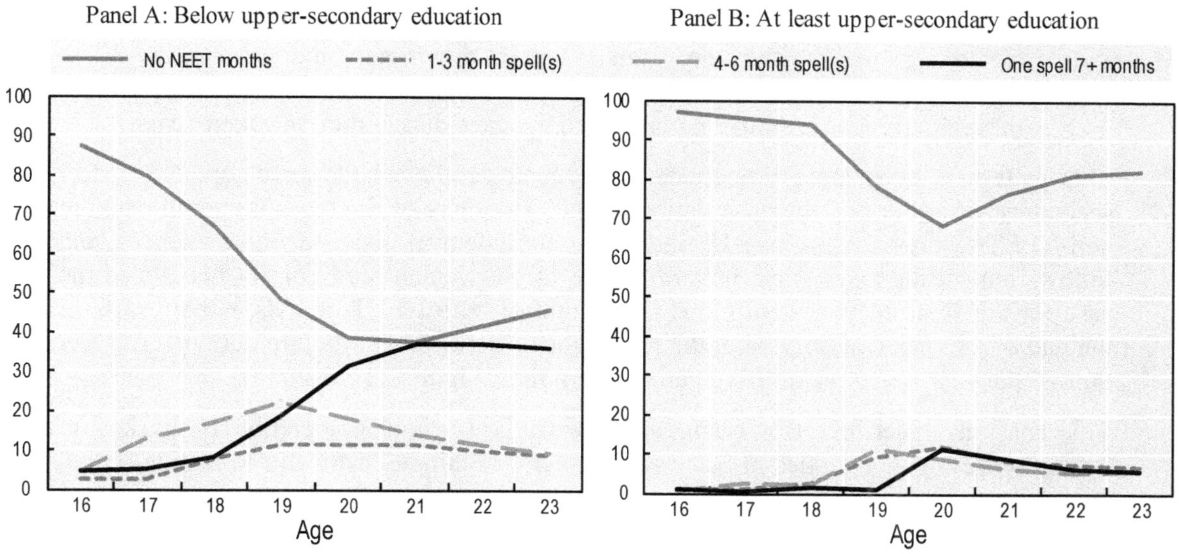

Note: The spell lengths refer to spells *during the calendar year*, that is, they are right- and left-censored.
Source: OECD calculations based on register data delivered by SSB.

Female upper-secondary graduates experience a smoother labour market transition than their male peers: a higher share directly transition from school to work; and at around 21, the share of male upper-secondary graduates who are long-term NEETs is nearly twice as high as the share among their female peers (Figure 2.A2.2, Panel B). This could reflect more young men than women taking extended "breaks" before embarking on work or further study: at the end of the observation period, the share of men and women who experience NEET spells reverts back to being almost identical.

Young people who were born abroad are almost 50% more likely to be long-term NEETs than their Norwegian-born peers: half of them are NEET for 13 or more months between the ages of 16 and 23, compared to a third of Norwegian-born youth (Figure 2.12, Panel A). By construction, this cohort only includes foreign-born young people who came to Norway before the age of 16.

While in the snapshot analysis of Section 2.1, young migrants who came as children and young adolescents only had a slightly elevated NEET rate, the longitudinal analysis reveals that they are more likely to be long-term NEETs. This difference is driven by two factors:

1. Young people born abroad are more likely to reach the age of 24 without an upper-secondary degree: 39% compared to 24% among their Norwegian-born peers. This difference explains about 60% of the Norwegian-foreign-born gap in long-term NEET rates.
2. Foreign-born youth are also more likely to be long-term NEETs holding education constant. However, the timing of these additional periods indicates that this might be driven by recent arrivals not having started upper-secondary school yet. Among those who have at most compulsory education at age 23, 90% of Norwegian-born youth are non-NEET for the entire calendar year at age 16 (Figure 2.12, Panel B) – this is because most compulsory graduates *start* upper-

secondary school in Norway (see Chapter 4). This share is a lot lower for foreign-born youth – at age 16, many are long-term NEETs, but this share drops in the next year at the expense of short- and medium-term NEET spells, indicating that they start school at the beginning of the academic year. By age 18 the share of young people who are non-NEET during the entire year is practically identical for the two groups, so they drop out at school at virtually the same rates. While Norwegian-born youth seem to have higher employment rates in their early 20s, these differences are small compared to the gaps during their late teen years.

This pattern is even more pronounced for young people who have completed upper-secondary school during the observation period. The share of foreign-born youth who are non-NEETs increases until age 18, indicating enrolment in upper-secondary school, and follows almost the exact same pattern as that of Norwegian-born youth (this is also the case for the share of youth with long- or medium-length NEET periods, not shown). At the end of the observation period, the gap in the share of those who are not NEET at any time of the year is very small (five percentage points, Figure 2.12, Panel B).

This analysis underlines that rising upper-secondary school completion is the key to further reducing NEET rates in Norway. Chapter 4 highlights pathways to raising school completion.

Figure 2.12. Young people born abroad are NEET before starting school

Cohort of 16-year-olds in 2006, by place of birth, in percentages

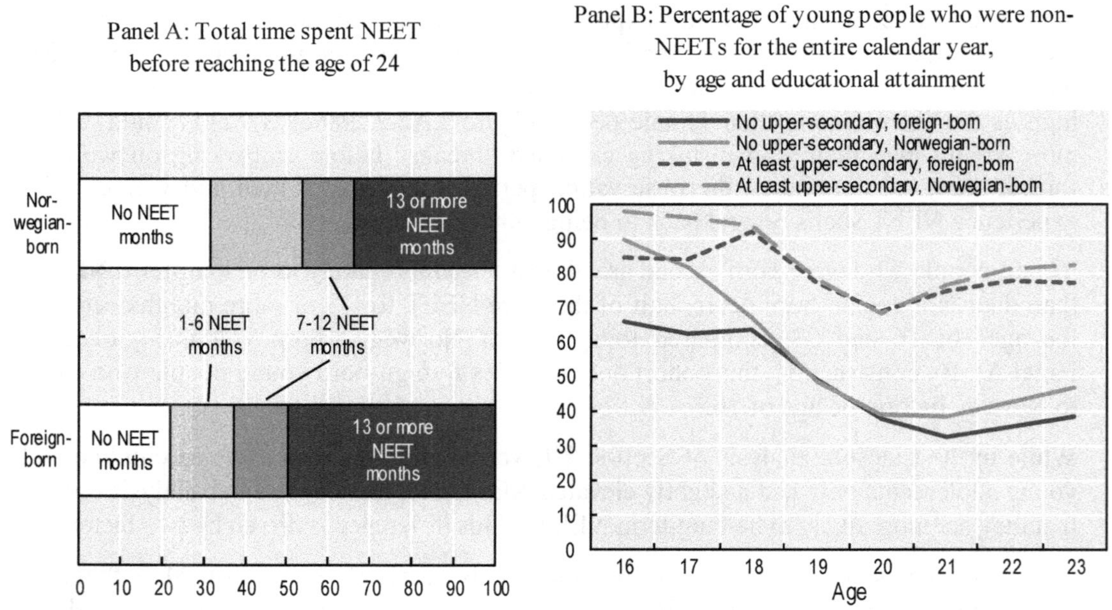

Note: In Panel B, educational attainment is measured at age 23.
Source: OECD calculations based on register data delivered by SSB.

Round-up

Spells of NEET status are generally not an unusual feature of a young person's transition from school into the labour market, and more than two-thirds of all young people in Norway spend at least some time out of school or work between the ages of 16 and 24. But while short NEET spells do not necessarily indicate problems with labour market integration, longer stretches out of education and employment can prevent young people from building up skills, work experience and professional networks and cause lasting "scarring" effects on future employment opportunities and earnings.

The low incidence of NEETs in Norway is associated with a higher concentration among those who are educationally disadvantaged, who come from low socio-economic backgrounds and who suffer from (mental) health problems. Many were not born in Norway, and a high share of them is detached from the labour market:

- *Low education is the most important risk factor*: 56% of NEETs in Norway have not completed upper-secondary education, compared to 36% across the OECD on average. Those without an upper-secondary qualification are seven times more likely to be NEET than university graduates, the largest gap across the OECD. This is concerning in particular as a much greater share of young people in Norway leave school without an upper-secondary degree than in the OECD on average.
- *There is no significant gender NEET gap*: Norway is one of the few OECD countries where young women are not more likely to be out of education or work than young men. Thanks to the widespread availability and acceptance of institutionalised childcare, only 17% of all mothers below the age of 30 are NEET, compared to nearly half across the OECD on average;
- *Immigrants face a much greater risk:* Young people born outside of Norway are more than twice as likely to be NEET as their Norwegian-born peers (16 vs. 7.5%). One reason is that young migrants have lower education levels than their native-born peers. Young migrants' age of arrival however makes an important difference: those who have come to Norway as children do significantly better than those who arrived in late adolescence or early adulthood. In particular, completing at least some education in Norway seems to somewhat protect young immigrants from becoming NEETs later on: young people who arrived in Norway before turning 16 are only 30% more likely to be NEET than Norwegian-borns.
- *(Mental) health problems are widespread:* Norwegian NEETs are nearly six times as likely to feel depressed, and more than four times as likely to feel nervous, than other young people. These risk ratios are much higher than in the EU average, where frequent feelings of depression and nervousness are only twice as prevalent among NEETs as among the general youth population. Also the ratio of NEETs to other young people who report poor self-assessed health is much higher in Norway than in the OECD on average (9 to 1 and 5 to 1, respectively).

NEET status moreover tends to be much more *persistent* for more disadvantaged young people:

- While upper-secondary graduates typically only experience short bouts of unemployment or inactivity upon labour market entry, many upper-secondary drop-outs become NEETs in their teens and remain NEET for longer. Young people who have not graduated from upper-secondary school by age 24 are more than three times as likely to be long-term NEETs: 70% of drop-outs vs. 22% of upper-secondary graduates are NEET for over a year.

- Young people born abroad are 50% more likely to be long-term NEETs than their Norwegian-born peers. More than half of this difference is caused by higher rates of upper-secondary drop-out – the remainder can likely be attributed to the fact that recently arrived young migrants tend to start upper-secondary school at a later age.

Raising upper-secondary school completion is hence essential for lowering the NEET rate in Norway.

Notes

1. Only Nordic countries (Finland, Iceland, Norway and Sweden) show no gender gap in NEET rates (not shown).

2. The effects of the 2007/08 financial crisis hit the Norwegian Labour Market in late 2008 (Bratsberg, Raaum and Røed, 2014[6]), so taking 2008 as a reference point might overstate the effect of the 2009/10 economic downturn, as the labour market was likely overheated in 2008. However, because of time-series breaks in Norwegian administrative data, it is difficult to build consistent pre-2008 time-series.

3. The share of refugees among all immigrants remained constant between 2008 and 2014.

4. Data on reason of migration and age at migration presented in Figure 2.4. is not linked. However, in 2016, less than a third of 18-29 year-old new arrivals came as refugees (the majority came to work or study), whereas 43% of under-17 year-olds did (the remainder to join their families) (SSB, 2017[22]). While stock and flow data cannot be compared, and foreign students are most likely to leave after a couple of years (Bratsberg, Raaum and Røed, 2017[8]), it is unlikely that these fluctuations would change the composition dramatically in the few years people who entered Norway aged 18 or older remain under 30 years old.

5. Shares refer to 15-34 year-olds in 2012, OECD calculations based on admin data prepared by SSB.

6. Unfortunately, there is no information on educational attainment by immigration status in the administrative data, and the Norwegian LFS is not reliable because of non-response bias (see note 2).

7. This section is based on the 2013 EU-SILC ad hoc module on well-being and life satisfaction, which is why only EU comparisons are possible.

8. That is, young people who attend upper-secondary school and go on to University between the ages of 16 and 24 would be non-NEET during the entire observation period.

References

Bratsberg, B., O. Raaum and K. Røed (2014), "Labour migrant adjustments in the aftermath of the financial crisis", *Discussion Paper Series*, No. 19, Centre for Research and Analysis of Migration Department of Economics, University College London, http://www.cream-migration.org. [6]

Bratsberg, B., O. Raaum and K. Røed (2017), "Immigrant Labor Market Integration across Admission Classes", *Nordic Economic Policy Review*, Vol. 7, pp. 17-54. [8]

Bratsberg, B., O. Raaum and K. Røed (2017), "Job Loss and Immigrant Labour Market Performance", *Economica*, http://dx.doi.org/10.1111/ecca.12244. [4]

Clark, G. (2014), *The son also rises : Surnames and the history of social mobility*, Princeton University Press. [13]

Diekman, A. and K. Schidheiny (2013), "The Intergenerational Transmission of Divorce: A fifteen-country study with the fertility and family survey", *Comparative Sociology*, Vol. 12/2, pp. 211-235, https://doi.org/10.1163/15691330-12341261. [11]

Friberg, J. (2017), "New patterns of labour migration from Central and Eastern Europe and its impact on labour markets and institutions in Norway: Reviewing the evidence", in Jon Erik Dølvik, L. (ed.), *Labour Mobility in the Enlarged Single European Market, Comparative Social Research*, Esmerald Group Publishing Limited, http://dx.doi.org/10.1108/S0195-631020160000032002. [3]

Heckman, J. (2008), "The case for investing in disadvantaged young children", *CESifo DICE Repor*, Vol. 06/2, http://hdl.handle.net/10419/166932, pp. 1613-6373. [15]

Kautz, T. et al. (2014), "Fostering and Measuring Skills: Improving Cognitive and Non-cognitive Skills to Promote Lifetime Success", *OECD Education Working Papers*, No. 110, OECD Publishing, Paris, http://dx.doi.org/10.1787/5jxsr7vr78f7-en. [16]

Kornstad, T., T. Skjerpen and L. Stambøl (2017), "Why Do Immigrants to Norway Leave the Country or Move Domestically? Some Important Facts", in Ingrid Muenstermann (ed.), *People's Movements in the 21st Century - Risks, Challenges and Benefits*, InTech, http://dx.doi.org/10.5772/66951. [7]

Lee, K. (2008), "The Effects of Children's Head Start Enrollment Age on Their Short- and Long- Term Developmental Outcomes", *Social Service Review*, Vol. 82/4, pp. 663-702, http://dx.doi.org/10.1086/597018. [14]

Min, J., M. Silverstein and J. Lendon (2012), "Intergenerational transmission of values over the family life course", *Advances in Life Course Research*, Vol. 17/3, pp. 112-120, http://dx.doi.org/10.1016/j.alcr.2012.05.001. [12]

Möller, J. and M. Umkehrer (2015), "Are there Long-Term Earnings Scars from Youth Unemployment in Germany?", *Journal of Economics and Statistics (Jahrbuecher fuer Nationaloekonomie und Statistik)*, Vol. 235/4-5, pp. 474-498, https://doi.org/10.1515/jbnst-2015-4-509. [19]

OECD (2013), *Mental health and work: Norway*, OECD Publishing, Paris, http://dx.doi.org/10.1787/9789264178984-en. [17]

OECD (2015), "Young people with a migrant background", in *Indicators of Immigrant Integration 2015: Settling In*, OECD Publishing, Paris, http://dx.doi.org/10.1787/9789264234024-16-en. [5]

OECD (2015), *Indicators of immigrant integration 2015: Settling in*, OECD Publishing, Paris, http://dx.doi.org/10.1787/9789264234024-en. [10]

OECD (2016), *Society at a Glance 2016: OECD Social Indicators*, OECD Publishing, Paris, http://dx.doi.org/10.1787/9789264261488-en. [1]

OECD (2017), *OECD Family Database - OECD*, Family Database, http://www.oecd.org/social/family/database.htm (accessed on 10 August 2017). [2]

Schmillen, A. and M. Umkehrer (2013), "The scars of youth - Effects of early-career unemployment on future unemployment experience", *IAB-Discussion Paper*, No. Nüremberg, Institute for Employment Research, http://doku.iab.de/discussionpapers/2013/dp0613.pdf (accessed on 03 October 2017). [18]

SSB (2017), *Table: 06313: Immigrations, by reason for immigration, sex and age*, Statbank, https://www.ssb.no/statistikkbanken/selectvarval/Define.asp?subjectcode=&ProductId=&MainTable=InnvBef04&nvl=&PLanguage=1&nyTmpVar=true&CMSSubjectArea=befolkning&KortNavnWeb=innvgrunn&StatVariant=&checked=true (accessed on 18 August 2017). [21]

SSB (2017), *Table: 07113: Immigrations, by reason for immigration, first citizenship and year of immigration*, Statbank, https://www.ssb.no/statistikkbanken/selectvarval/Define.asp?subjectcode=&ProductId=&MainTable=InnvBef05Ny&nvl=&PLanguage=1&nyTmpVar=true&CMSSubjectArea=befolkning&KortNavnWeb=innvgrunn&StatVariant=&checked=true (accessed on 18 August 2017). [9]

Umkehrer, M. (2015), "The impact of changing youth employment patterns on future wages", *IAB Discussion Paper*, No. 31, Institut für Arbeitsmarkt- und Berufsforschung (IAB), http://dx.doi.org/scarring. [20]

Annex 2.A. NEET rates and gender: Additional statistics

Figure 2.A1.1. NEET rates for young men in Norway have converged upwards towards those for young women

Unemployed and inactive NEETs as percentages of all 15-29 year-olds, by gender, OECD and Norway 2015

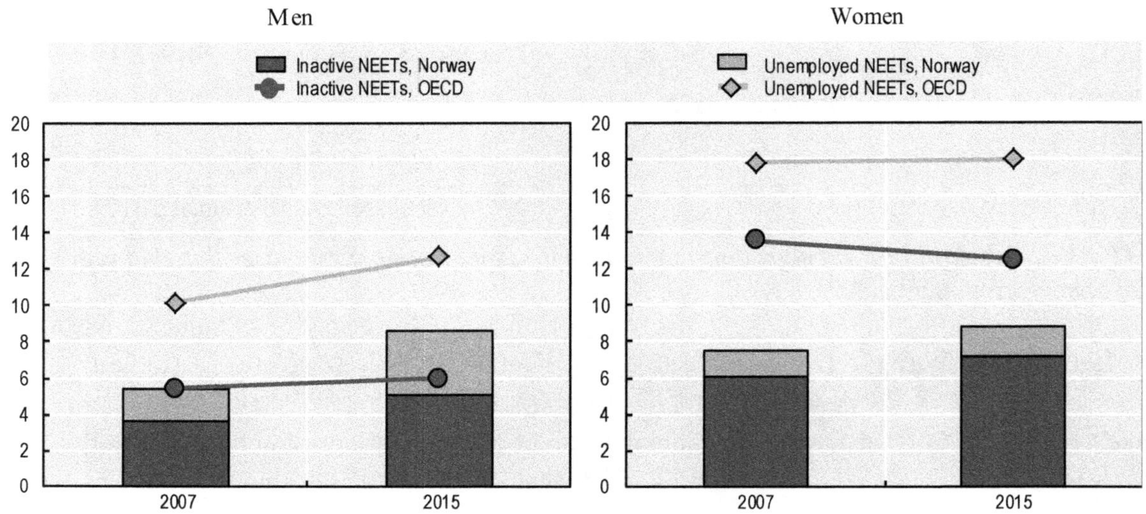

Note: Data for Korea refer to 2014, and for Mexico to 2016.
Source: OECD calculations based on national labour force surveys, the OECD Education Database (2016, Australia, Germany, Israel, Korea and New Zealand).

Annex 2.B. Time patterns of NEET status: Additional statistics

Figure 2.A2.1. Many NEETs remain NEET for long stretches of time

Cohort of 16 year-olds in 2006, by gender and number and length of (uninterrupted) NEET spells before reaching the age of 24

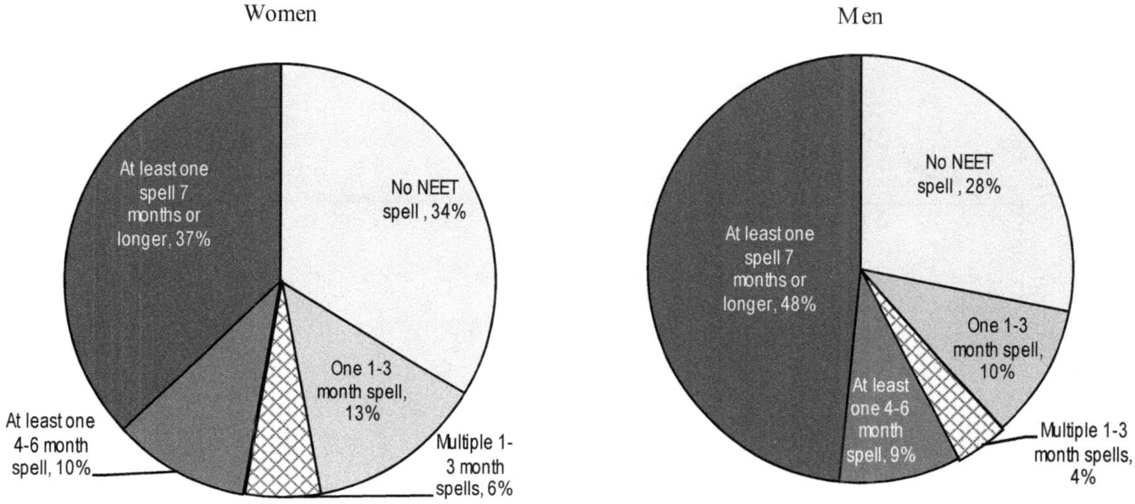

Source: OECD calculations based on register data delivered by SSB.

Figure 2.A2.2. Female upper-secondary graduates experience smoother labour market transitions

Timing of NEET spells by age, as percentages of the cohort of 16-year-olds in 2006, by educational attainment and gender

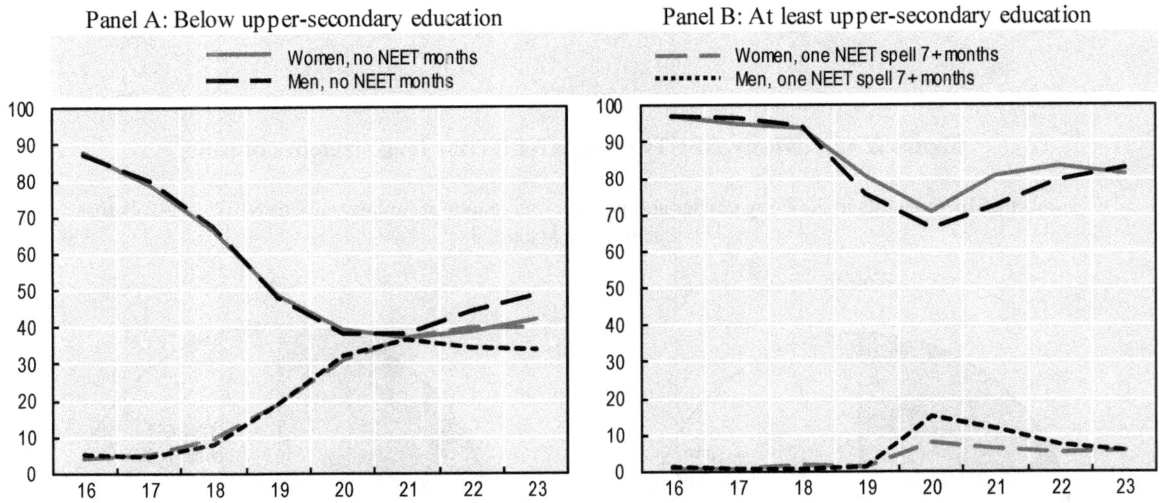

Note: The share of young people who were NEETs for under six months during the year are not shown. Educational attainment is measured at age 23.

Source: OECD calculations based on register data delivered by SSB.

Chapter 3. Benefit receipt and youth poverty in Norway

This chapter studies incomes and benefit receipt of youth, and particularly NEETs, in Norway. It sets off by describing the social safety net in Norway, providing a brief analysis of the benefits available for young people in the case of unemployment, disability or caring responsibilities. It then discusses trends in benefit receipt rates among young people since the start of the economic crisis. The final section provides evidence on benefit adequacy by looking at youth poverty.

The statistical data for Israel are supplied by and under the responsibility of the relevant Israeli authorities. The use of such data by the OECD is without prejudice to the status of the Golan Heights, East Jerusalem and Israeli settlements in the West Bank under the terms of international law.

Introduction

While the main goal of public policies for disadvantaged young people must be to help them on the path to self-sufficiency, those on low incomes – including the NEETs – may require support to avoid poverty. Income support schemes such as unemployment benefits, social assistance, housing benefits or family benefits play an important role for ensuring decent incomes of young people and their families. They also act as automatic macroeconomic stabilisers, alleviating income shocks for households affected by joblessness or a decline in earnings and hence bolster aggregate demand.

Norway devotes considerable resources to income support for working-age households, though substantially less than the OECD countries with the highest spending levels. Public social expenditures on cash income support for working-age household declined over the last years from their crisis peak to reach 5% of GDP in 2013, the same level as in 2008. Preliminary more recent results however suggest an uptick to 5.4% in 2015. This is above the OECD average (4.2%) and the level in Sweden (4.3%), but considerably less than for instance in Belgium (8%), Ireland or Finland (both around 7%) or Denmark (6.5%, Figure 3.1). A large part of these expenditures – 63% – are devoted to incapacity-related benefits (primarily disability pensions and sick leave payments), much more than in most other OECD countries. Meanwhile, the share devoted to unemployment benefits and social assistance is among the lowest across the OECD.

Figure 3.1. Public social expenditures are relatively high in Norway, but the bulk of it goes to incapacity benefits

Public social expenditure on cash income support to the working-age population as a percentage of GDP, by broad policy area, 2013 or latest year (2015 for Norway)

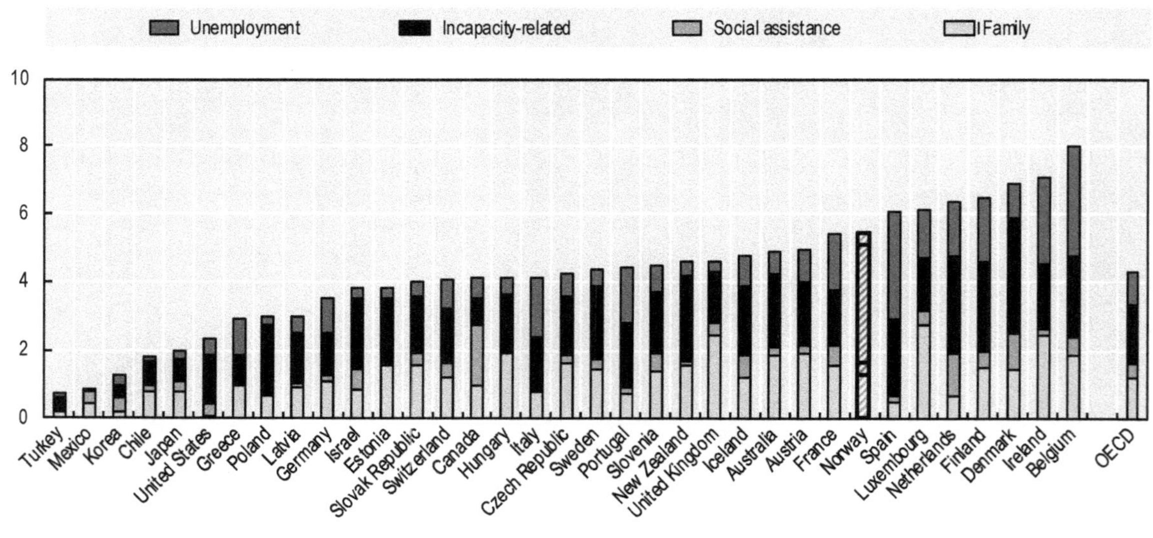

Note: Data are for 2013 except for Mexico (2011), Greece and Poland (2012), Australia, Canada, Korea and New Zealand (2014), Chile, Israel and Norway (2015). Results for Norway are preliminary. Those for Denmark include expenditures on unemployment insurance that are categorised as private.
Source: OECD (2016), OECD Social Expenditure Database, (www.oecd.org/social/expenditure.htm)

This chapter presents an analysis of the income situation of young people in Norway and the income support they receive. It sets off by describing the social safety net providing a brief analysis of the benefits available for young people in different life circumstances and assessing their generosity (Section 3.1). It then looks at benefit receipt rates among young people and at coverage rates for those who are unemployed (Section 3.2). The chapter concludes by studying youth poverty (Section 3.3).[1]

3.1. The income support system

The Norwegian income support system for jobseekers comes with a two-tiered structure: insurance-based Unemployment Benefits are available for a limited time for jobseekers with a sufficient earnings history; persons in low-income households, including those without unemployment benefit entitlements, can apply for the minimum-income Social Assistance. Those with reduced work capacity receive a Work Assessment Allowance, which is paid during vocational rehabilitation or medical treatment, or Disability Benefits if they are permanently unable to work full-time because of a disability. Separate benefits exist for jobseekers who participate in labour market measures and for single parents. This section gives a short overview of the eligibility criteria of different types of income support for young people and their families and assesses their generosity.

3.1.1. Unemployment benefits for young jobseekers with a work history

Young people in Norway face relatively low hurdles to accessing Unemployment Benefits (*Dagpenger*) in case of job loss or an involuntary reduction in working hours. Unlike in most OECD countries, where minimum contribution periods apply (OECD (2016[1]), Figure 1.20), Norway ties eligibility to Unemployment Benefits to a minimum *earnings record*: to qualify, a jobseeker must have earned at least 1.5 times the National Insurance Basic Amount "G" in the last calendar year (about one-quarter of the annual average wage), or 3G over the last three calendar years.[2] Even young people with low earnings or patchy employment records hence often have access to Unemployment Benefits in case of job loss. To receive payments, they have to be registered with the Norwegian Labour and Welfare Administration (NAV), actively look for work and be willing and able to take up any work anywhere in the country. There is no minimum age for receiving Unemployment Benefits.

Unemployment Benefits can moreover be received for relatively long. Jobseekers who earned at least 2G (about one-third of the annual average wage) are entitled to benefits for up to 24 months; those with lower previous earnings still qualify for up to 12 months.[3] Even for jobseekers with low previous earnings, the maximum receipt duration is hence longer than in most OECD countries (OECD average of eight months for a young jobseeker after one year of employment, see Figure 3.2).

Payment levels are lower than in many OECD countries, however: recipients are entitled to 62.4% of previous gross annual earnings throughout their benefit spell.[4] The share of previous *net* earnings replaced through benefits, the so-called net replacement rate (NRR), hence lies a little below the OECD average at 67% for a person with annual earnings of 50% of the average wage (Figure 3.3). This is substantially lower than in the more generous OECD countries, where jobseekers see over 80% of their previous earnings replaced in the initial months of unemployment. In some countries, jobseekers with previous earnings at 50% of the average wage moreover qualify for a top-up on unemployment benefits in the form of means-tested social assistance or housing benefits.

Figure 3.2. Young jobseekers in Norway may receive unemployment benefits for longer than in most OECD countries

Maximum duration of unemployment insurance benefit payments in months for a 20-year-old after one year of employment, 2015

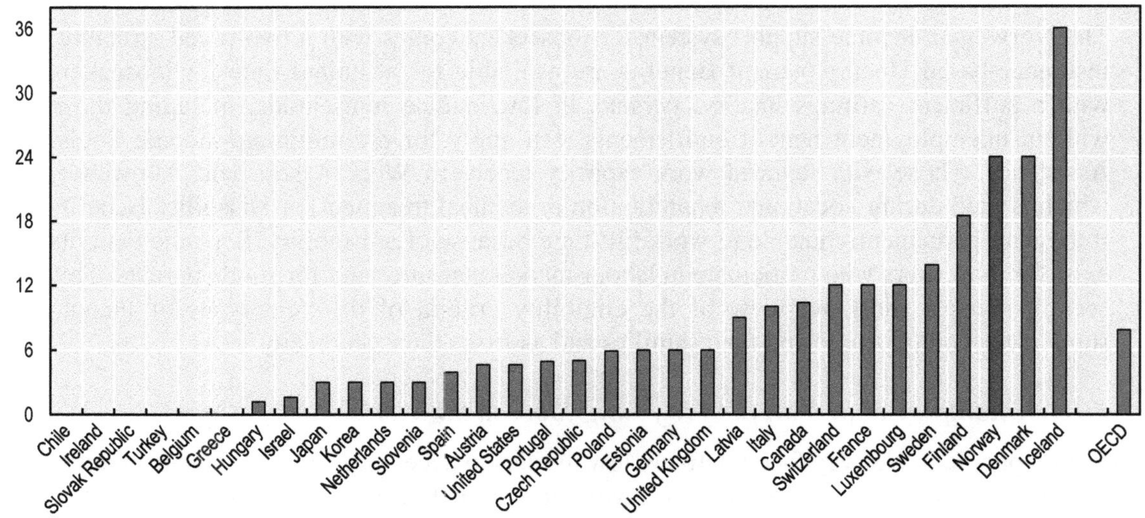

Note: In Belgium, Ireland, the Slovak Republic and Turkey, 20-year-olds with a one-year contribution record do not qualify for unemployment insurance benefits. In Greece, social insurance contributions in each of the previous two years are required. No maximum benefit duration applies in Chile. Results for the United States are for the State of Michigan. No results are available for Mexico. There are no unemployment insurance schemes in Australia and New Zealand. The OECD average for the maximum benefit duration is calculated for the countries where such a limit exists.
Source: OECD Tax-Benefit models, www.oecd.org/social/benefits-and-wages.htm.

Long-term unemployed youth with the required earnings history tend to be better off than in most OECD countries in spite of these modest payment rates. The reason is that they continue to receive benefits at the same NRR as early on in their benefit spell until exhausting their entitlements after 24 months. In countries with shorter maximum unemployment benefit durations, jobseekers often face substantial declines in their NRRs once they exhaust their benefit entitlements and are moved to minimum-income benefits (Figure 3.A.1). Long-term unemployment is rare in Norway, however: only 3.8% of 15-24 year-olds had been unemployed for over 12 months in 2016, the fourth-lowest rate across the OECD (OECD average of 17.8%, (OECD, 2018[2])).

Figure 3.3. Unemployment benefits in Norway are less generous than in many OECD countries

Net replacement rates in the 2nd month of unemployment for a 20-year-old jobseeker with previous earnings at 50% of the average wage, as a percentage of previous net income, 2016

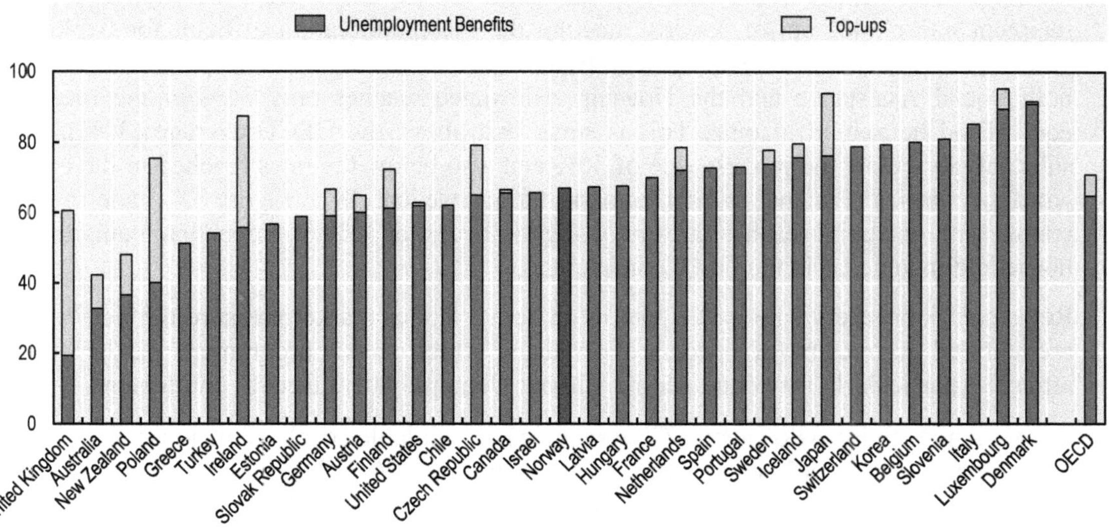

Note: The net replacement rate is that of a single, childless person who has been in continuous employment for 24 months. The average wage is not available for Turkey, such that calculations are based on wages for the Average Production Worker in the manufacturing sector. Top-ups may consist of social assistance and housing benefits, with housing costs being assumed to equal 20% of the average wage. Where receipt of social assistance or other minimum-income benefits is subject to activity tests, such as active job search or being "available" for work, these requirements are assumed to be met. No results are available for Mexico.
Source: OECD Tax-Benefit models, www.oecd.org/social/benefits-and-wages.htm.

3.1.2. Minimum-income benefits for young people on low incomes

Young people with low income, including jobseekers without Unemployment Benefit entitlements, may qualify for last-resort Social Assistance benefits (*Økonomisk sosialhjelp*), which is tax-financed and paid by the municipalities through NAV (see Chapter 5 for information on NAV's structure). The scheme is means-tested at the household level, and payments are fully withdrawn against any income from work or other benefits. Young people above the age of 18 years living alone on low incomes may qualify for Social Assistance irrespective of their parents' income level; those below the age of 18 years normally have to rely on support from their parents.

Payment levels vary locally: each municipality sets their own guidelines, taking into account a non-binding recommendation by the Ministry of Labour and Social Affairs.[5] Caseworkers moreover enjoy a considerable discretion in adjusting payments to the recipients' personal circumstances.

Unemployed Social Assistance claimants and possibly their employable spouse have to register as jobseekers with NAV, where they generally face the same activity requirements as Unemployment Benefit recipients (see Chapter 5). Households can in principle receive Social Assistance for an unlimited duration – actual receipt durations tend to be short, however (Königs, 2017[3]).

A separate Housing Allowance (*Bostøtte*) is available for low-income youth with high housing expenses from rent or mortgage payments and taxes in case of owner-occupied housing. It is administered by the Norwegian State Housing Bank (*Husbanken*) and paid out by local offices, often by the local NAV office. Under-18 year-olds can only claim this allowance if they have children; students qualify only if a child lives in the same household.

Minimum-income benefits in Norway are generally far from generous enough to lift recipient households out of poverty, making the income situation difficult for workless young people without Unemployment Benefit entitlements. A single person receiving both Social Assistance and the Housing Allowance reaches only 35% of the median equivalised household income. This is somewhat above the OECD average (30%), but substantially below the poverty line of 50% and also below the rates reached in the other Nordic countries (Finland, 54%; Denmark, 50%; Sweden, 48%; Figure 3.4, Panel A). A couple with one child reaches fares only slightly better, at 37% of the median equivalised household income, as in the OECD on average.

Registered jobseekers who participate in an active labour market measure through NAV are entitled to receipt of special allowances, which make programme participation attractive particularly for young people without Unemployment Benefit entitlements:

- An Activity Allowance (*Tiltakspenger*) is available to all adult jobseekers who participate in a labour market measure through NAV. The monthly payment rate lies about 40% above the national social assistance norm for a single person; it is typically below the level of Unemployment Benefits, however, such that jobseekers with Unemployment Benefit entitlements would usually not claim it.[6] Norway recently introduced a minimum-age threshold of 18 years for the Activity Allowance such as not to create incentives for young people to quit school to participate in a labour market measure.
- A Qualification Benefit (*Kvalifiseringsstønaden*) is paid to jobseekers who participate in the Qualification Programme (*Kvalifiseringsprogrammet*), a training programme with intensive support of typically up to two years for jobseekers with severely reduced earnings capacity without entitlements to insurance-based out-of-work benefits (see Chapter 5). Payments amount to 2G (i.e. one-third of the average wage) plus potential supplements including for recipients with children. Under-25 year-olds receive only two-thirds of the full Qualification Benefit.

Figure 3.4. Minimum-income benefits in Norway are too low to prevent poverty

Net income from social assistance benefits and cash housing assistance
as a percentage of median household incomes, 2016

Panel A. Single, childless person

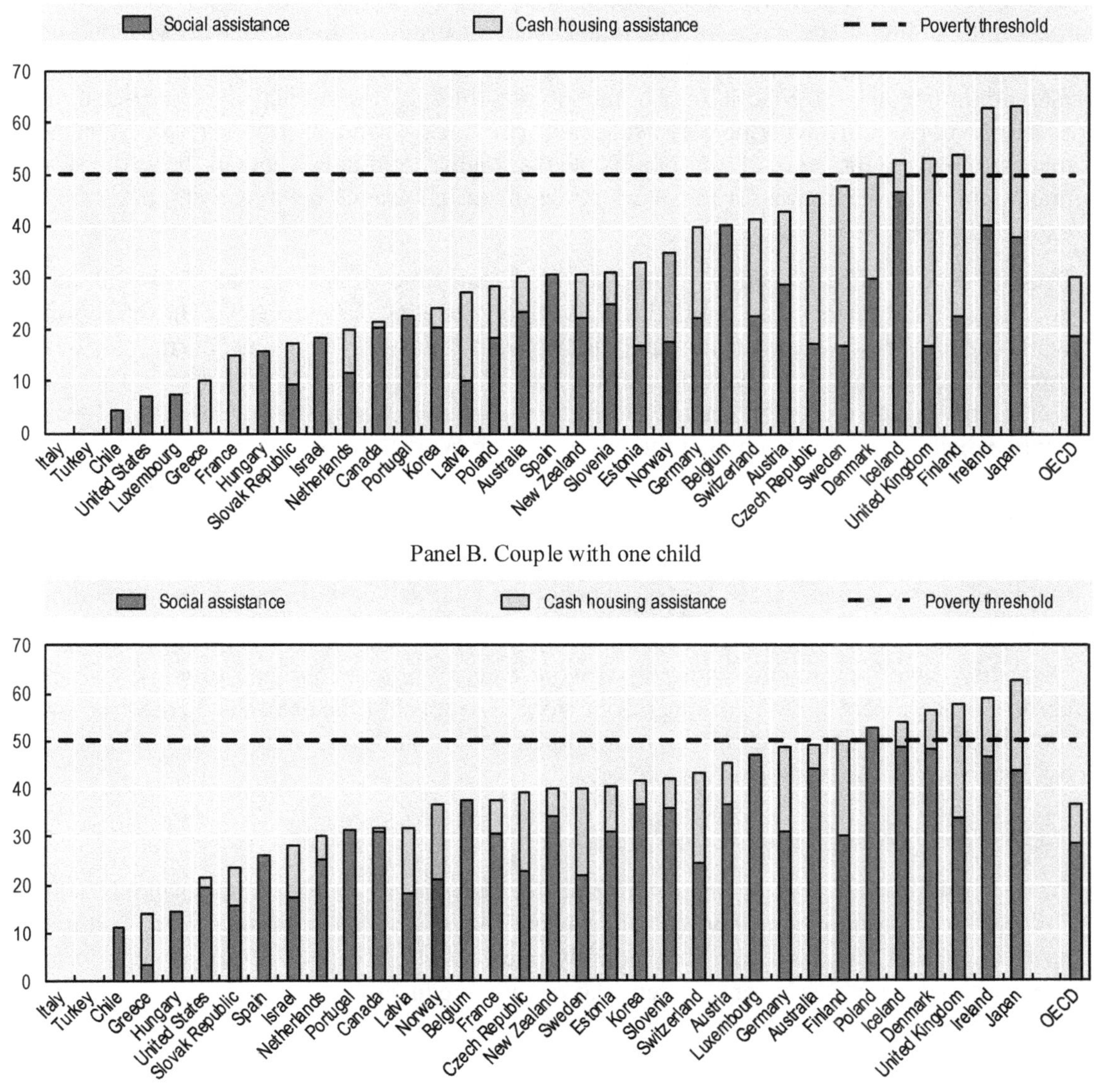

Note: The poverty threshold is defined as 50% of the median household income. Income levels are shown on an equivalised basis and account for all cash benefit entitlements of a family with no other income sources and no entitlements to primary benefits such as unemployment insurance. They are net of any income taxes and social contributions. "Cash housing assistance" represents cash benefits for a household in privately-rented accommodation with rent plus other charges amounting to 20% of average gross full-time wages. Calculations for families with children assume a child aged 4 and consider neither childcare costs nor benefits. Where benefit rules are not determined on a national level but vary by region or municipality, results refer to a "typical" case (e.g. Michigan in the United States, the capital in some other countries). US results include Food Stamps. No results are available for Mexico.

For Norway, cash housing assistance includes the part of social assistance that is earmarked for housing, heating and electricity expenses.

Source: OECD Tax-Benefit models, www.oecd.org/social/benefits-and-wages.htm.

3.1.3. Income support for young people with reduced work capacity

Working-age persons from the age of 18 whose work capacity is reduced by at least 50% because of illness or injury qualify for receipt of a Work Assessment Allowance (*Arbeidsavklaringspenger*). To be eligible, they have to be undergoing medical treatment and/or vocational rehabilitation and receive follow-up from NAV with a view to restoring the employability.[7] The payment rate equals 66% of insurable income in the year before work capacity dropped below 50%, or during the last three years if this is higher. A flat-rate minimum annual benefit of 2G (about one-third of the annual average wage) is available to persons with no or insufficient previous earnings; persons who became disabled before the age of 26 qualify for a higher minimum annual benefit.[8] The maximum receipt duration for the Work Assessment Allowance is three years, but can be extended by up to two years.

Persons who are permanently unable to work full-time after medical treatment and vocational rehabilitation are entitled to Disability Benefits (*Uføretrygd*).[9] Those without work capacity receive payments equalling 66% of the average income during the best three out of the last five years before the loss of work capacity;[10] persons with partial work capacity see their payments reduced proportionally. Again, minimum benefit levels apply, which are somewhat higher than those for the Work Assessment Allowance.[11]

When awarding disability benefits, caseworkers determine an upper limit for any additional earnings that recipients may have (i.e. an "earnings disregard"). It equals the person's expected income given the remaining work capacity (if any) plus 0.4G. Above that limit, every *kroner* earned leads to a benefit reduction – with the exact rate depending on the ratio of benefit to income before the loss of work capacity.

Disability Benefit recipients with partial work capacity are encouraged to work and are entitled to keep part of their earnings from work. The level of the earnings disregards, and the reduction in benefits for every *kroner* earned above that level, is determined on a case-by-case basis by the NAV caseworker.

3.1.4. Family benefits for young people

Family benefits can play an important role for bolstering incomes of households with children. Norway grants a universal child benefit (*Barnetrygd*) to families with children up to the age of 18 years, paid at a monthly rate of NOK 970 (EUR 100) per child. The age threshold is not raised for children who remain in education beyond this age, unlike in many OECD countries (OECD, 2016[11]).

Young parents are eligible for parental-leave benefits (*Foreldrepenger*) after childbirth if they have been employed with an insurable income for at least six out of the ten months prior to the start of the parental leave.[12] Benefits cover 100% of the previous income for a total period of 49 weeks, or 80% for 59 weeks. This period includes three weeks of maternity leave before childbirth and two "quotas" of ten weeks each reserved specifically for the mother and the father – the parents can share the remaining 26 or 36 weeks freely.[13] A lump sum grant is paid to parents who do not qualify for parental-leave benefits.

Single parents qualify for additional support. A special minimum-income scheme, the Transitional Benefit (*Overgangsstønad*), covers the living expenses of sole carers of young children on low-incomes. Payments amount to up to 2.25G per year (a little over one-third of the average annual wage) and are generally available for a maximum of three years as long as the child is below the age of eight.[14] Once the youngest child reaches the age of one, recipients have to register as jobseekers with NAV unless if they engage in part-time work or study or run their own business. Single parents also qualify for higher child benefits.[15]

Parents of one-year-old children who do not send their child into kindergarten receive a Cash-for-care benefit (*Kontantstøtte*) of NOK 6 000 (about EUR 620), or half that amount if the child attends kindergarten part-time.

3.2. Benefit receipt and coverage

Eligibility rules say only little about the actual coverage of income support programmes. This section looks at how many young people – and NEETs in particular – receive benefits in Norway, how long they typically remain on these benefits, and how benefit receipt has evolved over the last decade.

3.2.1. Benefit receipt rates

The Norwegian income support system stands out for the widespread receipt of incapacity-related benefits. While the overall share of young people who receive out-of-work benefits is close to the OECD average at around 17% in 2016 (15% in the OECD Figure 3.5, Panel A), receipt rates of incapacity benefits – primarily the Work Assessment Allowance and Disability Benefits – are the highest across the OECD. Over 6% of young people received such benefits in 2016, more than three times the OECD average. Nearly half of all young people live in households that receive some other kind of household-level benefit, typically family benefits (Figure 3.5, Panel B).

High receipt rates of incapacity benefits are not a new phenomenon, and Norway has undertaken significant efforts in recent years to tackle the issue. In a 2015 reform, Norway merged three earlier schemes into current Disability Benefit introducing a finer distinction between partially reduced work capacity levels and facilitating recipients' take-up of employment. Evidence suggests that the reform indeed led to an increase in hours worked among recipients with fully reduced work capacity (Alne, 2016[4]). In early 2018, Norway tightened access to the Work Assessment Allowance, specifying more clearly the medical requirements that permit access, shortening the maximum receipt duration by a year and restricting the reasons that justify an extension of payments beyond three years. There have also been efforts to regulate more strictly the access to Sickness Benefits as the main gateways to the Work Assessment Allowance for senior persons (OECD, 2018[5]).

Evidence indeed suggests that Norway has thus far been insufficiently restrictive in granting access to incapacity benefits. The counter-cyclical receipt pattern indicates that these benefits have partly served as income support for difficult-to-employ young people in times of labour market slack. As the receipt rates of Unemployment Benefits and Social Assistance surged during the economic crisis, the rate of incapacity benefit receipt followed suit rising by two percentage points between 2008 and 2011 (Figure 3.5, Panel B). Receipt rates for all three types of benefits showed a similar decline thereafter, an uptick following the 2014 oil price shock, and they remain above their (immediate) pre-crisis levels.

The high responsiveness of incapacity benefit receipt rates in Norway to economic conditions is corroborated by academic research. Using data on firm closures, Bratsberg et al. (2013[6]) show that job displacement can drive Disability Benefit receipt. Working in a firm that will go bankrupt within the next four years more than doubles the risk of transitioning into Disability Benefits for men, and increases it by 50% for women, compared to employees of firms which do not experience bankruptcy.

Disability Benefit recipients moreover strongly react to economic incentives. Exploiting a large-scale reform in the (now discontinued) Temporary Disability Benefit, Fevang et al. (2017[7]) show that a 10% cut in benefit levels for fully disabled recipients increases the likelihood of transitioning into regular employment by 3.3% – approximately half of the response estimated for Unemployment Benefit recipients. This is a substantial response given that these recipients are considered seriously disabled. Tightening access to Disability Benefits also influences the uptake of other benefits: Fevang et al. (2017[7]) find that a 10% drop in the Disability Benefit amount leads to a 4% increase in Unemployment Benefit receipt. Autor et al. (2014[8]) show that having a Disability Benefit claim denied increases the likelihood of labour force participation by 16 percentage points, and it significantly increases the receipt of benefits other than Disability Benefit, particularly immediately after the appeal, though most claimants divert to other incapacity-related programmes rather than to Social Assistance.[16]

High receipt rates of incapacity benefits in times of weak labour market demand risk further diminishing young people's employability, extending periods out of work and reducing incentives to use this time for skill development.

A concern is moreover that within the branch of incapacity benefits, there has been a gradual shift away from the temporary Work Assessment Allowance – which is geared towards restoring recipients' employability – towards the more permanent Disability Benefit. Young people's Disability Benefit receipt rate doubled over the last ten years. The pattern is particularly pronounced for 25-29 year-olds: NAV administrative data show that the share of young people receiving Disability Benefits rose by 1.3 percentage points to 2.7% since 2010; meanwhile, the share of those receiving the Work Assessment Allowance dropped by nearly one percentage point (NAV, 2018[9]; NAV, 2018[10]).[17]

Mental disorders have become a primary cause of Disability Benefit receipt among young people. This may reflect higher demands on young employees in the daily working life, stricter activation requirements in other benefit schemes, but also an apparent rise in the incidence of mental health problems in the general population. It is unclear, however, to what extent this latter trends reflects an actual rise in the share of young people with mental health problems as opposed to being primarily the consequence of improvements in detecting and diagnosing such problems (Brage and Thune, 2015[11]; Folkehelseinstituttet, 2016[12]; Grødem, Nielsen and Strand, 2014[13]; Sommar, 2016[14]). An ongoing research project is looking into the reasons for the rising Disability Benefit receipt among young people (Frisch Centre, 2017[15]).

These figures highlight the importance of curtailing receipt of incapacity-related benefit in Norway. This will likely have to imply further efforts to improve gatekeeping, i.e. through more rigorous work capacity assessments. There may moreover be scope for Norway to reduce incentives to transfer young people with poor labour market perspectives onto the Work Assessment Allowance by strengthening the available support – and possibly raising payment levels – of Social Assistance.

Figure 3.5. Receipt rates of incapacity-related benefits are high and counter-cyclical

Panel A: Percentage of 16-29 year-olds receiving out-of-work benefits, 2016

Panel B: Benefit receipt rates in Norway, as a percentage of all 16-29 year-olds, 2007-16

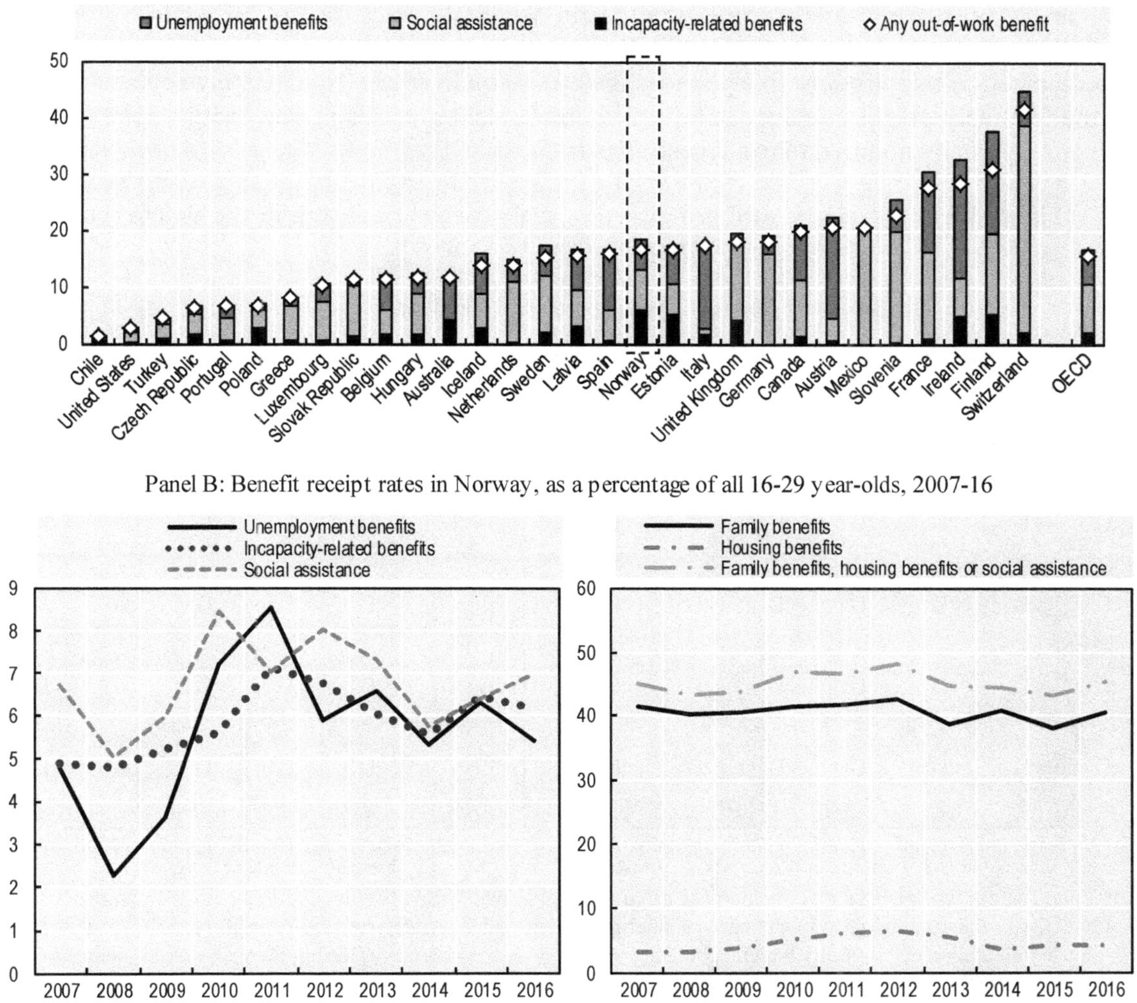

Note: Benefit receipt rates give the number of young people who report having received a positive amount of benefits (either individually in the case of unemployment and incapacity-related benefits, or who live in a household that received family benefits, housing benefit or social assistance) during the past year as a share of all 16-29 year-olds.

Panel A: Data on Canada refer to 2011, for Australia, Germany, Mexico and Switzerland to 2014, and for Chile, Iceland, Ireland, Italy, Luxemburg and Turkey to 2015.

Source: OECD calculations based on the European Union Statistics on Income and Living Conditions (EU-SILC) survey, Household, Income and Labour Dynamics in Australia (HILDA) Survey, Chiles National Socio-Economic Characterisation Survey (CASEN), and the US Current Population Survey (CPS).

3.2.2. Targeting and benefit coverage

NEETs are more likely to be covered by benefits in Norway than across the OECD on average: four-fifths of all NEETs receive some kind of benefit, compared to only two-thirds across the OECD on average. In light of overall benefit receipt rates that are very similar to the OECD average (Figure 3.6), this implies better targeting: NEETs in Norway are 60% more likely to receive income support than other young people, compared to a gap of 30% across the OECD on average.

The difference in coverage is mainly driven by the high share of youth and NEETs who receive incapacity-related benefits: nearly one-quarter of all NEETs in Norway, compared to just 8% across the OECD on average (Figure 3.6, Panel B).

Social Assistance also contributes to the high benefit coverage rate of NEET in Norway, and is highly targeted: NEETs are almost four times as likely to receive Social Assistance, compared to two times as likely across the OECD on average. This is likely connected to the fact that Social Assistance is fully withdrawn against earnings (see Section 3.1.2) and hence typically not used to top-up earnings from work.

Figure 3.6. Incapacity-related benefits and social assistance account for the high benefit coverage of NEETs in Norway

Benefit receipt rates for all young people and NEETs, as percentages, 2016

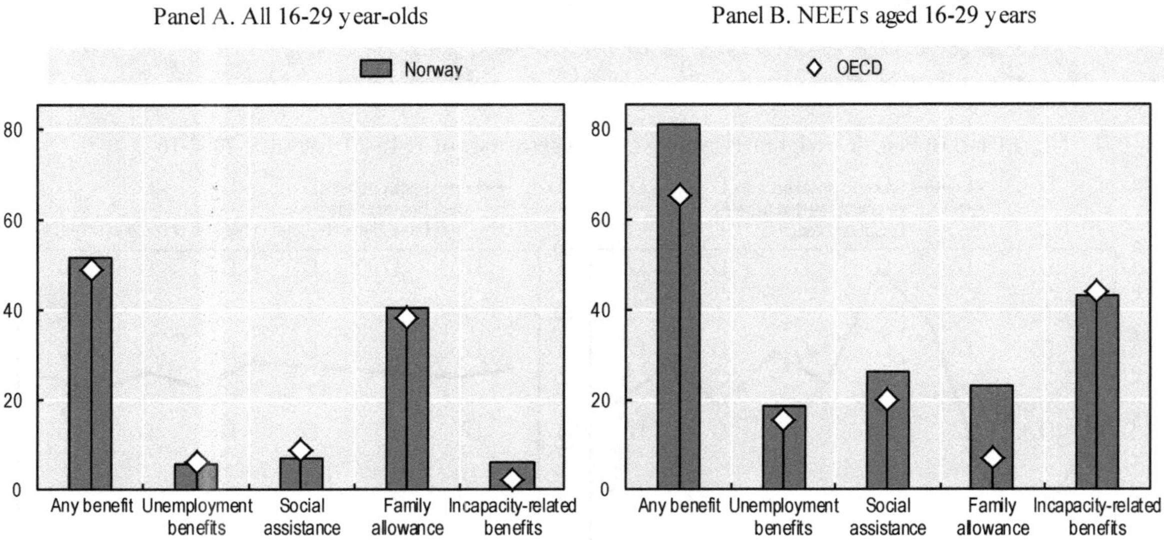

Note: Benefit receipt rates give the number of young people who report having received a positive amount of benefits (either individually in the case of unemployment and incapacity-related benefits, or who live in a household that received family benefits, housing benefit or social assistance) during the past year as a share of all 16-29 year-olds or the NEETs in that age group. Data on Canada refer to 2011, for Australia, Germany, Mexico and Switzerland to 2014, and for Chile, Iceland, Ireland, Italy, Luxemburg and Turkey to 2015.

Source: OECD calculations based on the European Union Statistics on Income and Living Conditions (EU-SILC) survey, Household, Income and Labour Dynamics in Australia (HILDA) Survey, Chiles National Socio-Economic Characterisation Survey (CASEN), and the US Current Population Survey (CPS).

3.2.3. Benefit receipt durations

The previous two subsections gave an overview of the broad trends in income support benefit receipt in Norway, and how receipt rates in Norway compare to those in other OECD countries. This subsection looks at the benefit dynamics: how long do young people remain on benefits, and how do durations vary by age, gender or education?

This analysis is based on an administrative data set that links several sources: the Social Security Database *FD-Trygd*, containing detailed information on benefit receipt, the National Education Database for information on the highest level of education and monthly register files from NAV for information on the cash-for-care benefit. The dataset collects all benefit spells of Norwegian residents aged 15 to 29 years starting between January 2008 and December 2011, and tracks them for up to three years – that is, the analysis includes benefit spells reaching into November 2014 for spells starting in

December 2011 and lasting three years or longer. Annex 3.B provides more detail on the methodology as well as on the benefits covered.

OECD (2016[16]) presents a similar analysis of benefit receipt durations for Sweden, so that Swedish results can be contrasted for some parts of the analysis.[18] The observation period for the Swedish analysis is 2009 to 2011, the period that saw the largest fall in youth employment in Sweden as a consequence of the Great Recession (OECD, 2016[16]). In Norway, the crisis hit the youth labour market in 2009 as well, such that the Norwegian analysis contains a boom year, which should depress spell durations in Norway as compared to Sweden.

Table 3.1. Benefit durations among young people in Norway and Sweden

	Unemployment Benefits				
	Duration in months		Percentage of spells		
	Median	Mean	> 6 months	> 12 months	Censored
Norway	5	7	35	14	0
Sweden	4	7	33	14	1
	Social Assistance				
	Duration in months		Percentage of spells		
	Median	Mean	> 6 months	> 12 months	Censored
Norway	3	7	31	17	3
Sweden	5	10	42	27	6
	Incapacity-related benefits				
	Duration in months		Percentage of spells		
	Median	Mean	> 6 months	> 12 months	Censored
Norway	36	25	85	76	51
Sweden	24	32	98	72	35

Note: Spells starting in 2008-11 (Norway) and 2009-11 (Sweden), young people aged 15-29 (Norway) and 16-29 (Sweden). Spells are tracked for a maximum of 36 months, at which point they are censored – the share of censored spells is therefore the share of spells lasting longer than 36 months. Interruptions of spells of SA and DB benefit receipt (Norway) and UB, SA and DB benefit receipt (Sweden) are ignored if the interruptions are not longer than two months. These short interruptions count toward the benefit receipt spell in Norway, but not in Sweden. See Annex 3.B for a detailed description of the methodology and the specific benefits covered.
Source: SSB calculations based on administrative data from *FD-Trygd* (Norway), SCB calculations based on administrative data from *Flödesdatabasen* (Sweden) as presented in OECD (2016[16]) *Investing in Youth: Sweden*.

Young people usually do not receive Unemployment Benefits for extended periods of time: 50% of all receipt spells were shorter than five months, and only about one-third of were longer than six months. Unemployment Benefit receipt durations are also almost identical in Norway and Sweden (Table 3.1).

Also Social Assistance receipt spells among young people are short – half of all spells are shorter than three months, and only about every sixth spell is longer than one year. They are both shorter than Unemployment Benefit receipt spells and Social Assistance spells among Swedish youth (Table 3.1). This is probably due to two factors: firstly, payment levels are comparatively low in Norway and do not provide a long-term sustainable income source for recipients, see Figure 3.4. Second, the least employable young people, who would constitute the social assistance recipient base in other countries, have access to other benefits such as the Transitional Allowance for single parents or incapacity-related benefits for those who suffer from physical or mental health issues (Königs, 2015[17]).

Receipt of incapacity-related benefits, in contrast, is prevalent (in line with the receipt rates shown in Figure 3.5) and very persistent. There are only about twice as many Unemployment Benefit as incapacity benefit spells (*not shown*), compared to 350 Unemployment Benefit spells for every incapacity benefit spells in Sweden (OECD, 2016[16]). More than half of all spells last longer than three years, and over three-quarters are longer than 12 months. In Sweden, only about one-third of spells were longer than three years (Table 3.1).

Benefit receipt and education are closely related. In line with the results of the NEET profiling exercise in Chapter 2, young people who did not obtain an upper-secondary qualification are more likely to receive out-of-work benefits, and remain on these benefits for longer, than young people with upper-secondary or tertiary education. Specifically:

- Unemployment Benefits are the most diverse benefit in terms of recipient education: for over half of all spells, the recipient had at least upper-secondary education (Figure 3.7, Panel B.1). Those with below-upper secondary education have lower exit rates from unemployment, however (Figure 3.7, Panel A.1) – over 40% remain on Unemployment Benefits for six months or longer, compared to just 30% for those with upper-secondary education.
- For Social Assistance, this picture is very stark: for nearly four in five Social Assistance receipt spells, the recipient does not have upper-secondary education. Those without upper-secondary education also leave the benefit more slowly, but as mentioned above, Social Assistance spell durations are relatively short overall (Figure 3.7, Panel A.2).
- Two-thirds of incapacity-related benefit spells are associated with recipients without upper-secondary education (Figure 3.7, Panel B.3). While exit rates from incapacity benefits are low in general, young people without upper-secondary education are particularly likely to remain on these benefits for an extended period of time: after three years, more than half of these spells are on-going, compared to less than a third for recipients with upper-secondary education (Figure 3.7, Panel A.3). The number of spells for higher educated young people is negligible.
- Ongoing health issues could of course drive both low educational attainment and receipt of incapacity-related benefits. However, nearly half of all incapacity benefit spells start when the recipient is between 25 and 29 years old, so clearly after the typical age of upper-secondary education. However, those 12% of spells that start at the at ages 18 or 19, so immediately upon the recipient reaching the minimum age to be eligible for the benefit (see Annex 3.B) have the longest median duration and the highest share of censored spells (not shown).

Benefit receipt durations are remarkably similar for men and women. While men account for two-thirds of all Unemployment Benefit spells, they exit the benefit at virtually the same rate as women (Panel 1, Figure 3.C.1). For Social Assistance and incapacity-related benefits, the number and duration of spells nearly coincide for men and women (Panels 2 and 3, Figure 3.C.1).

Figure 3.7. Young people without upper-secondary education are more likely to receive benefits, and receive them for longer

Panel A. Percentage of benefit spells that are longer than 6 months, 12 months and 3 years, by benefit type and education

Panel B. Percentage breakdown of the total number of benefit spells by benefit type and education

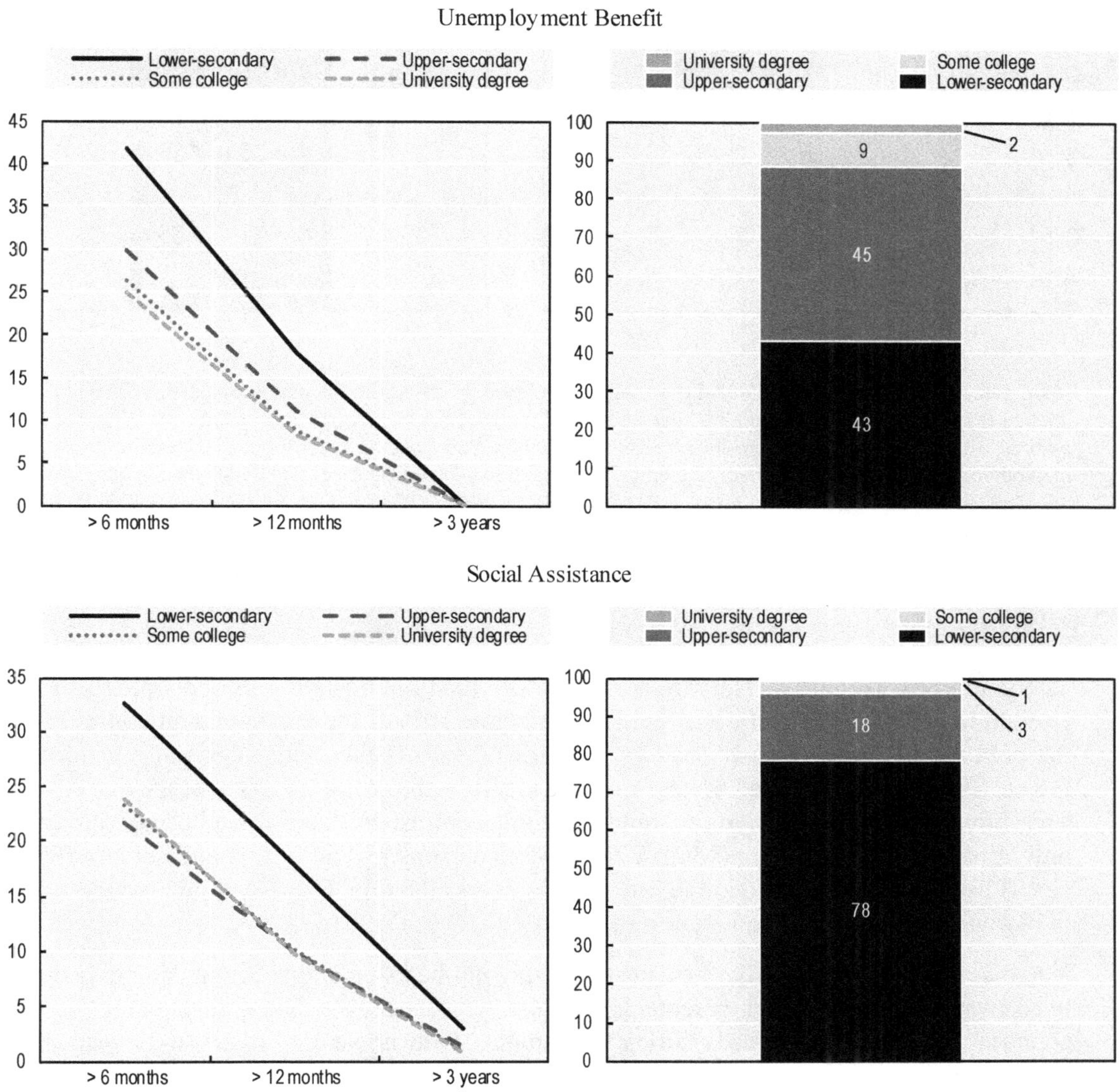

Incapacity-related benefits

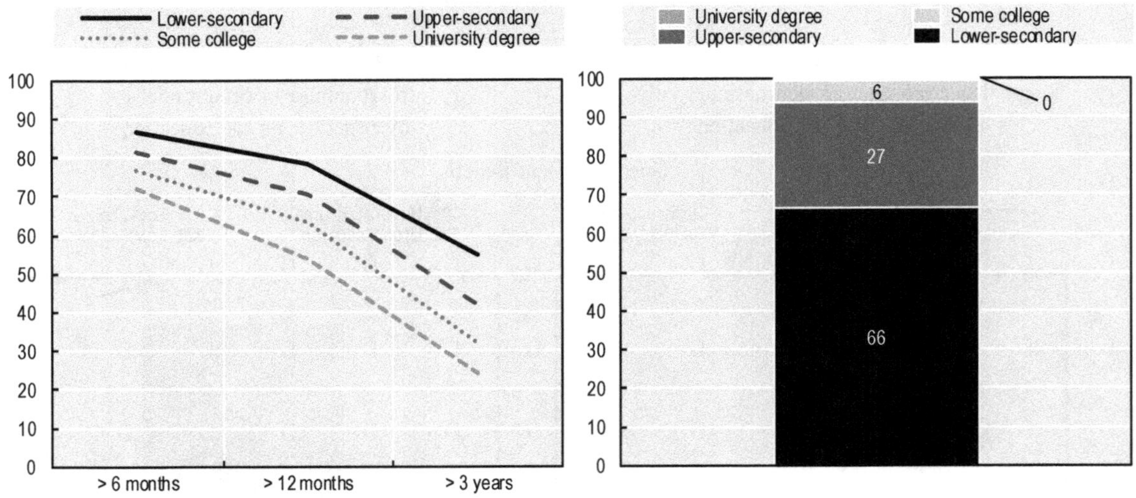

Note: Benefit spells starting in 2008-11, young people aged 15-29 at the beginning of the spell. Spells are tracked for a maximum of 36 months. Interruptions of spells of SA and incapacity-related benefit receipt are ignored if the interruptions are not longer than two months. See Annex 3.B for a detailed description of the methodology and the specific benefits covered. The breakdown of spells (Panel B) refers to spells with known recipient education – the education of 2% of all UB recipients, 6% of all SA recipients and 3% of all incapacity benefit recipients is not known.
Source: SSB calculations based on administrative data from *FD-Trygd* and the National Education Database.

3.3. Youth poverty

The youth poverty rate in Norway is high. More than one-in-five young people, 22.8%, lived in households with an equalised income below 50% of the median income in 2016 – the poverty measure typically used by the OECD. This is the second-highest rate across the OECD behind the United States, and considerably above the OECD average of 12.8%. This high poverty rate for youth stands in stark contrast to those for other age groups: only around 4% of both non-youth working-age persons (30-64 years) and seniors (65+ years) live in poverty – among the lowest rates across the OECD. Also child poverty rates in Norway are among the lowest across the OECD (OECD, 2016[1]).

Yet, these high youth poverty rates must probably not be taken at face value. Young people in Norway tend to leave their parental homes at much earlier ages than in most other OECD countries, in many cases already during their studies. Only about 40% of all 16-29 year-olds in Norway live with their parents, compared to around 60% across the OECD (OECD, 2016[1]). After having moved out, they often finance their living through student loans from the Norwegian State Educational Loan Fund (*Lånekassen*). These loans are not considered part of income, however (unlike study *grants*). Young people living on student loans are hence often classified as poor even though they are not cash-strapped. The data match this explanation: youth poverty in Norway is very much concentrated among young people no longer living with their parents (Figure 3.8, Panel A). At the same time, Norway has one of the highest youth poverty rates for non-NEETs (i.e. young people who are studying or working) across the OECD (Figure 3.8, Panel B).[19]

Poverty rates for NEETs in Norway are only a little higher than for non-NEETs, but nonetheless above the OECD average (26 vs 24% in 2016). This likely reflects comparatively low payment levels of social assistance benefits for out-of-work young people.

Figure 3.8. Youth poverty rates in Norway are high because many young people leave their parental homes already during their studies

Panel A: Poverty rates of 16-29 year-olds living with and without their parents, as percentages, 2016

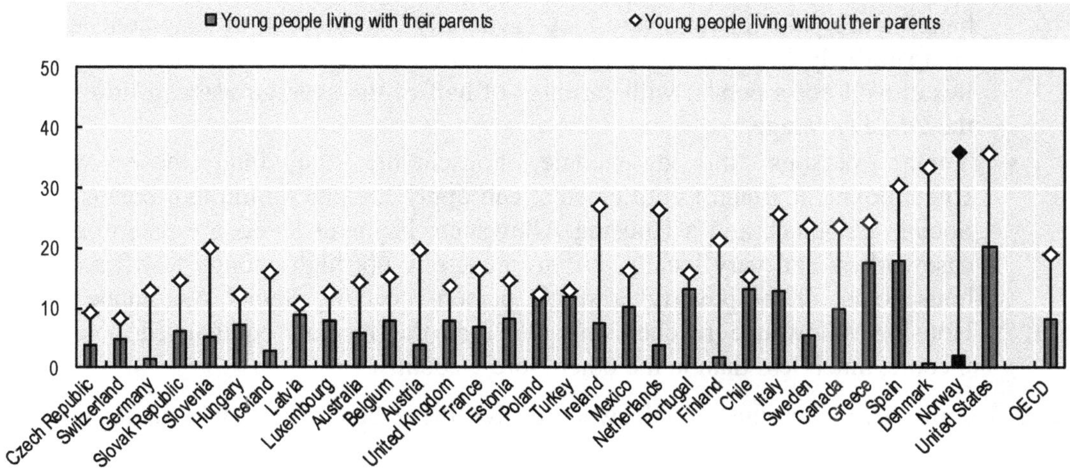

Panel B: Poverty rates of 16-29 year-olds by NEET status, as percentages, 2016

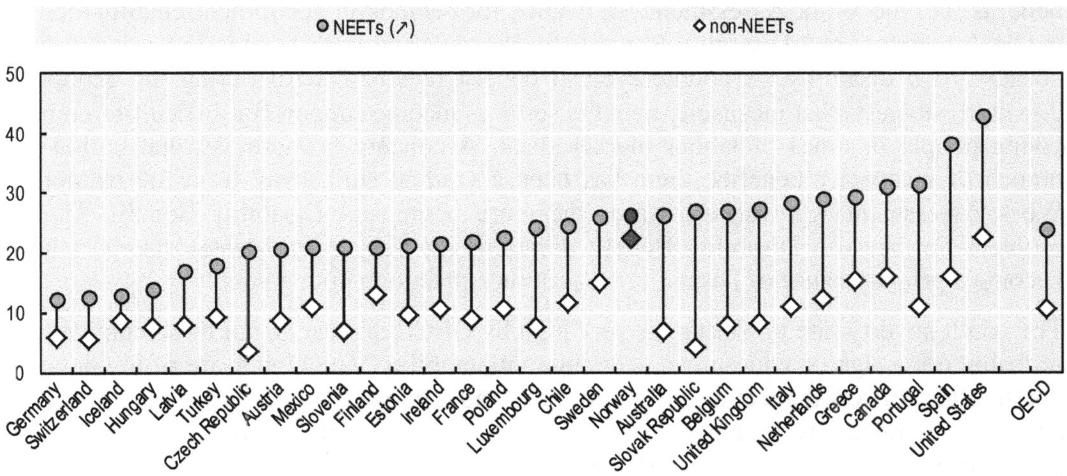

Note: Individuals are defined as poor if they live in a household with an equvalised household income (household income adjusted by the number of household members) below 50% of the median income. The poverty rate of seniors in Australia is high because many retirees draw their pensions as a lump sum instead of receiving monthly payments, which is why they "appear poor" in income statistics. Data on Canada refer to 2011, for Australia, Germany, Mexico and Switzerland to 2014, and for Chile, Iceland, Ireland, Italy, Luxemburg and Turkey to 2015. In both panels, countries have been ordered by the youth poverty rate in ascending order.

Source: OECD calculations based on the European Union Statistics on Income and Living Conditions (EU-SILC) survey, Household, Income and Labour Dynamics in Australia (HILDA) Survey, Chiles National Socio-Economic Characterisation Survey (CASEN), and the US Current Population Survey (CPS).

Round-up

While the main goal of public policies for disadvantaged young people must be to help them on the path to self-sufficiency, those on low incomes – including the NEETs – may require support to avoid poverty.

The Norwegian income support system for jobseekers has a two-tiered structure:

- Earnings-related Unemployment Benefits are available for young jobseekers with an earnings record of at least around one-quarter of the annual average wage in the last calendar year, or half the annual average wage of the last three years. While benefits are paid for relatively long (generally 24 months), the payment level is comparatively low: the share of previous net earnings replaced through benefits lies at 67% for a person with earnings of half of the average wage, a little below the OECD average.
- Young persons in low-income households, including those without Unemployment Benefit entitlements, can apply for time-unlimited, means-tested Social Assistance and a Housing Allowance. Payment levels are determined by caseworkers and vary locally, but are generally not high enough to lift recipient households out of poverty: a single person receiving Social Assistance and a Housing Allowance reaches only 35% of the median equivalised household income, much less than in the other Nordic countries.

The overall share of young people who receive these benefits is close to the OECD average, and benefit spell durations tend to be short.

Meanwhile, Norway has the highest receipt rate across the OECD for incapacity-related benefits, i.e. the Work Assessment Allowance for persons in vocational rehabilitation or medical treatment and Disability Benefits for those permanently unable to work full-time because of a disability. A countercyclical benefit receipt pattern during the economic downturn suggests that incapacity benefits serve as income support for difficult-to-employ young people in times of labour market slack. A concern is moreover that within the branch of incapacity benefits, there has been a gradual shift away from the temporary Work Assessment Allowance towards the more permanent Disability Benefit. This is problematic, because Disability Benefit durations are very long. Mental disorders have become a primary cause of Disability Benefit receipt among young people.

The youth poverty rate in Norway is very high by OECD standards, but these numbers are probably not a sign of widespread economic vulnerability. The high share of low-income youth rather reflects the fact that young people tend to move out of their parents' home for studies at a relatively young age; many of them finance their studies through loans provided by the Norwegian State Educational Loan Fund, which are not considered part of income. However, also the poverty rate for NEETs is somewhat higher than in the OECD on average, which reflects the low generosity of Social Assistance.

Notes

1. For further information on the Norwegian tax-benefit system, see the country chapters on the webpage of the OECD Tax-Benefit model (http://www.oecd.org/els/soc/benefits-and-wages-country-specific-information.htm) and the recent overviews by the European Commission (2017[19]) and the Ministry of Labour and Social Affairs (2017[20]).

2. The National Insurance Basic Amount G is updated annually and has stood at NOK 93 634 since May 2017, or about EUR 9 700. Jobseekers may hence be entitled to Unemployment Benefits if they have had earnings of NOK 140 451 (about EUR 14 600) in the previous year.

3. Basis for the calculation are the earnings during the last calendar year or average earnings during the last three calendar years, whichever is higher.

4. Earnings above a ceiling of six times G (i.e. the equivalent of a full annual average wage) are not considered for the calculation of benefit entitlements. Meanwhile, there is no upper limit to the social insurance contributions.

5. The Ministry recommends for 2018 a payment level of NOK 6 050 (EUR 630) per month for a single person, and an additional 66% of this amount for a two-person household. Expenses for housing, electricity and heating are not included in this amount. The payment rate for children varies between a little below 40% of the rate of a single for a below-6 year-olds to 65% an 11-17 year-old.

6. Programme participants are entitled to NOK 375 (EUR 40) per day, i.e. about NOK 8 250 (EUR 860) for a full month of programme participation. A reduced rate of NOK 271 (EUR 28) per day applies for 18-year-olds. Top-ups are available to cover the costs of travel or of living away from home to participate in the programme as well as for recipients with children and those requiring childcare.

7. Norway introduced the Work Assessment Allowance in 2010 by merging three existing benefit schemes, the vocational and medical rehabilitation benefits and the temporary disability benefit. See (OECD, 2013[21]) for further details. The Work Assessment Allowance is often paid after previous episodes of Sickness Benefit (*Sykepenger*) receipt.

8. For these persons, the minimum annual benefit is 2.44G.

9. Recipients of the work assessment allowance already qualify for a disability pension if their income capacity is reduced by 40%.

10. An assessment ceiling of 6G applies.

11. The minimum annual disability benefit is 2.48G for singles and 2.28G for partnered persons; persons who became disabled before the age of 26 receive 2.91G for singles and 2.66G if they are partnered, but not before the age of 20 years.

12. The annual income must exceed at least 0.5G (i.e. about one average *monthly* wage per year), and an assessment ceiling of 6G applies.

13. To be eligible for a maternal quota, the mother must have accumulated individual rights to parental benefits. The paternal quota is conditional on both parents having accumulated individual rights.

14. Single parents with an income of at least 0.5G see their payment reduced by 45% for every *kroner* earned above that threshold. The maximum payment duration is extended by two years for single parents who participate in education to increase their chances of finding work and by three years for single parents with three or more children and those who became single parents as minors.

15. All single parents receive a supplement to their child benefit equal to the standard child benefit paid for one child (i.e. they receive the same benefit as a couple with one child more), and an additional infant supplement is available for single parents receiving the Transitional Allowance if their child is below the age of four.

16. Benefit claimants can appeal a negative decision on their Disability Benefit application, and are randomly assigned judges, some of whom are significantly more lenient than others. Autor et al. (2014[8]) use the average acceptance rate of randomly assigned judges to instrument for the acceptance of a claim to look at outcomes of Disability Benefit claimants who have been rejected "at the margin" (i.e. who have similar characteristics to claimants who had their applications accepted).

17. The Eurostat version of the EU-SILC data used for this analysis unfortunately do not permit further breaking down receipt rates into the distinct benefit schemes.

18. The analysis on Swedish youth benefit receipt is based on administrative data from *Flödesdatabasen*. The age-group is slightly different (16-29 instead of 15-29). However, given that most benefits covered in this analysis have a minimum age of 18, this should not cause big divergences. Spells are equally censored at three years, and the same "chain rule" applies (see Annex 3.B), but short breaks between benefit spells (shorter than two months) are not added to the total spell duration (they are in the case of Norway), and UB benefits are also "chained". This slight difference in the chain rule should work in the following direction: SA and DB benefits would look *longer* for Norwegian youth, because breaks of up to two months would count towards the total benefit duration; but UB benefits would look *shorter* for Norwegian youth. However, because of the relative length of the benefit durations in the two countries, these (most likely quite slight) differences would work to *mitigate*, not exaggerate, the differences between the two countries, see Table 3.1.

19. For this reason, Norway excludes young people in student households from its national income statistics.

References

Alne, R. (2016), "Jobber de uføretrygdede mer etter uførereformen i 2015? [Do the disabled work after the disability benefit reform of 2015]", *Arbeid og velferd*, Vol. 3, https://www.nav.no/no/NAV+og+samfunn/Kunnskap/Analyser+fra+NAV/Arbeid+og+velferd/Arbeid+og+velferd/jobber-de-uf%C3%B8retrygdede-mer-etter-uf%C3%B8rereformen-i-2015. [4]

Autor, D., A. Kostøl and M. Mogstad (2014), "Economic Consequences of Tightening the Disability Screening *", *NBER Working Papers*, NBER, Cambridge, MA, http://www.nber.org/aging/drc/papers/odrc14-11.pdf (accessed on 22 February 2018). [8]

Brage, S. and O. Thune (2015), "Ung uførhet og psykisk sykdom [Disability among youth and mental illness]", *Arbeid og velferd*, Vol. 1, https://www.nav.no/no/NAV+og+samfunn/Kunnskap/Analyser+fra+NAV/Arbeid+og+velferd/Arbeid+og+velferd/ung-uf%C3%B8rhet-og-psykisk-sykdom, pp. 37-49. [11]

Bratsberg, B., E. Fevang and K. Røed (2013), "Job loss and disability insurance", *Labour Economics*, Vol. 24, http://dx.doi.org/10.1016/j.labeco.2013.08.004. [6]

European Commission (2017), *Your social security rights in Norway*, Directorate-General for Employment, Social Affairs and Inclusion, http://ec.europa.eu/social/main.jsp?catId=1123&langId=en. [19]

Fevang, E., I. Hardoy and K. Røed (2017), "Temporary Disability and Economic Incentives", *Economic Journal*, Vol. 127/August, pp. 1410-1432, http://dx.doi.org/10.1111/ecoj.12345. [7]

Folkehelseinstituttet (2016), *Barnehelserapporten [Child health report]*, Folkehelseinstituttet, Oslo, https://www.fhi.no/nettpub/barnehelserapporten/. [12]

Frisch Centre (2017), *Årsaker til økt tilstrømming til uføretrygd blant unge [The reasons for increased access to disability benefits of young people]*, https://www.frisch.uio.no/prosjekter/?view=project&pid=1377 (accessed on 09 March 2018). [15]

Grødem, A., R. Nielsen and A. Strand (2014), *Unge mottakere av helserelaterte ytelser - Fordelingen mellom offentlig og familiebasert forsørgelse av unge NEET [Young recipients of health-related benefits - The distribution between public and family-based care of young NEETs]*, Fafo, Oslo, http://www.fafo.no/images/pub/2014/20384.pdf. [13]

Hetland, A. (2016), *Benefit Analysis - Documentation for the benefit analysis component of the OECD data table delivery*, SSB, Oslo-Kongsvinger, https://www.ssb.no/sosiale-forhold-og-kriminalitet/artikler-og-publikasjoner/benefit-analysis. [18]

Königs, S. (2015), "Micro-level dynamics of social assistance receipt. Evidence from 4 European countries", *Discussion Papers - Statistics Norway Research Department*, No. 797, SSB, Oslo, http://www.ssb.no/en/forskning/discussion-papers/_attachment/217410 (accessed on 20 February 2018). [17]

Königs, S. (2017), "Micro-level dynamics of social assistance receipt: Evidence from four European countries", *International Journal of Social Welfare*, http://dx.doi.org/10.1111/ijsw.12279. [3]

Ministry of Labour and Social Affairs (2017), *The Norwegian Social Insurance Scheme*, https://www.regjeringen.no/contentassets/03b0e088c8f44a8793ed0c0781556b11/a-0008-e_the-norwegian-social-insurance-scheme_web-samlet.pdf (accessed on 31 January 2018). [20]

NAV (2018), *Mottakere av arbeidsavklaringspenger. Alder og kjønn. Desember 2010 - 2017*, https://www.nav.no/no/NAV+og+samfunn/Statistikk/AAP+nedsatt+arbeidsevne+og+uforetrygd+-+statistikk/Arbeidsavklaringspenger/_attachment/535977?_download=true&_ts=161091080e0 (accessed on 21 February 2018). [9]

NAV (2018), *Mottakere av uføretrygd, etter kjønn og alder. Pr. 31.12.2008-2017*, https://www.nav.no/536879/mottakere-av-uf%C3%B8retrygd-etter-kj%C3%B8nn-og-alder.pr.31.12.2008-2017.antall (accessed on 21 February 2018). [10]

OECD (2013), *Mental Health and Work: Norway*, Mental Health and Work, OECD Publishing, Paris, http://dx.doi.org/10.1787/9789264178984-en. [21]

OECD (2016), *Investing in Youth: Sweden*, Investing in Youth, OECD Publishing, Paris, http://dx.doi.org/10.1787/9789264267701-en. [16]

OECD (2016), *Society at a Glance 2016: OECD Social Indicators*, OECD Publishing, Paris, http://dx.doi.org/10.1787/9789264261488-en. [1]

OECD (2018), *Labour force statistics - incidence of unemployment by duration*, http://stats.oecd.org/Index.aspx?DataSetCode=DUR_I. [2]

OECD (2018), *OECD Economic Surveys: Norway 2018*, OECD Publishing, Paris, http://dx.doi.org/10.1787/eco_surveys-nor-2018-en. [5]

Sommar, M. (2016), *Mental health among youth in Norway : Who is responsible? What is being done?*, Nordic Council of Ministers, Stockholm, http://www.diva-portal.org/smash/record.jsf?pid=diva2%3A1071160&dswid=422. [14]

Annex 3.A. Unemployment benefit replacement rates: Additional statistics

Figure 3.A.1. Income support for the long-term unemployed is relatively high in Norway

Net replacement rates in the 13th month of unemployment for a 20-year-old jobseeker with previous earnings at 50% of the average wage, as a percentage of previous net income, 2016

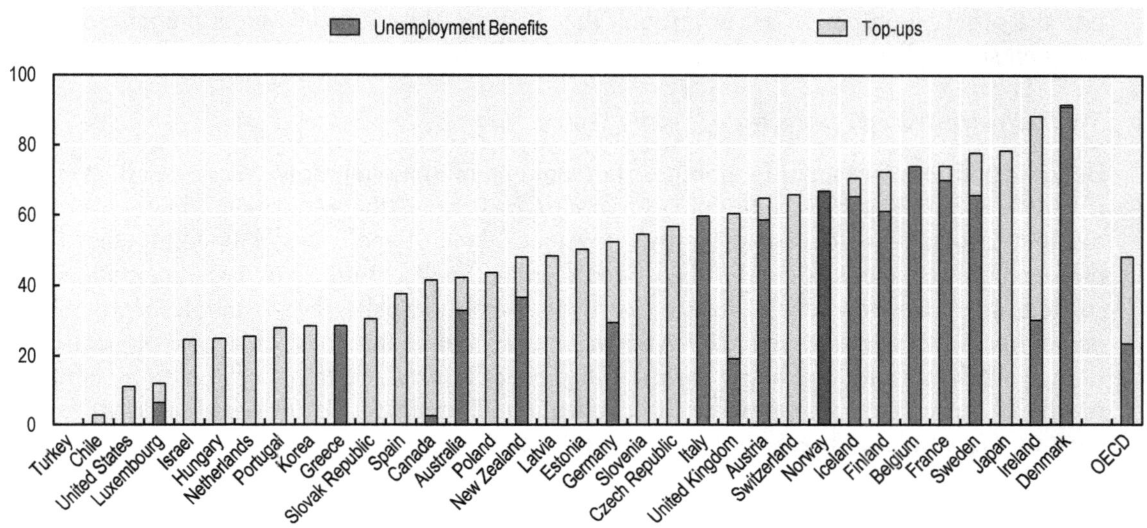

Note: The net replacement rate is that of a single, childless person who has been in continuous employment for 24 months. The average wage is not available for Turkey, such that calculations are based on wages for the Average Production Worker in the manufacturing sector. Top-ups may consist of social assistance and housing benefits, with housing costs being assumed to equal 20% of the average wage. Where receipt of social assistance or other minimum-income benefits is subject to activity tests, such as active job search or being "available" for work, these requirements are assumed to be met. No results are available for Mexico.
Source: OECD Tax-Benefit models, www.oecd.org/social/benefits-and-wages.htm.

Annex 3.B. Benefit spell analysis: Methodology

Target population

All Norwegian residents who *start* receiving one of the benefits considered in this analysis between January 2008 and December 2011, and who are 15-29 years old in the month they start receiving this benefit. Benefit spells that started before 2008, but reach into the observation period are not part of this analysis. Age is measured at the month of the spell start; education is measured on 1 October in the year the spell starts.

Spell duration and chaining of spells

Benefit spells are measured in months. Start and end month count towards the spell, even if benefit receipt starts in the middle of a month for benefits that are counted in days. For disability, social assistance and family allowances, benefit spells are chained together if the gap between spells is shorter than three months. Spells of the same type are chained so administrative procedures do not artificially shorten spells. For example, a young person receiving Work Assessment Allowance may realise that they have a permanently limited work capacity and apply for disability benefit, but there may be a gap in benefit receipt because NAV is reviewing the application. The chain rule ensures that short (at most two-month long) breaks do not interrupt factually longer spells.

Benefits covered

Unemployment Benefit

- Unemployment Benefit

Incapacity-related benefits

- Disability Benefit (pension)
- Work Assessment Allowance
- Temporary Disability Benefit (now discontinued)
- Time-limited Disability Benefit (now discontinued)
- Rehabilitation Benefit (now discontinued)

Social Assistance

- Social Assistance
- Qualification Programme

Family Benefits

- Parental-leave benefit
- Single-parent benefits (Transitional Allowance, child care benefit for working single parents, supplemental benefits and tuition support)
- Cash-for-care benefit

Source: Hetland (2016[18]).

Annex 3.C. The length of benefit receipt spells: Additional statistics

Figure 3.C.1. Benefit receipt durations of men and women are remarkably similar

Panel A. Percentage of benefit spells that are longer than 6 months, 12 months and 3 years, by benefit type and education

Panel B. Percentage breakdown of the total number of benefit spells by benefit type and education

Unemployment Benefit

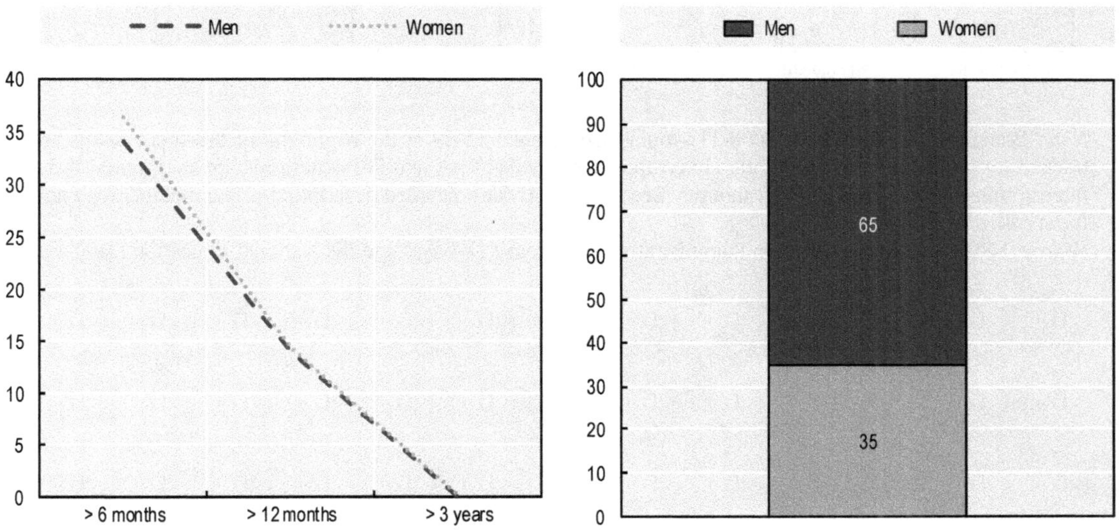

Social Assistance

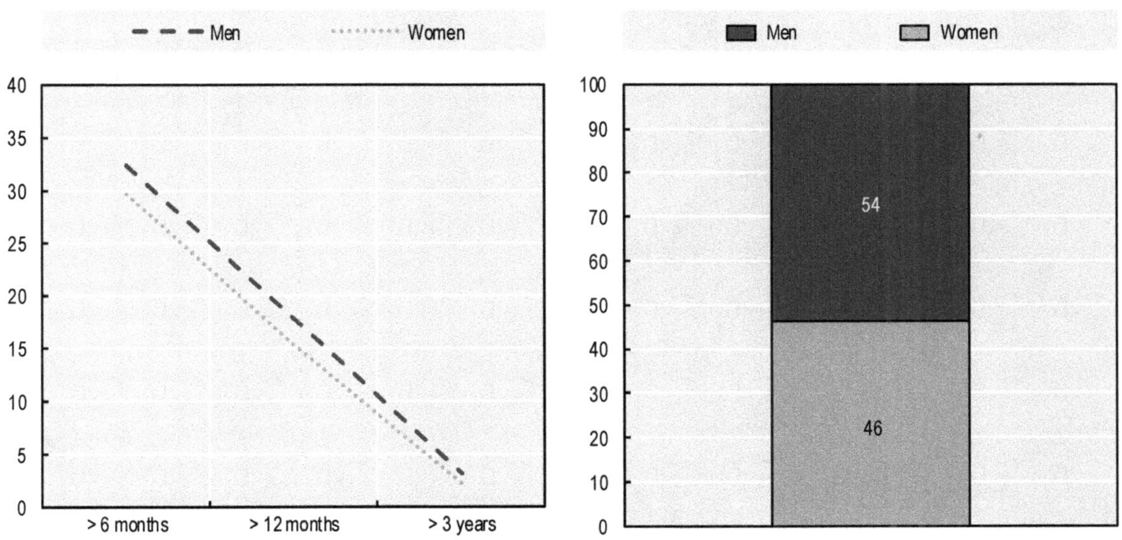

Incapacity-related benefits

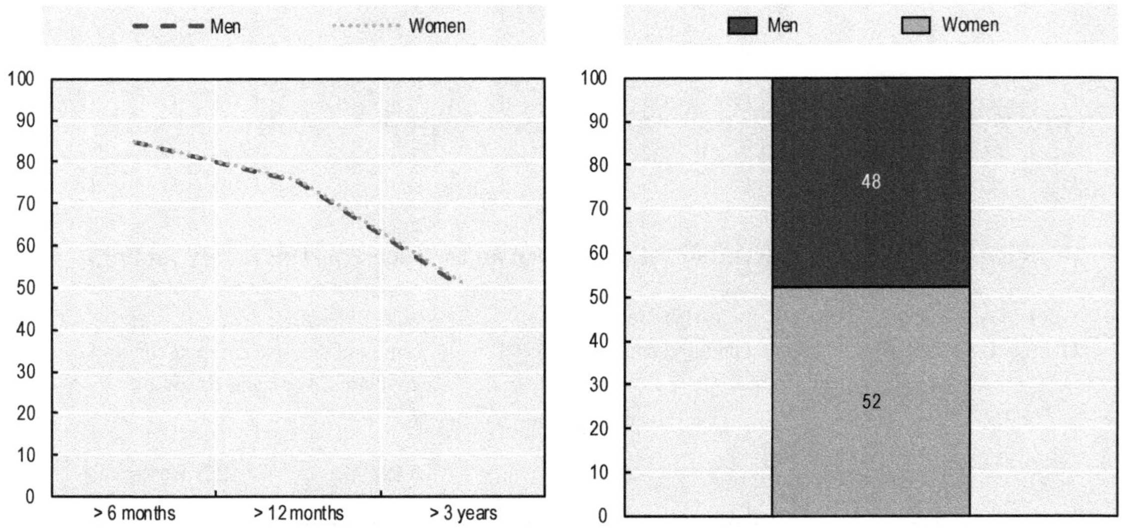

Note: Benefit spells starting in 2008-11, young people aged 15-29 at the beginning of the spell. Spells are tracked for a maximum of 36 months. Interruptions of spells of SA and DB benefit receipt are ignored if the interruptions are not longer than 2 months. See Annex 3.B for a detailed description of the methodology and the specific benefits covered.

Source: SSB calculations based on administrative data from *FD-Trygd* and the National Education Database.

Chapter 4. Raising school completion rates and providing high-quality professional training in Norway

This chapter discusses Norway's upper-secondary education system, especially its performance for disadvantaged and at-risk youth. It looks at early school leaving in Norway, policies aimed at combating school drop-out, and ways of designing education programmes for students who are not successful in the mainstream school system. It then examines vocational education and training in Norway, with a focus on workplace-based training programmes, and career guidance at school. Finally, it gives an overview of social services offered in school, and the co-ordination of these services.

The statistical data for Israel are supplied by and under the responsibility of the relevant Israeli authorities. The use of such data by the OECD is without prejudice to the status of the Golan Heights, East Jerusalem and Israeli settlements in the West Bank under the terms of international law.

Introduction

In a labour market that demands ever higher levels of qualifications and skill, ensuring that all young people achieve a level of education that allows them to gain a foothold in the labour market is essential. This is especially true for those young people who do not plan to continue on to higher education, and for highly skill-based (and high-wage) economies such as Norway.

Upper-secondary non-completion is the single most important predictor of NEET status among young people in Norway: those without upper-secondary education account for 56% of all young NEETs in Norway, and upper-secondary non-completion is the strongest predictor of being NEET as a young adult: 25-29 year-olds with at-most compulsory school are seven times more likely to be NEET than those with upper-secondary or tertiary education, the highest gap across the OECD (see Chapter 2).

Combatting early school leaving has been a policy priority in Norway for decades, but the challenge remains. Almost one in five young people between the ages of 25 and 34 has not completed upper-secondary education, which puts Norway well above the OECD average of 16%, and far above best-performers such as Korea (2%), Slovenia and Poland (6%), but also peer countries such as Finland (10%) or Sweden (13%, Figure 4.1, Panel A). Even more worryingly, while upper-secondary non-completion is on the decline across the OECD on average, it is stagnating in Norway, and even increasing among young men (Figure 4.1, Panel B).

Figure 4.1. Many young people in Norway leave school without an upper-secondary degree

Percentage of 25-34 year-olds without upper-secondary qualification

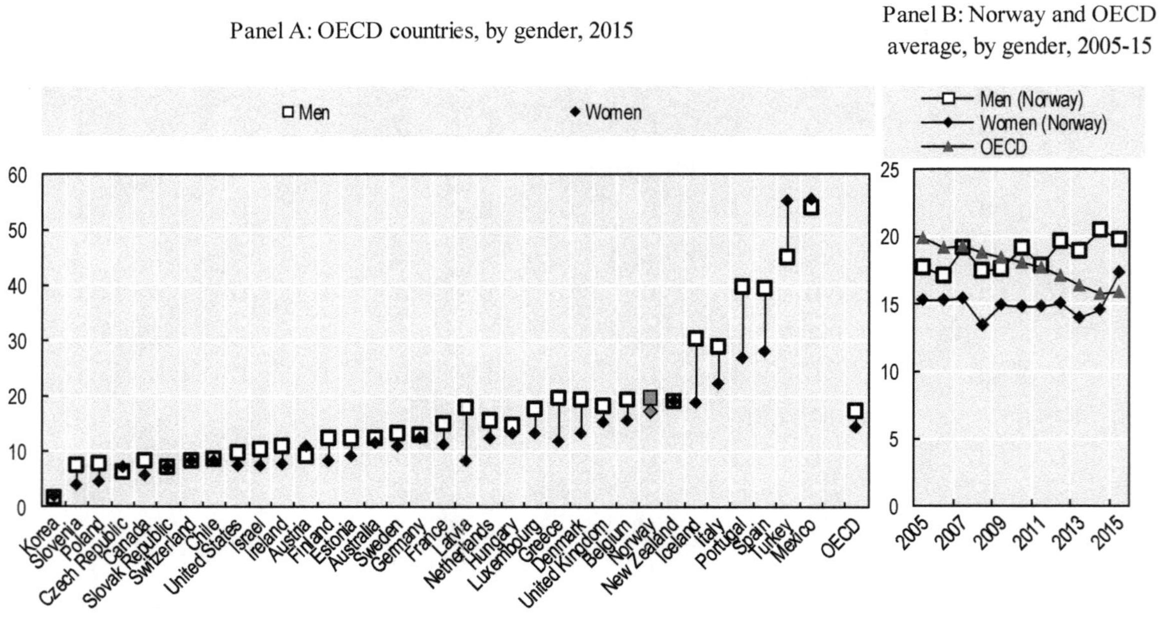

Note: There are no data on Japan. Data on Korea refer to 2013, data on Mexico to 2016. In Panel B, the OECD average excludes Australia, Chile, Israel, Korea, Mexico and New Zealand from 2000-2014.
Panel A is sorted by the overall NEET rate in ascending order.
Source: OECD calculations based on National Labour Force Surveys and the 2016 NEAC database (Australia, Germany, Israel, Korea and New Zealand).

Low returns to education as well as a tight labour market lower young people's motivation to complete upper-secondary school (OECD, 2015[1]). Reiling and Strøm (2015[2]) show that upper-secondary completion rates in Norway are counter-cyclical using regional data on unemployment rates for the years 1981-2004. They find that high unemployment rates at the time of starting upper-secondary school motivate students to complete, and this effect is strongest for VET students.[1]

This chapter takes an in-depth look at the Norwegian upper-secondary school system, focusing on how well it serves students who are at-risk of dropping out, and how well it prepares those who do not aim for tertiary education for the labour market. It is structured as follows: Section 4.1 presents the overall architecture and governance of the education system, Section 4.2 examines early school leaving in Norway and policies aimed at monitoring and improving school attendance, as well as alternative pathways in Vocational Education and Training (VET). Section 4.3 discusses the Norwegian VET system and investigates strategies to promote quality vocational training and career guidance. Section 4.4 focuses on the support available to at-risk students and their families.

4.1. General architecture and governance

The education system in Norway is highly decentralised. Primary and lower-secondary schools are run by municipalities, while upper-secondary schools are run by counties, who are also responsible for apprenticeship training. The central government has the overall responsibility for the education system, its contents (through the National Curriculum) and its funding, but schools have a lot of leeway regarding the use of their resources, and are free to make their own hiring decisions. Teachers are responsible for the technical organisation of their lessons, and the choice of teaching methods (Werler and Sivesind, 2008[3]). Because municipalities and counties have the operational responsibility for primary and secondary education, the majority of programmes for disadvantaged young people under the age of 18 are run by municipality and/or country authorities.

Funding is generous: overall expenditure on education from primary through to tertiary education is among the highest in the OECD (OECD, 2016[4]). Public education is generally free, except at kindergarten level, and also private schools derive most of their resources from public subsidies (OECD, 2013[5]). A national quality assessment system is in place to provide data and tools to evaluate school performance.

The architecture of the system is divided into three levels:

- Compulsory education (ages 6-16) is provided in comprehensive schools. It is divided into two levels, the primary level (grades 1-7) and the lower-secondary level (grades 8-10).
- Upper-secondary education (ages 16-19) is voluntary, but it is national policy that all students should attain an upper-secondary school diploma.
- Higher education follows the Bachelor-Masters-PhD model of the Bologna system.

4.1.1. Compulsory schooling

Compulsory schooling in Norway is inclusive in that students are not tracked according to ability,[2] there is no grade repetition, and students are assigned to schools by catchment area rather than school choice (OECD, 2013[5]). Over 96% of compulsory students attend public schools (SSB, 2016[6]). Norway has one of the lowest student-to-teaching-staff ratios in the OECD: around ten in both primary and lower-secondary education, compared to an OECD average of 15 in primary and 13 in secondary education (OECD, 2017[7]).

Students score above average in all three core competencies of the OECD Programme for International Student Assessment PISA, i.e. in Mathematics, Reading and Science. Norway scores well on equity in student performance across socio-economic backgrounds, but the performance gap between immigrant and non-immigrant students after accounting for socio-economic background and language spoken at home is slightly above the OECD average, and shows an upward trend. As in many OECD countries, girls outperform boys on average, but the gap in reading proficiency is among the highest in the OECD. Girls also achieve higher scores in mathematics, whereas boys perform better in this subject across the OECD on average (OECD, 2016[8]).

While subject content in lower-secondary school emphasises basic skills, the new subject "work-related training" (*Arbeidslivsfag*) was piloted with the 2006 Knowledge Promotion Reform and became a permanent part of the curriculum in the academic year 2015/16. Its goal is to give students insights into the available vocational education pathways and first practical occupational experience, which should also motivate students in their academic endeavours.

4.1.2. Upper-secondary education including VET

Compulsory school graduates have the statutory right to upper-secondary education in the regular upper-secondary school system irrespective of their grades until the age of 24; this turns into a right to upper-secondary education in the adult education system from the age of 25 onwards (Education Act, 2016[9]).[3] Almost all adolescents enrol in upper-secondary school upon leaving compulsory school (The Norwegian Directorate for Education and Training, 2016[10]).

Students can choose between three general programmes that prepare for tertiary education and nine VET programmes that are offered nationwide – students rank the programmes according to their preferences, and have to be offered a place in one of their three preferred programmes. Upper-secondary education is inclusive in that all compulsory graduates can participate irrespective of their academic performance; general and vocational programmes are taught in the same schools.

General study programmes take three years and are entirely school-based. They lead to a certificate of upper-secondary education, which grants admission to tertiary education.

VET programmes typically take four years, two years at school (the Vg1 and Vg2 level, from *Videregående skole*, i.e. upper-secondary school), followed by a two-year apprenticeship with a private business or public institution (Vg3) – this is known as the "2+2" model (Figure 4.2). Not all programmes follow this model, however – some are entirely school-based and others are based on a 1+3 model (one year in school and three years of apprenticeship).

Figure 4.2. The structure of compulsory and upper-secondary education in Norway

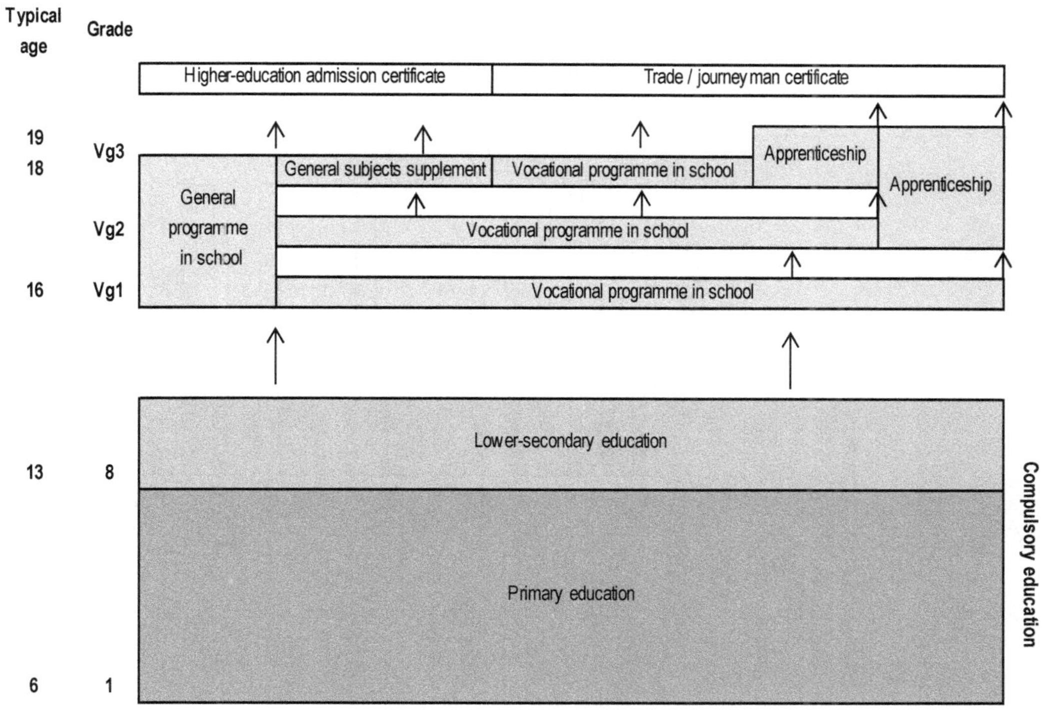

Source: OECD adaptation based on Utdanningsdirektoratet (2016[11]) and Cedefop (2014[12]).

The apprenticeship period is supposed to be split roughly evenly between work-based training and "productive work". Graduates receive a trade's or journeyman's certificate. Students who are unsuccessful in securing an apprenticeship can spend an additional year at school (Vg3 level), after which they may take the same exam as apprentices and obtain the same craft or journeyman certificate. Students who have completed the second year of their vocational education may choose to take a "supplementary programme" in grade 3 to obtain a certificate of upper-secondary education.[4]

In 2016, 53% of all first-year upper-secondary students enrolled in VET programmes – well above the OECD average of 46%, but down from nearly 60% in the early 2000s (Figure 4.3).

Figure 4.3. The share of VET students is high but declining

Panel A: First-year VET students as a percentage of all first-year upper-secondary students, 2001-16

Panel B. Percentage of students by programme type, all grades and age groups, Norway and selected OECD economies, 2015

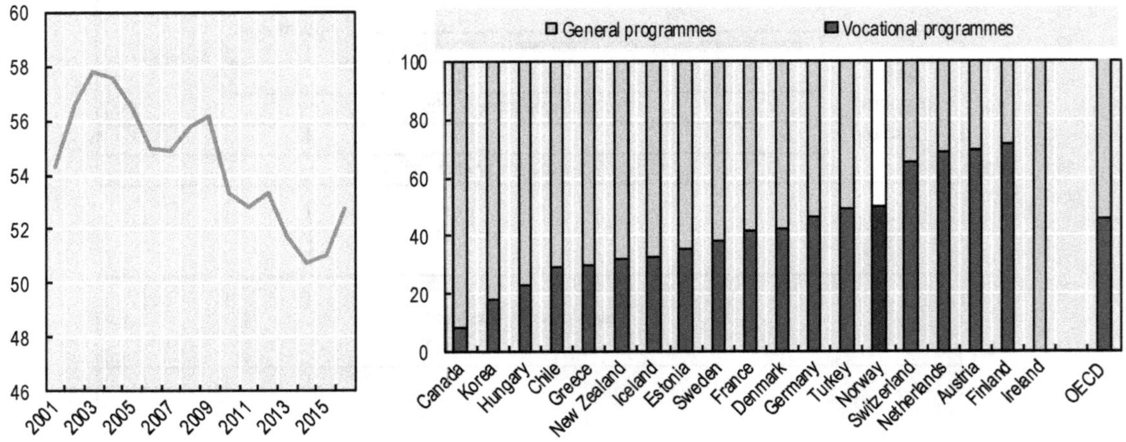

Note: No data for the US. Countries are ordered by the share of upper-secondary students in ascending order.
Source: (SSB, 2017[13]), (OECD, 2017[7])

4.1.3. Offers for special-needs students

Students with learning difficulties generally benefit from attending mainstream schooling along with other students all the way to upper-secondary education (OECD, 2012[14]). To the extent possible, learning environments should be flexible and supportive enough to cater to special-needs students in standard schools and to minimise the share of students taught in separate special education programmes. In some cases, it will however remain very difficult to integrate students who require special attention into mainstream schooling – not least because creating such an environment is very costly. Young people with severe learning difficulties or social problems may then be served best by being taught in special classes with smaller class-sizes, an adjusted and more practically-oriented curriculum and specially-trained teachers and support staff.

In Norway, the explicit policy aim is for pupils with learning difficulties to attend mainstream schooling. There is no grade retention in primary and lower-secondary school, such that students with poor marks remain in the same class with the other students of their cohort. However, pupils who do not, or cannot, benefit from mainstream education because of learning difficulties or other impairments have a right to special-needs education following a professional assessment. Special-needs education is provided in kindergartens and at all levels of schooling, including VET.

Municipalities receive an allowance to cover the additional costs of working with compulsory-school students who have learning difficulties. These funds can be used to hire assistants who help teachers working in a class with a student with a physical or mental illness or language problems. In 2016, 8% of all compulsory school students received special education (SSB, 2017[15]).

Upper-secondary school students may also receive special education, either within ordinary or adapted study programmes at school, or in workplace training; however, the right to special education does not apply to apprentices. Students who are recognised as having special needs are preferentially admitted to their choice of upper-secondary programme; furthermore, their right to upper-secondary education can be extended from three to five years to give them more time to complete their education. In 2012, 6% of all upper-secondary school students received special-needs education, a lower percentage than in primary and lower-secondary school (The Norwegian Directorate for Education and Training, 2014[16]).

Special-needs students may study to obtain a full diploma or a so-called basic qualification. A basic qualification does not lead to a full university admissions certification or to a full vocational qualification. Instead, graduates receive a training certificate that indicates which competencies they have attained. In 2013, 2.8% of all students studied for a basic qualification (The Norwegian Directorate for Education and Training, 2014[16]). Special-needs students in vocational programmes may also complete their education as training candidates, see the following section. Businesses taking on apprentices/training candidates with special needs can apply for an additional subsidy. In 2017, 959 subsidies were granted, most of them for training candidates. The average subsidy was NOK 62 000 (around EUR 6 500).

4.2. Pathways to improving school attendance

The fact that almost all young people make the transition from compulsory to upper-secondary school is a great success of the Norwegian education system. High rates of upper-secondary school dropout are a major concern, however, especially for VET programmes.

4.2.1. Early school leaving in Norway

Of the cohort who enrolled in a VET programme in 2009, only four out of ten graduated within the regular four-year programme duration. Even two years after their expected graduation, only 63% had successfully graduated, compared to an average of 70% in selected OECD and emerging economies for which data are available. Almost nine out of ten general programme students graduate within the same time frame (Figure 4.4).

Completion rates for VET programmes have been relatively stable since the late 1990s, although an upward trend is discernible in recent years (Figure 4.A1.1). This increase might have been driven by improving primary school results and an increasing share of students with well-educated parents who are more likely to complete upper-secondary school. Labour market slack might also have played a role (Huitfeldt et al., 2018[17]).[5]

Figure 4.4. Fewer than half of all VET students finish their programme within four years

Graduation rates in upper-secondary programmes within the regular programme duration and two years later, by programme orientation, in percentages, 2015

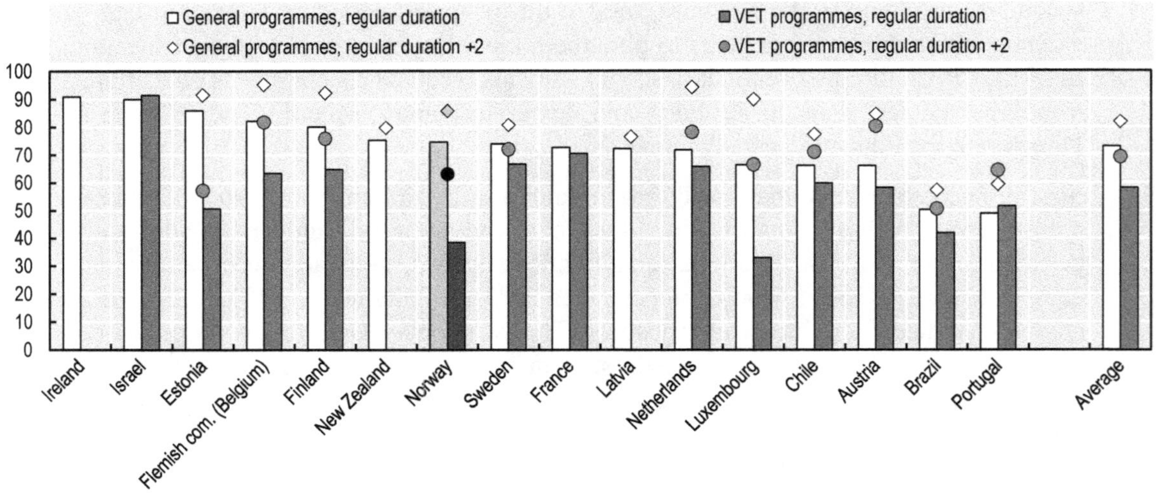

Note: Data refers to full-time students who entered upper-secondary education for the first time. Completion rates are measured at the end of the standard programme duration and two years later. These are "true cohort data", meaning that the same students are tracked and completion rates are measured at the expected graduation date and two years on. Since expected durations of general and VET programmes differ in Norway, data refer to the cohort who started a general programme in 2010 and a VET programme in 2009.
Source: Figure A2.3 in: OECD (2017), *Education at a Glance 2017: OECD Indicators*.

Completion rates vary with academic performance in compulsory school, socio-economic characteristics, region and gender:

- As there is no grade retention in Norway, students who completed compulsory school with low marks still advance to upper-secondary school. In the 2011 cohort of first-year upper-secondary students, 13% of students had a grade point average of below 30 points (out of 60) in compulsory school, indicating a low or very low level of competence in at least some subjects.[6] Only 30% of them completed upper-secondary school within five years. Students sort into upper-secondary programmes according to academic performance – over 90% of those with below 30 points in lower-secondary school chose a VET programme, compared to under 10% of those who scored 50 points and higher (SSB, 2017[18]). These weaker students have a slightly higher chance of completing VET than general programmes, but the success rate remains low (Figure 4.5, Panel A).

- Young people born abroad are less likely to graduate from upper-secondary school within five years than their Norwegian-born peers (Figure 4.5, Panel B). However, this is probably at least partly driven by young people who arrived in Norway in their late teens and might take longer than five years to graduate (see also Chapter 2). The difference in completion rates between foreign- and native-born students is wider in Norway than in other countries with available data, however in the context of low completion rates overall.

- Young people whose parents do not have upper-secondary education are less likely to graduate themselves in all countries for which data are available. In

Norway, however, only half of them achieve an upper-secondary degree within five years, compared to 56% in Sweden and 57% in Finland. The gap between the completion rates of the children of tertiary and lower-secondary educated parents is higher than in any other country for which data are available (Figure 4.5, Panel C).

- Completion rates are lower in more remote areas. The three northernmost counties of Finnmark, Troms and Nordland have the lowest completion rates (64-67%), the more densely populated areas in the south-east have the highest one (e.g. 77% in Oslo, 79% in Akershus)
- The share of students completing within the regular programme duration is higher among girls than among boys. While this is the case in all OECD countries with available data, the gender completion gap is particularly stark in Norway (14 percentage points, compared to an OECD average of 8 percentage points; it falls to 7 percentage points, in line with the OECD average, two years after the end of the programme (OECD, 2017[7])). This is consistent with better school performance among girls: PISA results show that the share of students who are low-achievers in all tested subjects (Mathematics, Reading and Science) is higher for boys than for girls in virtually all countries. For Norwegian boys, it coincides with the OECD average (14%), while Norwegian girls perform somewhat above the OECD average (8 vs. 9%; OECD, (2015[19])).

The most difficult transition for VET students is moving from the second year of school-based VET training (Vg2) to an apprenticeship (The Norwegian Directorate for Education and Training, 2016[10]). Of the cohort of students enrolling in a VET programme for the first time in 2014, only about one in three were apprentices in 2016, while 20% had left school without completing upper-secondary education. The remainder switched to a general programme, or continued their vocational education in school (Figure 4.6). These transition outcomes point to the importance of creating additional apprenticeship places, although the share of Vg2 graduates who started an apprenticeship has increased somewhat in recent years (The Norwegian Directorate for Education and Training, 2017[20]). Section 4.3.1 presents policy options to encourage employer engagement in apprenticeships.

Those who fail to secure an apprenticeship are entitled to another year of upper-secondary education, after which they can sit the same exams as apprentices ("Vg3 in school"). This alternative is not very attractive, however, because of its short duration and lack of work-based training (Aspøy and Nyen, 2015[21]).[7]

Only 30% of the 2011 VET cohort had attained a journeyman's or craft certificate one year after the end of the regular four-year programme period in 2016, and an additional 3% had attained a VET qualification with diploma. Nearly as many, 27%, had attained a university admissions certification, and 31% had dropped out of school (SSB, 2017[22]). VET students who secured an apprenticeship place are much more likely to obtain their trade certificate – over 80% of all apprentices who started their workplace training in 2011 did so within five years of starting an apprenticeship (The Norwegian Directorate for Education and Training, 2017[23]).

Figure 4.5. Completion rates vary by academic success in lower-secondary, migration background and socio-economic status

Panel A: Five-year completion rate, by grade point average in compulsory school and programme type, as percentages, young people starting upper-secondary school in 2011

Panel B: Completion rates two years after the end of the regular programme duration, as percentages, by migration background, in percentages, 2015

Panel C: Completion rates two years after the end of the regular programme duration, as percentages, by parents' educational attainment, 2015

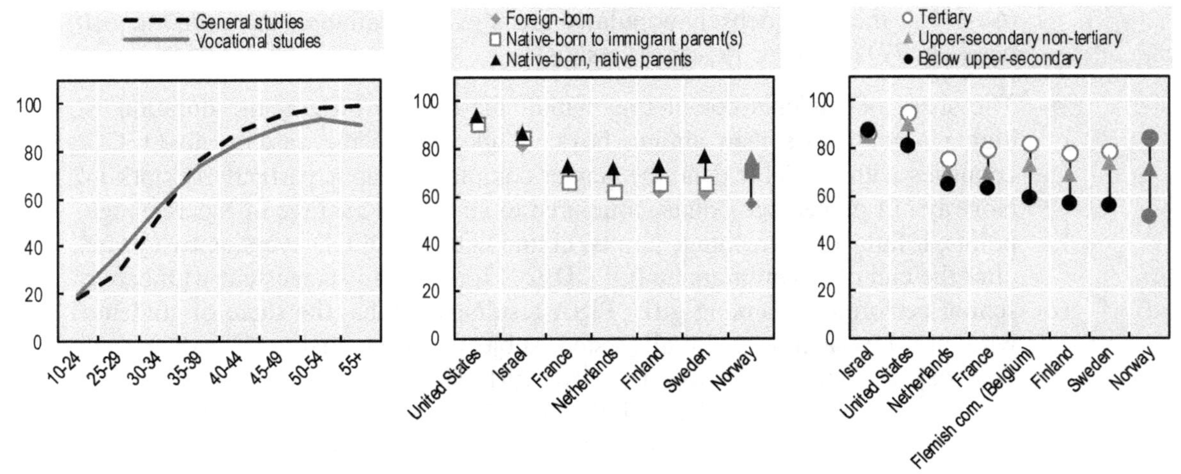

Source: Panel A: SSB (2017[18]); Panels B and C: OECD (2017[7]).

While the transition to apprenticeships is the biggest leak in VET students' progression through the system, the relatively academic nature of upper-secondary VET also contributes to the high drop-out rates. The first two years are mainly school-based (see Section 4.3), with about 25-30% of the teaching hours conducted at workplaces. General subjects account for about one-third of the curriculum, which may be overly academic for some young people; a further 50% are vocational subjects common to all students in a given VET programme without a possibility of specialisation. Around 14% of VET drop-outs never progress beyond grade one (Huitfeldt et al., 2018[17]).

Raising academic expectations in VET programmes can improve their status and facilitate transitions to tertiary education, but it can also discourage low performing students from completing upper-secondary school. Norway introduced a set of measures to combat school drop-out 2010 under the label *Ny Giv* (see Box 4.1), which acknowledged this trade-off by piloting lower-level VET pathways featuring more practical training (Section 2.2.3).

The fact that counties are responsible for the development and implementation of measures against drop-out furthermore creates a fragmented landscape of multiple interventions that complicates the diffusion of effective programmes and their consistent implementation. Over the past decade, Norwegian councils have implemented literally hundreds of measures (see Huitfeldt et al. (2018[17]) for a recent overview), very few of which have been rigorously evaluated.

Figure 4.6. Only a third of all VET students start an apprenticeship

Transitions of VET students after the end of Vg2, in percentages, 2016

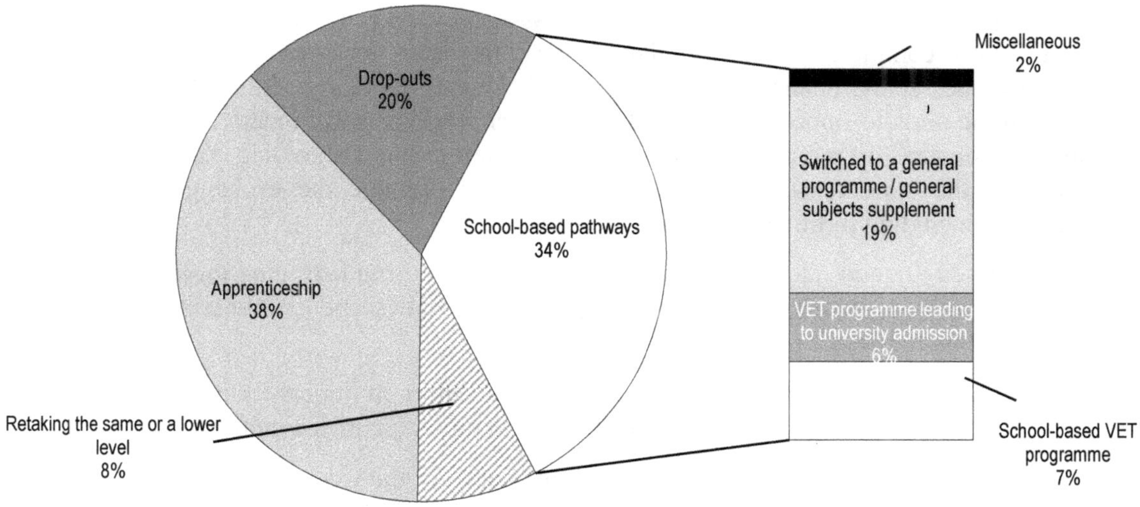

Source: The Norwegian Directorate for Education and Training (2017).

Norway is taking important steps, however, to submit local projects to more rigorous evaluation to be able to identify and scale the most successful programmes. Under the Programme for Enhanced Completion of Upper-secondary Education (Box 4.1), municipalities and research organisations can apply for funding to trial methods that have the potential to raise upper-secondary completion. The aim is to build a body of knowledge of "what works" in different locations. Four research consortia have been granted funding so far, and all of them use experimental randomised controlled trial (RCT) techniques to evaluate their programmes. Similarly, the Research Council of Norway will establish an Innovation Fund to finance consortia of councils and research institutions that carry out trials to improve the quality of kindergartens and schools, up to upper-secondary education.

Norway also tries to improve the coordination of programmes for young people at-risk of dropping out through better coordination of government services within the "0-24" agreement, see Section 4.4.3.

The youth guides project (*Losprosjektet*) also aims to reduce upper-secondary drop out by offering youth more guidance and personalised follow-up, see Section 4.4.

Box 4.1. *Ny Giv* and beyond

Ny Giv (New Possibilities) was a 2010-13 cross-agency effort to increase the share of youth who complete upper-secondary education, later renewed under the title "Programme for Enhanced Completion of Upper-secondary Education". The programme aims to improve collaboration between various stakeholders dealing with upper-secondary drop-outs – municipalities, counties, the Follow-Up Service (see below in the main text), NAV and schools – and promote the exchange of best practices, including through research and evaluation.

Between 2010 and 2013, the central government funded the project with NOK 611 million, which can be supplemented by counties and/or municipalities. It consists of three parts:

- **Statistics**: develop a standardised set of indicators to improve the consistency of information about school drop-out across municipalities/counties.
- **Additional instruction** (7.5 hours each week) for the weakest 10% of students in the last semester of lower-secondary school. At-risk students may also be offered summer jobs or courses to ease the transition from lower to upper-secondary school. Over 12 000 students benefitted from this programme, funded at EUR 4 000 per student.
- **Improve follow-up** for NEETs, mostly through improved coordination between agencies to reduce the time between school drop-out and offer of an activity, but also through increased additional funding for psychologists and counsellors in schools.

Ny Giv also introduced two new VET pathways to make VET more attractive for school-tired youth: the Certificate of Practice and the Training Candidature Scheme (see Section 2.2.3).

Huitfeldt et al. (2018[17]) estimate the impact of the additional basic skills courses for the weakest students in the last year of lower-secondary school, exploiting a gradual phase-in across regions. The authors find no effect of the additional courses on upper-secondary completion, such as grades in the last year of lower-secondary or the first year of upper-secondary, or transitions to the second year of upper-secondary school. One reason for these weak outcomes could be that the additional lessons took place during regular class hours, meaning that students would miss their regular classes to attend – this led to high absence rates in additional instruction classes. Teachers also thought that the measure had been implemented too hastily, resulting in a lack of essential resources such as dedicated classrooms and suitable timeslots. Many teachers also found the measure came too late in students' school careers.

The fact that a majority of headmasters, teachers and students nevertheless assessed the measure as effective (Huitfeldt et al., 2018[17]) illustrates that stakeholder perceptions of a programme's success, that are normally the outcomes assessed by *ad hoc* programme evaluations, do not necessarily correlate with programme impacts (see also the discussion on the need for rigorous impact evaluation in Chapter 5).

2.2.2. Monitoring and reporting school attendance

School drop-out is typically not a sudden, unexpected event but the consequence of a longer process of gradual disengagement (Lyche, 2010[24]). This process can be driven by a range of different factors – learning difficulties, mental health issues, family problems, or a more general disappointment with the school experience – which tend to interact and accumulate over time (OECD, 2012[14]). To prevent a young person from dropping out, these challenges need to be addressed as soon as they arise.

School attendance is tightly monitored in Norway. Counties are legally obliged to track young people aged 16-21 who have not completed upper-secondary education and are neither in work nor attending school, to offer them guidance and interventions, such as educational or active labour market programmes with a view to bringing them back into upper-secondary school. To that purpose, each county has, since 1994, a "Follow-Up Service" that tracks those not in upper-secondary school to offer counselling, establish contact with the public employment and welfare office (NAV), or coordinate other services (such as health or social services).

The Follow-Up Service identifies young NEETs by comparing county-level population registries with lists of enrolled students; schools also notify them directly of drop-outs during the year. In the 2016/17 academic year, the Follow-Up Services identified around 18 000 young NEETs – 8% of all 16-21 year-olds – who had not completed upper-secondary education (The Norwegian Directorate for Education and Training, 2017[25]). They successfully established contact with 94% of them, up from 88% in 2012 (The Norwegian Directorate for Education and Training, 2018[26]).

Once contact is established, the Follow-Up Service collaborates with NAV and municipal and county authorities to provide tailored combinations of work practice and schooling to provide youth with alternative ways of completing their education. Young people may be registered as part-time students and part-time unemployed. In the 2016/17 academic year, nearly half of all identified young NEETs could be engaged in an activity, mostly NAV-run active labour market programmes, but also programmes offered by municipal or county authorities, as well as combinations of NAV and local authority measures (Figure 4.7).

In most counties, the Follow-Up Services as independent entities collaborate with schools and social services, but they may also be integrated with schools and the NAV. In Oslo, for instance, Follow-Up Service coordinators work both at schools and NAV offices; 110 counsellors work directly at Oslo's schools (both at the lower- and upper-secondary level) and an additional Follow-Up offices exist in each of the 15 district NAV offices.

Figure 4.7. Nearly half of the Follow-Up Services' target group are in active programmes

16-21 year-olds without upper-secondary education who are not enrolled in school or working, by status, academic year 2016/17

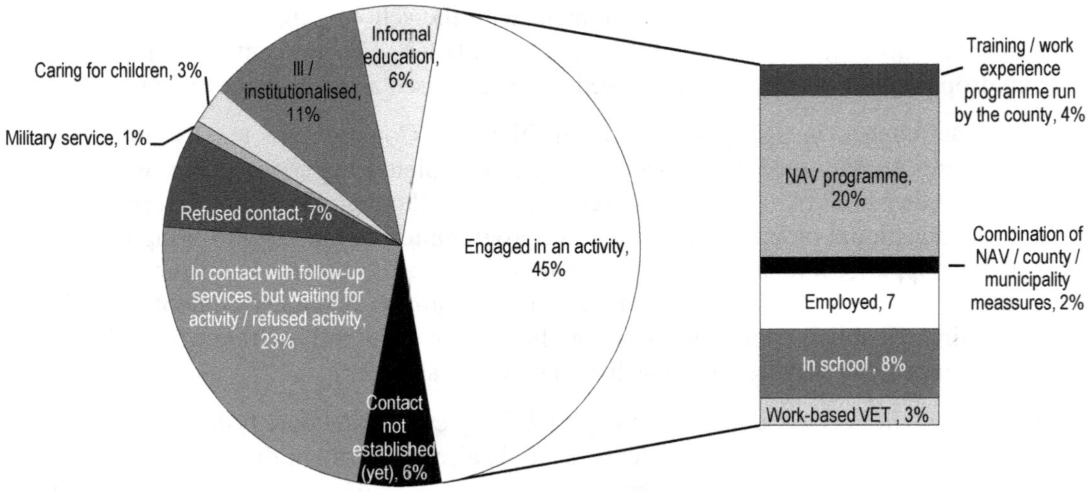

Source: The Norwegian Directorate for Education and Training (2018[26]) based on data from the Follow-Up Services.

2.2.3. Tailored learning options for at-risk students

School environments have to be tailored to students' individual needs to help all young people to attain their full potential and minimise the risk of school failure and dropout. In a step to raise upper-secondary completion rates, Norway introduced several alternative routes in the upper-secondary VET system that feature earlier and more work-based training than the regular 2+2 system, and are therefore interesting for students who are disenchanted with classroom-based instruction.

Two other alternative pathways in VET, the Certificate of Practice (*Praksisbrev*) and the Training Candidature Scheme gained relevance in recent years:

- The Training Candidature Scheme is a vocational track for special-needs students who cannot meet the requirements for a full vocational qualification. Curricula are student-tailored and can combine work- and classroom-based training. The programme does not have a set duration, and the final competence attained can vary across trainees. Graduates receive a "certificate of competence" detailing the level of competence / the parts of the regular curricula they have mastered (Høst, 2008[27]; Olsen et al., 2014[28]). Students may start their upper-secondary education in this scheme, or may transfer if they realise that they are unlikely to be able to achieve the "full competence" of the vocational certificate. There were 2 000 registered trainees in 2016, around 5% of all apprentices / trainees (SSB, 2018[29]).
- The Certificate of Practice is an alternative VET pathway for youth at risk of dropping out because they lack motivation for classroom-based learning. The programme is only two years long, and students spend four days a week training at the workplace (OECD, 2013[30]). Successful candidates are awarded a lower-level VET certificate, which they may top up with a regular

apprenticeship to obtain their full journeyman / craft certificate. In a 2008 small-scale pilot, 41 of 51 participants completed within two years, and around half went on to a regular apprenticeship after completing the programme with the goal of earning a full journeyman or craft certificate (Olsen et al., 2014[28]). It is not possible to draw firm conclusions on the success of this scheme because this pilot had a small number of participants and lacked a control group. However, the pilot participants had low grades from compulsory school and were thus at a high risk of dropping out (see Section 4.2.1), and transition rates to a regular apprenticeship were *higher* than among students in mainstream VET on average (although about a third of VET students transition to school-based pathways after two years, see Figure 4.6). Following the 2008 pilot, this scheme has been regularised in 2016. The Certificate of Practice has also a curriculum and competence requirements set at the county level, which should make the qualification standardised and recognisable for employers at least at the local level. To judge the impact of this alternative track, more research is needed on the long-term school-to-work pathways of young programme participants compared to similar other youth.

The question of expanding alternative pathways in VET is controversially discussed in Norway (e.g. Olsen et al. (2015[31])) – there is a concern that alternative, lower-level tracks could erode the inclusiveness of the education system, pushing disadvantaged young people into inferior pathways instead of offering them support to obtain a full diploma. Companies might also take advantage of shorter training contracts to further extricate themselves from their training responsibilities.

These concerns are not without merit: in countries that have strongly diversified educational options such as Austria and Germany, students with low socio-economic status backgrounds tend to sort into the less academically challenging pathways, with detrimental effects on their future school careers. However, in Austria and Germany, children are already tracked at age ten – providing lower-level options at age 16 should put students in a better position to choose the right educational path (OECD, 2012[14]).

Youth who might otherwise successfully complete a full upper-secondary school programme might also end up with a lesser qualification. More practically oriented programmes are, however, also more inclusive, especially to low-performing students and those from disadvantaged backgrounds. Holm et al (2013[32]) estimate that the introduction of vocational upper-secondary options in Denmark increased participation in upper-secondary education by around six percentage points, and that especially students from socio-economically disadvantaged families benefited from this increase. They do find, however, that some of these students are less likely to go on to university rather than to post-secondary VET. Similarly, Ichou and Vallet (2011[33]) show that while the differentiation of the French upper-secondary system did increase sorting into tracks based on socio-economic background it also lead to increased participation. Indeed, in countries with lower-level upper-secondary tracks, such as Austria, Germany and Switzerland, around 90% of all 25-34 year-olds have completed an upper-secondary degree, compared to only 81% in Norway (Figure 4.1).

At present, high drop-out rates, especially among disadvantaged young people, show that the standard upper-secondary programmes do not deliver for the weakest students. Offering them a lower-level option is preferable to leaving them without a qualification – too high standards can prevent some young people from getting the qualifications they need to make a smooth transition to work.

Also, as the Certificate of Practice shows, alternative pathways can be designed as stepping stones toward higher levels of qualification that seem more achievable for students who struggled in compulsory school and who find the perspective of two more years of schooling demotivating.

Besides continuing to expand alternative VET tracks, Norway should consider offering short courses to prepare those most at-risk of dropping out for upper-secondary school. Students who leave compulsory school with gaps in basic skills or who are not motivated for class-room based training could benefit from short pre-apprenticeship programmes that combine basic skills training with work experience, see Box 4.2.

Box 4.2. Offering pre-apprenticeship programmes to the weakest students

Pre-apprenticeship programmes are targeted at young people who lack the basic skills and motivation to complete a regular VET programme. They help young people close any basic skill gaps with additional training in literacy and numeracy; they build their motivation by offering them work experience that demonstrates how skills built at school can be used in practice; and they improve their non-cognitive and social skills by familiarising them with workplace routines and practices. The goal of pre-apprenticeship programmes is for young people to transition into a regular apprenticeship / VET programme.

In Germany, young people who cannot find an apprenticeship because of poor compulsory-school performance can apply for pre-vocational training. These programmes last up to one year and introduce trainees to various occupational fields, placing them in companies for subsidised internships. They teach the curriculum of the first year of the regular vocational pathway. Pre-vocational courses are also open to young people without a lower-secondary qualification, who can attend school part-time during the pre-apprenticeship to obtain their school-leaving certificate. Employment outcomes of the German pre-vocational training have been good, albeit not among the most disadvantaged students (Caliendo, Künn and Schmidl, 2011[34]).

In Australia, pre-apprenticeships seek to introduce young people to a trade before they commit to an apprenticeship, build their basic skills and motivation as well as their knowledge in the relevant profession to increase their chances of securing an apprenticeship. They typically involve both classroom-based VET courses and work placements, and students who are still at school can participate part-time. In 2010, an estimated 28% of all apprentices had completed a pre-apprenticeship (OECD, 2016[35]).

Source: OECD (2016[35]; 2016[36]), Caliendo et a. (2011[34]).

4.3. Promotion of quality vocational training and apprenticeships

Quality VET can play an important role in equipping young people with the mix of general and job-specific skills that they need to find stable employment. A combination of classroom-based learning and practical training in the workplace serves a dual role: it ensures the relevance of the training through the active participation of employers, and it is an attractive alternative to more academic, general education for practically minded young people.

VET at the upper-secondary level in Norway changed substantially over recent decades. A sweeping reform incorporated apprenticeships into upper-secondary VET programmes in 1994 and reduced the number of programmes significantly to delay students' choice of occupation and to make countrywide VET provision more homogenous. The reform also increased the emphasis on academic subjects in VET programmes, and established transitional pathways between VET and general upper-secondary education with the goal of making VET more equivalent to general upper-secondary school in both status and content. The number of VET programmes was further reduced in 2006, and even more emphasis was put on general subjects at the expense of vocational content.

The system's main problems today are low completion rates and weak ties to the labour market. Around 30% of applicants do not find an apprenticeship place (The Norwegian Directorate for Education and Training, 2016[10]), and the transition from school-based to workplace-based VET is the point at which most students drop out (see Section 4.2.1).

Three factors contribute to employers' reluctance to take on apprentices: the fact that VET provision is largely driven by student choice, the limited specialisation in the school-based part of training, as well as the relatively generous remuneration of apprentices in international comparison. The Norwegian Government, together with the social partners, is developing a new vocational programme framework that will permit students to specialise earlier, which will enter into force with the 2020/21 school year.

4.3.1. Providing youth with relevant practical skills

Student choice is an important value in Norwegian VET. All compulsory graduates are entitled to a place in one of their three preferred VET programmes. The late start of apprenticeship training in year three means that youth choose their vocational pathway before beginning to look for an apprenticeship; the extent to which businesses can steer youth towards occupations that they require through offering to train them is therefore limited. This *de facto* weakens the influence of the skill needs of local employers on VET, although the social partners are involved in its governance. In countries with strong apprenticeship traditions, apprentices choose a specific occupation from day one, and they are required to have secured an employer before starting their training, see Box 4.3 on the apprenticeship system in Austria.

The first two years of upper-secondary VET are school-based and offer limited scope for specialisation: about 30% of teaching time is devoted to general subjects, and a further 50% are common to all students in a given VET programme. The remaining 20% is devoted to the "in-depth study project", which is ideally carried out in cooperation with local businesses and supposed to enable students to learn more about specific vocations and connect with businesses earlier on (Michelsen, Olsen and Høst, 2014[37]). Schools have a lot of leeway in the realisation of this project – students may specialise in a specific occupation in their chosen programme, but they may equally pick a common core subject. In practice, during the first year, training mostly takes place in workshops in schools; schools and municipalities try to place students with local businesses in the second year. The institutional link to employers is weak, however, and student placements depend heavily on personal contacts of individual schools/teachers (Olsen et al., 2015[31]).

Students only pick a specific trade or occupation after completing the second year. The number of trades depends on the programme area, and varies between 50 (technical and industrial production) and three (media and communications, Olsen et al. (2014[28])).

VET programmes should offer earlier and deeper specialisation of students in specific occupations – VET tends to work best when it equips students with specialist, occupational knowledge and skills that are readily applicable in the workplace. Kreisman and Stage (2017[38]), for example, show for a sample of US high school students that taking advanced VET courses adds a wage premium of about 2% per year, while introductory courses do not carry a wage premium. A more specialised curriculum would make VET students more attractive apprentices for employers. The Norwegian Directorate for Education and Training also recommends more specialised VET training in a recent submission (The Norwegian Directorate for Education and Training, 2016[39]).

The relatively generous remuneration of apprentices likely contributes also to employers' reluctance to take them on. Apprentice salaries are part of collective agreements and hence vary across sectors and occupations, but typically start at 30% of a newly qualified worker's salary and increase to up to 75-80% at the end of the apprenticeship. In Germany and Switzerland, apprentices start at about 15% of a qualified worker's wage, and progress to 18-27% by the end of the apprenticeship period (Muehlemann et al., 2010[40]). German and Swiss apprentices spend 20-30% of the work week at school, while Norwegian apprentices work full-time and have already acquired theoretical training in the first two years of their VET programme. Thus, in the first year, Norwegian apprentices receive about the same relative wage as their German and Swiss counterparts, while working more hours. But their cost rises quickly: in the second year, their gross earnings more than double, while in Germany and Switzerland, earnings increase by less than a third.

This argument can also be made by comparing apprentices' salaries directly with those of skilled workers. Employers receive a government grant, NOK 153 053 (about EUR 16 000) per apprentice in 2018, to be distributed across the two years of training (The Norwegian Directorate for Education and Training, 2018[41]). The labour cost of an apprentice including this subsidy and employer contributions to social security is about 12% of that of a low-wage worker (67% of the average wage) at the beginning, and about 57% at the end of the apprenticeship.[8] Muehlemann et al. (2010[40]) estimate the relative productivity of apprentices to start at about 30% of a skilled worker's productivity, and to reach 50% by year two. Norwegian apprentice contracts stipulate that about half of their time should be spent on training and half on "productive work"; hence, 50% of their working time on training, their relative cost in the first year appears to be aligned with their relative productivity, but increases too sharply in the second year, when it should only increase to about 25%. This indicates that firms face comparatively relatively high costs in hiring apprentices, especially in the second year.

Box 4.3. The apprenticeship system in Austria

Austria is one of the countries with the highest overall participation in VET – 80% of all male and 70% of all female upper-secondary students participated in VET in 2012. Around 40% of each cohort chooses the traditional apprenticeship route, while the other 40% enrol in school-based VET or VET colleges (Dornmayr and Nowak, 2015[42]).

Apprentices can pursue 197 defined occupations as of 2015 (BMWFW, 2014[43]). Occupations are introduced or amended at the initiative of the social partners or individual businesses; the Ministry of Labour, in collaboration with the social partners, then fleshes out a detailed profile for the occupation, and develops the national curricula. Apprenticeships start after compulsory school (around age 15) and typically last three years. Young people must secure an apprenticeship slot to start training, although in some cases, they may start an apprenticeship at a publicly run workshop as part of the youth guarantee. The availability of apprenticeship places therefore acts as a link between the labour market and the training system, as young people cannot choose occupations that employers are not willing to train. Apprentices spend around 25% of their time in school and 75% in work-based training. They receive a salary determined by collective bargaining agreements that differs across sectors and occupations; it reaches an average of 80% of a skilled worker's starting wage in the last year of the apprenticeship.

Social security contributions are partly waived, and businesses receive a public subsidy covering 25% of the apprentice's salary in the first, and 8% in the last year of apprenticeship training. There are additional subsidies for the further qualification of VET trainers in businesses, taking on special-needs apprentices, or young people who were previously unsuccessful in finding a place. In 2013, 75% of all apprentices who ended their apprenticeship contract did so after successfully completing their final exams.[1] The median time graduates took to start their first job is shortest for apprentices (1.5 months) as compared to graduates of classroom based VET schools and colleges (around three months) and general upper-secondary programmes (four months, Statistik Austria, 2015).[2] Fersterer and Winter-Ebmer (2003[44]) find wage returns of 15% to a training period of three to four years. Fersterer, Pischke and Winter-Ebmer (2008[45]) find similar returns for apprentices in small firms.

1. This is not strictly equivalent to a drop-out rate, as it measures young people who successfully completed as a share of all apprentices who dissolved a contract and did not sign a new one within a year, i.e. this measure is not cohort-based. Apprenticeship contracts are most likely to be dissolved in the first couple of months; hence this measure of apprenticeship drop-out is upward-biased if the number of apprentices increases, and downward-biased if it decreases. Furthermore, apprentices who completed their work-based training, but failed or did not take their exam, may sit for it later, but are counted as drop-outs by this measure.

2. Training enterprises are obliged by law to keep on successfully graduated apprentices for at least three, but up to six months after their exam (depending on the collective bargaining agreement for the company's sector). To correct for this, only periods of employment starting after the first six months, or exceeding six months, are counted as first jobs. The numbers are furthermore corrected for young men serving their compulsory military service after completing their schooling / training.

Source: BMWFW and WKÖ (2015[46]), Hoeckel (2010[47]) , OECD (2016[48]).

The total cost of training apprentices does not only depend on wage costs and subsidies, however, but also on time spent training apprentices on the job, the skill demand of tasks apprentices perform (largely determined by regulations, and likely to differ across sectors and occupations) and the productivity of apprentices in the tasks they are assigned. In the long run, firms can recoup training costs through the retention of qualified apprentices, especially in the presence of significant hiring costs (Muehlemann and Wolter, 2014[49]). Many employers, especially small and medium enterprises, might not take these long-term considerations into account, however, and may be put off by relatively high wages for apprentices who require a lot of training.

Norway implemented a variety of measures to increase the number of apprenticeship places in recent years, including stepwise increases in the training subsidy, as well as the introduction and subsequent increase of a bonus for first-time training companies. All public agencies with over 100 employees have to train apprentices, and in 2017, a training clause was added to public tenders (The Norwegian Government, 2017[50]). A new website helps young people find employers that offer apprenticeship places.[9]

While these are important efforts, Norway could do more could to reduce the cost of apprentices, either through additional subsidies or through a slower pace of wage increases during the training. Public subsidies to firms are already quite generous and carry the risk of deadweight loss (of subsidising firms who would have trained apprentices even in the absence of government intervention). This is especially true in Norway, where detailed data on total costs of apprentices are lacking, and the amount of the subsidy would therefore be a shot in the dark (Muehlemann and Wolter, 2014[49]). One alternative would be to flatten the wage in the course of the apprenticeship bringing it on par with that in other countries; but government influence over collective bargaining is of course limited.

Other forms of incentives for firms are possible. A number of diverse financial incentives are in place in other OECD countries, from direct subsidies to tax and social security rebates to direct levy financing (see Box 4.4). Norway used a substantial subsidy for firms upon successful graduation of their apprentices in the late 1990s (Askilden and Øivind, 2005[51]), similar to a tax benefit now granted to employers when apprentices complete their training in Australia (OECD, 2016[35]). Norway could consider reintroducing this subsidy, which could also help improve training completion rates.

Box 4.4. Providing employers with incentive to offering apprenticeships

Direct subsidies

Several countries subsidise employers directly to take on apprentices. In the United Kingdom, the National Apprenticeship Service offers apprenticeship grants of GBP 1 500 to employers with up to 1 000 employees who recruit 16-to-24 year-olds. Eligible employers are those who have never before employed an apprentice and those who have not recruited one in the previous 12 months. Up to 10 grants can be made to any 1 employer. In Austria, companies are financially rewarded for every additional apprentice they take above the number hired in the previous year. They also receive a grant if they resume hiring apprentices after a break. Under the Australian Apprenticeships Incentives Programme, companies are eligible for incentive payments when their apprentices start and complete the programme – up to AUD 4 000 in total. Employers of apprentices and trainees who have faced particular barriers to training and employment can receive additional support.

Tax credits and social security rebates

Another way to subsidise the provision of apprenticeship places is to grant tax credits and/or social security rebates. The French government grants certain firms receive a tax credit of EUR 1 600 per apprentice, which increases to EUR 2 200 if the apprentice has a disability or is considered disadvantaged. Firms may are also exempted from social security contributions for the apprentices they take on. On top of the tax credits, each region offers additional subsidies for hiring apprentices. In Canada, employers can claim up to CAD 2 000 per year for each eligible apprentice under Apprenticeship Job Creation Tax Credit scheme.

Minimum wage

The cost of hiring apprentices can also be lowered by agreeing a special sub-minimum wage. Several countries make use of the practice. In France, the minimum wage for apprentices depends on their age and the year of training they are in, starting at 25% of the national minimum wage for 18-year-olds in their first year and rising to 93% for the over-2s in their fourth year. In Germany, a "training allowance" is agreed upon by the social partners, which also varies according to the apprentice's age and experience with the firm.

Levy financing

An interesting indirect mechanism for incentivising companies to offer apprenticeships is to require them to contribute to a special training fund, from which only firms who take on apprentices benefit. All companies in Denmark pay a yearly contribution of nearly EUR 400 per employee into the Employers' Refunds for Apprentices Fund (AER). The AER then compensates companies every 24 months for each apprentice hired. In France, workplace training is funded through an apprentice tax paid by all businesses. It is set at 0.05% of the payroll for firms with fewer than 250 employees and 0.06% for firms with more than 250 employees. Companies may be exempted from the tax if they train a certain number of apprentices.

Source: OECD ($2014_{[52]}$).

2.2.2. *Offering career guidance and counselling*

Career guidance can improve the match between youth and their chosen education or training path. It increases the likelihood of programme completion, links the labour market to the education system by encouraging young people to choose paths that are likely to lead to stable employment, and encourages social mobility by informing young people of career options that might not be suggested by their family and social networks. Career guidance is of particular importance for young people considering a VET programme, because these programmes affect students' career prospects more directly than general secondary tracks. As the Norwegian education system is based on student choice, with a limited input of employer's skills requirements in the funding of study places, steering young people towards programmes with attractive employment and earnings prospects is crucial.

Students in Norway are entitled to career guidance by law. Educational and vocational guidance should inform students of various educational pathways and their career options, and provide them with knowledge of the labour market. A digital career guidance portal[10], with descriptions of 600 different professions, is available as a resource for career guidance in the final grades of compulsory education.

Career guidance is implemented at the school level, and is thus under the purview of municipalities (for compulsory schools) and counties (for upper-secondary schools). As a consequence, the quality of the provision can be uneven – while the education act recommends minimum qualifications for counsellors, it does not mandate them (Vox, 2018[53]). A recent government report (NOU, 2016[54]) recommends consistent qualification requirements for career counsellors and a clearer differentiation between career guidance and social and pedagogical counselling at schools (see Section 4.4.1).

Because of the decentralised responsibility for career guidance, there are no harmonised statistics on the number of career counsellors – the government report (NOU, 2016[54]) estimates that there are about 1 500 career counsellors in compulsory and upper-secondary schools, implying a ratio of one to every 260 lower- and upper-secondary students.

In the last year of compulsory school, students may visit upper-secondary schools and do one-week internships, but they are not particularly encouraged to do longer internships (4-6 weeks) that would allow them to learn about work life or a specific occupation they are interested in.

The Follow-Up Service (Section 4.2.2) also offers career guidance to young people aged 16-21, and, since 2008, most counties established "regional partnerships" for career guidance involving schools, the local NAV office, county authorities and other stakeholders. The goal is to provide more coherent guidance to youth and improve the labour market knowledge of career advisors (Vox, 2018[53]). The "Programme for Enhanced Completion of Upper-secondary Education" (see Section 4.2.1) also provides additional funds for improving career guidance in upper-secondary school (Cedefop, 2017[55]). The "NAV counsellors in upper-secondary schools" project also aims to improve career guidance in upper-secondary schools, see Chapter 5, Box 5.3.

4.4. Support for at-risk students and their families

School absenteeism and low educational performance are often caused or reinforced by non-educational factors, such as family problems, health issues or substance abuse.

Young people suffering from these problems need comprehensive support – in addition to any help the school can offer, students may require support from specialised social and health service agencies that can help them navigate family problems, solve a difficult housing situation, or provide treatment for mental health or substance abuse problems. This section discusses the support available to troubled young people within and outside schools and looks at the coordination of these services.

4.4.1. Services offered within schools

Students with personal, family or health problems are entitled to "social and pedagogical" counselling at school. Counsellors should either assist students directly, or help them navigate other services. This type of guidance has strong links to the Pedagogical and Psychological Service (see below) and the school health service. Schools can autonomously decide how many counsellors to hire; funds from "Programme for Enhanced Completion of Upper-secondary Education" can be used for this purpose. About 1 500 social and pedagogical counsellors work in Norway's lower- and upper-secondary schools (NOU, 2016[54]).

Teachers and students can also access psychological counselling through the county-run Pedagogical and Psychological Service (*Pedagogisk-psykologisk tjeneste*, PPT). The PPT assesses students' need for special-needs education releasing federal funding, works with students suffering from mild learning disabilities or mental disorders such as dyslexia or anxieties, and helps with the referral of more serious cases. They can also support the school or individual teachers in dealing with students with emotional or behavioural problems (OECD, 2013[56]). At compulsory school level, the PPT had 1 861 staff in 2017; 1 480 of them professional psychologists, special-needs educators, and pedagogues, translating to a ratio of 425 compulsory school students to every specialist staff, down from 500 in 2012.

Students also have access to the school health services, which are part of the municipal health services. School nurses in upper-secondary school may also offer basic mental health services in the form of seminars or group discussions on stress management, body image, self-esteem and other mental-health topics. This is especially salient given that 15-20% of Norwegian adolescents struggle with mental-health problems, and mental-health problems are associated with school drop-out. Basic mental-health education by school nurses has been found effective in improving the mental health of upper-secondary students (Bjørnsen et al., 2017[57]).

4.4.2. Services provided outside of schools

Social services for young people up to the age of 18[11] are provided by the municipal Child Welfare Services, which are a separate entity from the municipal social services (sometimes offered jointly by municipalities). The Child Welfare Services work closely with the municipal health services, school nurses and the police. The organisation of service provision can differ across municipalities – in Sund, for example, the municipality set up a dedicated youth office to service 14-24 year-olds who are at-risk of school drop-out or have mental-health or substance abuse issues. The centre is funded jointly by the municipality, the Directorate for Children, Youth and Family Affairs and the Directorate for Health. The youth office offers diverse support to young people, including individual follow-up and vocational guidance, connecting young people to specialised health-care professionals and job search assistance (Nordic Centre for Welfare and Social Issues, 2016[58])

The Youth Guides Project ("*Losprosjektet*") was introduced in 2014 after a three-year pilot scheme (2010-13). The Norwegian Directorate for Children, Youth and Family Affairs endowed the project with NOK 12.3 million (about EUR 1.2 million) to be distributed among 50 municipalities, mostly over the period 2015-2018 – municipalities have to at least match the national funding to participate. The project provides young people aged 14-23 who are at-risk of dropping out of school or work with a designated guide or mentor. Guides should support young people both at school and in their home life, help them access public services and support their parents or guardians in their efforts to keep them in school or work. Backe-Hansen et al. (2014[59]) evaluated the pilot scheme. Over 400 young people in 15 municipalities participated in the pilot project, which funded 19 full-time counsellors, implying a caseload of about 21 young people per guide. While 68% of all project participants were at school, in employment or in a NAV measure at the end of the project, this result is difficult to interpret in the absence of a control group.

Well-designed leisure activities and after-school programmes can greatly contribute to the educational and social development of young people by building social and professional skills and countering the risk of isolation. Empirical evidence confirms the positive effects of participating in extracurricular activities on schooling outcomes and career prospects, especially for youth from disadvantaged backgrounds (see, e.g., Heckman (2008[60])). In Norway, the Education Act obliges all municipalities to run music and culture schools – either alone or in co-operation with other municipalities. These schools offer dance, music, theatre and arts classes for school aged children, with municipalities covering part of the costs. Since municipalities can decide autonomously how much they want to subsidise these schools, costs can vary locally, and can therefore discourage participation in some areas (Tchernoff, 2007[61]). Their lack of integration with schools also means that participation very much depends on the involvement of parents, a detriment to the participation of disadvantaged young people. Norway should consider offering afternoon activities that are of very low or no cost to families and integrated with the education system such that all children and young people can participate regardless of family income or parental involvement.

4.4.3. Coordination of services

Disadvantaged young people have multiple and diverse needs – meeting them requires careful coordination of public services. While this is a common problem, Norway's decentralised governance structure adds an additional layer to it, as public agencies do not only have to coordinate across providers – health-care providers, education system etc. – but also across levels of government.

To improve coordination in the provision of services for children and young people under the age of 25, the Ministry of Education launched the "0-24 cooperation" agreement in 2015, with a planned run to 2020. This is an agreement between four Directorates under the supervision of different Ministries – the Directorates for Education and Training, of Health, for Children, Youth and Family Affairs, and of Labour and Welfare (NAV) – to improve collaboration in the provision of services for vulnerable children and young people with the goal of reducing upper-secondary drop-out.

The Norwegian Directorate for Education and Training established a "0-24" unit, with designated funding of NOK 3 Million (about EUR 310 000) annually to coordinate efforts across the four Directorates, as well as with counties and municipalities. The Directorates formed cross-cutting working groups to propose measures to solve regulatory conflicts, improve the management of subsidies, and coordinate the provision of language training. County governors are heavily involved in this process.

A first assessment by the public management advisory body Difi (2016[62]) underlines the complexity of overlapping competences across agencies, while attesting all participating agencies and public bodies a commitment to improve collaboration. According to this report, cross-agency communication improved during the first two years of the agreement, and a common picture of the needs of disadvantaged young people, as well as the priority areas for intervention, has been established. Since 2016, the process is being observed by an external management consultancy.

Round-up and recommendations

Nearly all young people start upper-secondary education; a great strength of the Norwegian education system. Completion rates are below expectations, however: almost one in five young people aged 25-34 has not completed upper-secondary education, well above the OECD average of 16%. Students with poor marks from compulsory school are especially likely to drop out.

The relatively academic nature of VET contributes to these low completion rates. Links to the labour market are also weak, and about one-third of applicants could not find an apprenticeship place in 2016.

Norway could further promote school completion and expand good-quality vocational training along the following dimensions:

Strengthen the labour market ties of the VET system

- *Align VET provision more closely with labour market demand:* Combining school- and work-based training from day one is one way to ensure that young people acquire skills that are valuable on the local labour market.
- *Bring forward specialisation in the school-based part of VET*: School-based VET training is relatively broad, with students only settling on a specific occupation during the apprenticeship. Favouring depth instead of breadth earlier in the programme curriculum could make aspiring apprentices more attractive for employers.

Make hiring apprentices more affordable for employers

- *Encourage the social partners to reconsider apprentice remuneration:* A flatter wage increase in the second year would better align apprentice wages with their productivity.

Make the VET system more inclusive for the weakest students

- *Continue expanding lower-level tracks in VET:* Academically weak or practically minded young people can lack motivation to complete the two-year school-based component of VET training. Norway recently rolled out nationally a lower-level VET track. Norway should continue to promote alternative pathways in VET that enable those young people who otherwise would have dropped out to attain a qualification.

Consistently evaluate efforts against school drop-out

- *Make rigorous evaluations a pre-requisite for national funding for programmes:* Counties and municipalities have made considerable efforts to support drop-outs and at-risk students locally through a variety of measures – additional instruction, individualised follow-up, counselling – and these efforts are often supported by national funds. Without rigorous evaluations, it is hard to know which measures are effective, deliver value for public money, and deserve a broader roll-out. Conditioning funds on rigorous programme evaluations would help ensure that disadvantaged young people receive the best interventions.

Notes

1. They estimate the elasticity of the completion rate with respect to the local unemployment rate to be between 0.04 and 0.12.

2. The Education Act explicitly limits the segregation of students according to ability, sex or ethnicity to short periods of time when justified by pedagogical necessity. There are two exceptions: the Sami curriculum developed by the Sami parliament and the right of students with a mother tongue other than Norwegian to receive adapted education their native language.

3. Until recently, the right to upper-secondary education applied only to compulsory-school graduates aged 16-18, and for the duration of five or six years depending on the programme. There was hence an entitlement gap for 19-to-24 year-olds who had not started upper-secondary education yet, as the right to upper-secondary education in the adult system only started at age 25. This gap was closed in 2016, and young people up to the age of 24 may start upper-secondary education in the regular system, while those aged 25 and over are guaranteed a place in the adult education system.

4. Two VET programmes – Media and Communication and Agriculture, Fishing and Forestry – offer the option to choose general studies in year three, and thus lead directly to a university admissions certificate.

5. While Huitfeldt et al. (2018[17]) find no effects of intensive education within *Ny Giv* (see Box 4.1), they cannot reject the possibility that local efforts to increase completion rates might have been successful.

6. The grading system in compulsory education is on a scale from 1 (very low level of competence in the subject) to 6 (outstanding competence in the subject). For the "school points" measure, marks are averaged and multiplied by 10. Hence, to have below 30 school points, a student must have been graded with a 2, "low level of competence" in at least one subject.

7. Five counties piloted a reinforced alternative Vg3 that lasts 18 instead of 12 months in 2013, and that has students spend about four days a week in work-based training. An evaluation (Aspøy and Nyen, 2015[21]) found that of the 243 programme participants, about half became regular apprentices or obtained their craft certificate within 18 months. However, given the small number of participants and the lack of a control group the authors cannot assess whether the programme in fact increased the chances of youths to obtain an apprenticeship. They infer from qualitative interviews, however, that companies were more willing to hire apprentices through this alternative pathway because the contract period was shorter, enabling employers to use the programme much like a probationary period.

8. Total labour cost (gross earnings plus employer social security contributions) for a worker at 67% of average gross earnings were about EUR 45 000 in 2016 (OECD, 2018[65]). Assuming a wage progression from 30 to 75% of the low wage and taking into account the subsidy over two years implies an evolution of the apprentice labour cost from 12 to 57% of the low wage from year one to year two of the apprenticeship.

9. https://finnlarebedrift.no/

10. www.utdanning.no

11. For children in foster care, the services provided by the Child Welfare Services can be extended up to the age of 23 if the young person agrees ("after-care measures"). Social services for young people aged 18 years and older are provided by the municipal arm of NAV, see Box 5.3.

References

Askilden, J. and A. Øivind (2005), "Apprentices and young workers: a study of the Norwegian youth labour market", *Scottish Journal of Political Economy*, Vol. 52/1. [51]

Aspøy, T. and T. Nyen (2015), *Godt, men ikke for godt - evaluering av forsterket alternativ Vg3 for elever som ikke får læreplass. Sluttrapport*, Fafo, Oslo, http://www.fafo.no. [21]

Backe-Hansen, E. et al. (2014), *Til god hjelp for mange. Evaluering av Losprosjektet*, NOVA, Oslo, https://evalueringsportalen.no/evaluering/til-god-hjelp-for-mange-evaluering-av-losprosjektet/rapport_NOVA.pdf/@@inline (accessed on 11 February 2018). [59]

Bjørnsen, H. et al. (2017), "The Relationship Between Positive Mental Health Literacy and Mental Well-Being Among Adolescents: Implications for School Health Services", *The Journal of School Nursing*, http://dx.doi.org/10.1177/1059840517732125. [57]

BMWFW (2014), *Die Lehre – Duale Berufsausbildung in Oesterreich, Moderne Ausbildung mit Zukunft*, BMWFW, Vienna, http://www.bmwfw.gv.at/Berufsausbildung/LehrlingsUndBerufsausbildung/Documents/HP_Kern_Die%20Lehre_2014_311.pdf. [43]

BMWFW and WKÖ (2015), *Lehrberufe in Österreich – Ausbildungen mit Zukunft*, BMWFW, Vienna, https://www.bic.at/downloads/at/broschueren/lehrberufslexikon_2015.pdf (accessed on 09 February 2018). [46]

Caliendo, M., S. Künn and R. Schmidl (2011), "Fighting Youth Unemployment: The Effects of Active Labor Market Policies", *IZA Discussion Paper*, No. 6222, IZA, Bonn, http://ftp.iza.org/dp6222.pdf (accessed on 09 February 2018). [34]

Cedefop and Refernet Norway (2014), *Title: Norway VET in Europe – Country Report 2014*, Cedefop, http://www.cedefop.europa.eu/en/publications-and-resources/country-reports/vet-in-europe-country-reports. [12]

Cedefop (2017), *Norway - Leaving education early: putting vocational education and training centre stage*, Cedefop, Brussels, http://www.cedefop.europa.eu/en/publications-and-resources/country-reports/leaving-education-early-putting-vocational-education-a-10. [55]

Difi (2016), *Felles problem - felles løsning? Lærdommer fra 0-24-samarbeidet | Difi*, Direktoratet for forvaltning og ikt, Oslo, https://www.difi.no/rapport/2017/01/laeringsnotat-2016-felles-problem-felles-losning-laerdommer-fra-0-24-samarbeidet (accessed on 12 February 2018). [62]

Dornmayr, H. and S. Nowak (2015), *Lehrlingsausbildung im Überblick 2015 Strukturdaten, Trends und Perspektiven*, IBW, Vienna, http://www.ibw.at. [42]

Education Act (2016), *Lov om grunnskolen og den vidaregåande opplæringa (opplæringslova) [Law on primary and secondary education (education act)]*, https://lovdata.no/dokument/NL/lov/1998-07-17-61#KAPITTEL_5 (accessed on 01 February 2018). [9]

Fersterer, J. and R. Winter-Ebmer (2003), "Are Austrian returns to education falling over time?", *Labour Economics*, Vol. 10, http://citeseerx.ist.psu.edu/viewdoc/download?doi=10.1.1.504.1004&rep=rep1&type=pdf (accessed on 09 February 2018), pp. 73-89. [44]

Fersterer, J., J. Pischke and R. Winter-Ebmer (2008), "Returns to apprenticeship training in Austria: Evidence from failed firms", *Scandinavian Journal of Economics*, Vol. 110/4, pp. 733-753, http://dx.doi.org/10.1111/j.1467-9442.2008.00559.x. [45]

Heckman, J. (2008), "The case for investing in disadvantaged young children", *CESifo DICE Repor*, Vol. 06/2, http://hdl.handle.net/10419/166932, pp. 1613-6373. [60]

Hoeckel, K. (2010), *OECD Reviews of Vocational Education and Training: A Learning for Jobs Review of Austria 2010*, OECD Reviews of Vocational Education and Training, OECD Publishing, Paris, http://dx.doi.org/10.1787/9789264113695-en. [47]

Holm, A. et al. (2013), "Incomplete equalization: The effect of tracking in secondary education on educational inequality", *Social Science Research*, http://dx.doi.org/10.1016/j.ssresearch.2013.06.001. [32]

Høst, H. (2008), *Continuity and Change in Norwegian Vocational Education and Training (VET)*, Norwegian Institute for Studies in Innovation, Research and Education, http://www.nifustep.no. [27]

Huitfeldt, I. et al. (2018), *Fullføring av videregående opplæring og effekter av tiltak mot frafall [Completion of upper-secondary education and the effects of measures against drop-out]*, Statistics Norway, Oslo-Kongsvinger. [17]

Ichou, M. and L. Vallet (2011), "Do all roads lead to inequality? Trends in French upper secondary school analysed with four longitudinal surveys", *Oxford Review of Education*, Vol. 37/2, pp. 167-194, http://dx.doi.org/10.1080/03054985.2011.559350. [33]

Kreisman, D. and K. Stage (2017), "Vocational and Career tech education in American high schools: The value of depth over breadth", *NBER working paper series*, No. 23851, NBER, Cambridge, MA, http://www.nber.org/papers/w23851. [38]

Lyche, C. (2010), "Taking on the Completion Challenge: A Literature Review on Policies to Prevent Dropout and Early School Leaving", *OECD Education Working Papers*, No. 53, OECD Publishing, Paris, http://dx.doi.org/10.1787/5km4m2t59cmr-en. [24]

Michelsen, S., O. Olsen and H. Høst (2014), *Origins and development of VET 1850- 2008 - an investigation into the Norwegian case*, Nord-VET - The future of Vocational Education in the Nordic countries, http://nord-vet.dk/indhold/uploads/Norwegian-VET-historical-emergence-final-20141.pdf (accessed on 13 October 2017). [37]

Muehlemann, S. et al. (2010), "The financing of apprenticeship training in the light of labor market regulations", *Labour Economics*, Vol. 17, pp. 799-809, http://dx.doi.org/10.1016/j.labeco.2010.04.006. [40]

Muehlemann, S. and S. Wolter (2014), "Return on investment of apprenticeship systems for enterprises: Evidence from cost-benefit analyses", *IZA journal of Labour Policy*, Vol. 3/25, http://dx.doi.org/10.1186/2193-9004-3-25.. [49]

Nordic Centre for Welfare and Social Issues (2016), *In Focus: Mental Health among Young People*, Nordic Centre for Welfare and Social Issues , Stockholm, http://www.nordicwelfare.org/ (accessed on 11 February 2018). [58]

NOU (2016), "Norge i omstilling – karriereveiledning for individ og samfunn", No. 7, https://www.regjeringen.no/contentassets/05a79a5ed91e40e1a80e6f8028b21e3e/no/pdfs/nou201620160007000dddpdfs.pdf (accessed on 11 February 2018). [54]

OECD (2012), *Equity and Quality in Education: Supporting Disadvantaged Students and Schools*, OECD Publishing, Paris, http://dx.doi.org/10.1787/9789264130852-en. [14]

OECD (2013), *Education policy outlook*, http://www.oecd-ilibrary.org/docserver/download/9115011ec029.pdf?expires=1507744121&id=id&accname=ocid84004878&checksum=77337B1D826E20BF44644739C964E317 (accessed on 11 October 2017). [5]

OECD (2013), "Education policy outlook Norway", *Education Policy Outlook* , OECD, Paris, http://www.oecd.org/education/policyoutlook.htm. [30]

OECD (2013), *Mental Health and Work: Norway*, Mental Health and Work, OECD Publishing, Paris, http://dx.doi.org/10.1787/9789264178984-en. [56]

OECD (2014), *Investing in Youth: Brazil*, Investing in Youth, OECD Publishing, Paris, http://dx.doi.org/10.1787/9789264208988-en. [52]

OECD (2015), *The ABC of Gender Equality in Education: Aptitude, Behaviour, Confidence*, PISA, OECD Publishing, Paris, http://dx.doi.org/10.1787/9789264229945-en. [19]

OECD (2015), "Norway", in *Education Policy Outlook 2015: Making Reforms Happen*, OECD Publishing, Paris, http://dx.doi.org/10.1787/9789264225442-29-en. [1]

OECD (2016), *Education at a Glance 2016: OECD Indicators*, OECD Publishing, Paris, http://dx.doi.org/10.1787/eag-2016-en. [4]

OECD (2016), *PISA 2015 Results (Volume I): Excellence and Equity in Education*, PISA, OECD Publishing, Paris, http://dx.doi.org/10.1787/9789264266490-en. [8]

OECD (2016), *Society at a Glance 2016: OECD Social Indicators*, OECD Publishing, Paris, http://dx.doi.org/10.1787/9789264261488-en. [36]

OECD (2016), *Investing in Youth: Sweden*, Investing in Youth, OECD Publishing, Paris, http://dx.doi.org/10.1787/9789264267701-en. [48]

OECD (2016), *Investing in Youth: Australia*, Investing in Youth, OECD Publishing, Paris, http://dx.doi.org/10.1787/9789264257498-en. [35]

OECD (2017), *Education at a Glance 2017: OECD Indicators*, OECD Publishing, Paris, http://dx.doi.org/10.1787/eag-2017-en. [7]

OECD (2018), "Taxing Wages: Comparative tables", *OECD Tax Statistics* (database), http://dx.doi.org/10.1787/data-00265-en.
(accessed on 11 February 2018) [65]

Olsen et al. (2014), *Key challenges for Norwegian VET: the state of play*, Nord-VET – The future of Vocational Education in the Nordic countries, Roskilde, http://nord-vet.dk. [28]

Olsen, O. et al. (2015), *Institutional innovations in Norwegian VET – responses to key challenges*, Nord-VET – The future of Vocational Education in the Nordic countries, Roskilde, http://nord-vet.dk. [31]

Reiling, R. and B. Strøm (2015), "Upper Secondary School Completion and the Business Cycle", *Scandinavian Journal of Economics*, Vol. 117/1, pp. 195-219, http://dx.doi.org/10.1111/sjoe.12088. [2]

SSB (2016), *Table: 05232: Pupils in primary and lower secondary school, by class level, tenure status and type of institution*, https://www.ssb.no/statistikkbanken/SelectVarVal/Define.asp?MainTable=ElevarGrunnSk&KortNavnWeb=utgrs&PLanguage=1&checked=true (accessed on 12 October 2017). [6]

SSB (2017), *Table: 05430: Pupils in upper secondary education, by grade and area of study*, Statbank, https://www.ssb.no/statistikkbanken/selectvarval/saveselections.asp (accessed on 12 October 2017). [13]

SSB (2017), *Table: 08624: Pupils who receive special training, by grade*, Statbank, https://www.ssb.no/statistikkbanken/selectvarval/saveselections.asp (accessed on 12 October 2017). [15]

SSB (2017), *Table: 09326: Completion rates of pupils in upper secondary education, by sex, area of study/education programme and degree of completion*, Statbank, https://www.ssb.no/statistikkbanken/selectvarval/saveselections.asp (accessed on 13 October 2017). [63]

SSB (2017), *Table: 11592: Completion rates of pupils in upper secondary education, by sex, lower secondary school points, area of study/education programme and degree of completion*, Statbank, https://www.ssb.no/statistikkbanken/selectout/pivot.asp?checked=true (accessed on 18 October 2017). [18]

SSB (2017), *Tabell: 08777: Gjennomføring i videregående opplæring, etter alder, studieretning/utdanningsprogram (todelt) og sluttkompetanse*, Statbank, https://www.ssb.no/statistikkbanken/selectvarval/Define.asp?subjectcode=&ProductId=&MainTable=GjennomVGSKomp&nvl=&PLanguage=0&nyTmpVar=true&CMSSubjectArea=utdanning&KortNavnWeb=vgogjen&StatVariant=&checked=true (accessed on 20 October 2017). [22]

SSB (2018), *Table 09262: Completion rates of pupils in upper secondary education, by parental education and degree of completion*, Statbank Norway, https://www.ssb.no/en/statbank/table/09262/?rxid=c7e464ae-385a-42d9-81ea-ed59beed1677 (accessed on 25 January 2018). [64]

SSB (2018), *09378: Pupils, apprentices and trainees in upper secondary education, by education programs (C) 2010 - 2016.*, Statbank, https://www.ssb.no/en/statbank/table/09378/?rxid=95ffc339-3c57-4659-b8d8-a3057e0d1c6e (accessed on 05 February 2018). [29]

Tchernoff, E. (2007), "Part B: National Information - country overviews", in *Music Schools in Europe*, Association Européenne des Conservatoires, Académies de Musique et Musikhochschulen (AEC), https://www.aec-music.eu/ (accessed on 12 February 2018). [61]

Digre, K. and T. Haugberg (eds.) (2014), *The Education Mirror 2014 Facts and analysis of kindergarten, primary and secondary education in Norway*, The Norwegian Directorate for Education and Training, Oslo, https://www.udir.no/Upload/Rapporter/EducationMIrror/The%20EducationMIrror_english.pdf?epslanguage=no (accessed on 12 October 2017). [16]

The Norwegian Directorate for Education and Training (2016), *Gjennomgang av det yrkesfaglige utdanningstilbudet. Utdanningsdirektoratets anbefalinger til Kunnskapsdepartementet*, The Norwegian Directorate for Education and Training, Oslo, https://www.udir.no/globalassets/filer/fag-og-yrkesopplering/gjennomgang-av-det-yrkesfaglige-utdanningstilbudet.pdf (accessed on 11 February 2018). [39]

The Norwegian Directorate for Education and Training (2016), *Norwegian vocational education and training (VET)*, https://www.udir.no/in-english/norwegian-vocational-education-and-training/ (accessed on 12 October 2017). [11]

The Norwegian Directorate for Education and Training (2016), *The Education Mirror 2016*, The Norwegian Directorate for Education and Training, Oslo, http://utdanningsspeilet.udir.no/2016/wp-content/uploads/2016/10/Utdanningsspeilet_2016_en.pdf (accessed on 12 October 2017). [10]

The Norwegian Directorate for Education and Training (2017), *Overgangar*, Skoleporten, https://skoleporten.udir.no/omskoleporten/ (accessed on 25 October 2017). [20]

The Norwegian Directorate for Education and Training (2017), *Utdanningsspeilet 2017 [The education mirror 2017]*, The Norwegian Directorate for Education and Training, Oslo, http://utdanningsspeilet.udir.no/2017/ (accessed on 02 February 2018). [25]

The Norwegian Directorate for Education and Training (2017), *Udir.no - Skoleporten - Gjennomføring av læretiden - Nasjonalt*, https://skoleporten.udir.no/rapportvisning/fag-og-yrkesopplaering/gjennomfoering/gjennomfoering-av-laeretiden/nasjonalt?enhetsid=00&vurderingsomrade=37&underomrade=53&skoletype=6&skoletypemenuid=2&sammenstilling=1 (accessed on 18 October 2017). [23]

The Norwegian Directorate for Education and Training (2018), *Statistikportalen*, https://statistikkportalen.udir.no/vgs/Pages/Statusgruppe.aspx (accessed on 02 February 2018). [26]

The Norwegian Directorate for Education and Training (2018), *Satser lærlinger, praksisbrevkandidater og lærekandidater – 2018*, https://www.udir.no/om-udir/tilskudd-og-prosjektmidler/tilskuddssatser/satser-larlinger-praksisbrevkandidater-og-larekandidater-2018/ (accessed on 10 February 2018). [41]

The Norwegian Government (2017), *Yrkesfagløftet*, https://www.regjeringen.no/no/om-regjeringa/solberg/Regjeringens-satsingsomrader/Regjeringens-satsingsomrader/kunnskap-gir-muligheter-for-alle1/Yrkesfagloftet/id753135/ (accessed on 11 February 2018). [50]

Vox (2018), *Guidance System in Norway | Euroguidance Network*, https://www.euroguidance.eu/guidance-systems-and-practice/national-guidance-systems/guidance-system-in-norway (accessed on 11 February 2018). [53]

Werler, T. and K. Sivesind (2008), “Norway”, in Hörner, W. et al. (eds.), *The Education Systems in Europe*, Springer International Publishing. [3]

Annex 4.A. Additional statistical results on VET completion

Figure 4.A1.1. VET completion rates are slowly rising

Status of VET students five years after programme start, by start year, in percentages

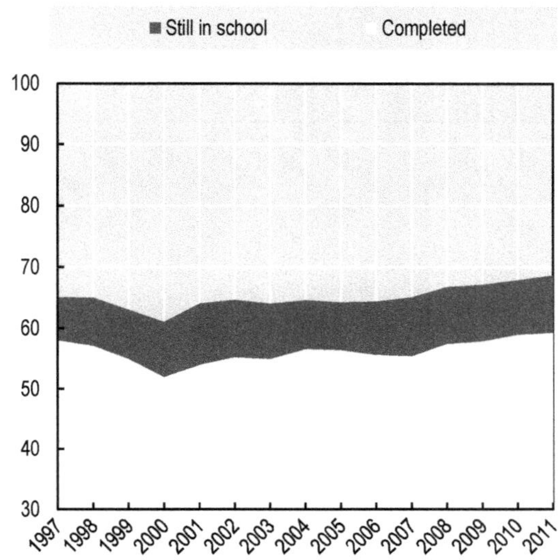

Note: Completion rates are measured five years after each cohort enrolled (one year after the end of the regular programme duration). Only first-time enrolees are counted.
Source: SSB (2017[63])

Figure 4.A1.2. Completion rates are lower in more remote areas

Status of the 2011 cohort of first-time upper-secondary enrolees in 2016, by county, in percentages

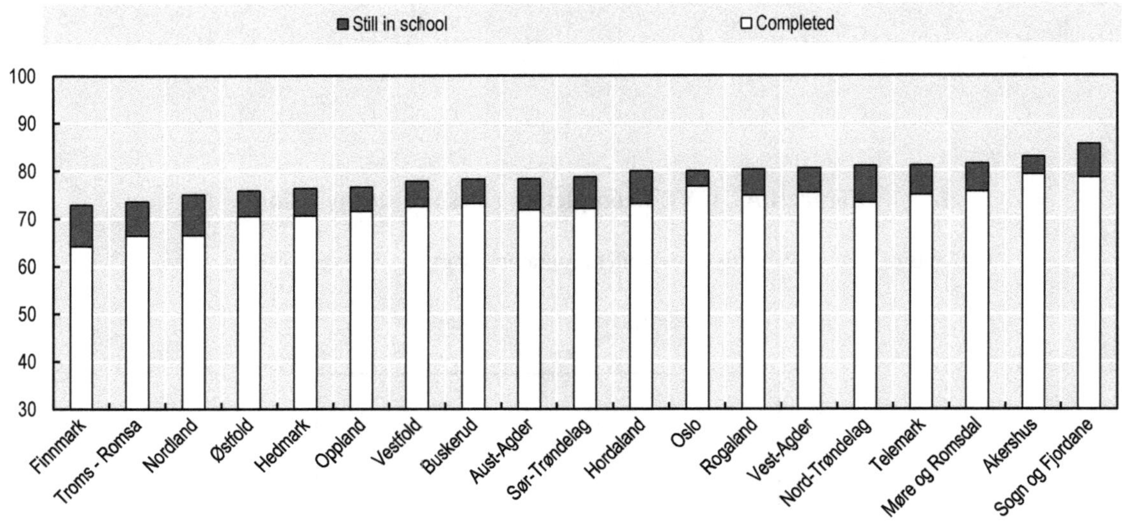

Source: SSB (2018[64]).

Chapter 5. Guaranteeing employment or training options for NEETs in Norway

This chapter looks at Norway's policies and programmes to bring NEETs into education or employment. It starts by describing the current architecture of employment and social service delivery, and by discussing the challenge of co-ordinating services for at-risk young people. The chapter presents Norway's strategies and solutions for reaching out to disengaged young people. It then assesses the coverage and adequacy of programmes aimed at re-engaging young jobseekers in employment, education or training, and to provide them with comprehensive social support. The chapter ends with a discussion of the political framework for ensuring that the impact of programmes targeted at NEETs in Norway is rigorously evaluated.

The statistical data for Israel are supplied by and under the responsibility of the relevant Israeli authorities. The use of such data by the OECD is without prejudice to the status of the Golan Heights, East Jerusalem and Israeli settlements in the West Bank under the terms of international law.

Introduction

Labour market conditions for young people in Norway are among the most favourable across OECD countries: Youth employment rates are high at 59% (52% in the OECD on average), 22% of young people combine studies and work (OECD average of 13%), and the NEET rate of 9% is one of the lowest across OECD countries (OECD average of 14%, see Chapter 1).

The developments over the last decade have been somewhat less positive, however. The youth employment rate has declined substantially since 2008, and its 2016 value was seven percentage points below the pre-crisis peak (see Chapter 1). This does not so much reflect effects of the Great Recession, as in other OECD countries, but rather the rise in the increase in the youth population because of migration. The NEET rate has risen by two percentage points since 2008, which reflects higher rates of both inactivity and unemployment. The number of registered jobseekers (of all ages) more than doubled between 2008 and 2010 and has stagnated on this higher level since, whereas the vacancy count declined by 40% (Figure 5.1).

Figure 5.1. Registered unemployment remains substantially higher than in 2008

Monthly number of 15-29 year-olds who are registered as unemployed and number of vacancies in Norway

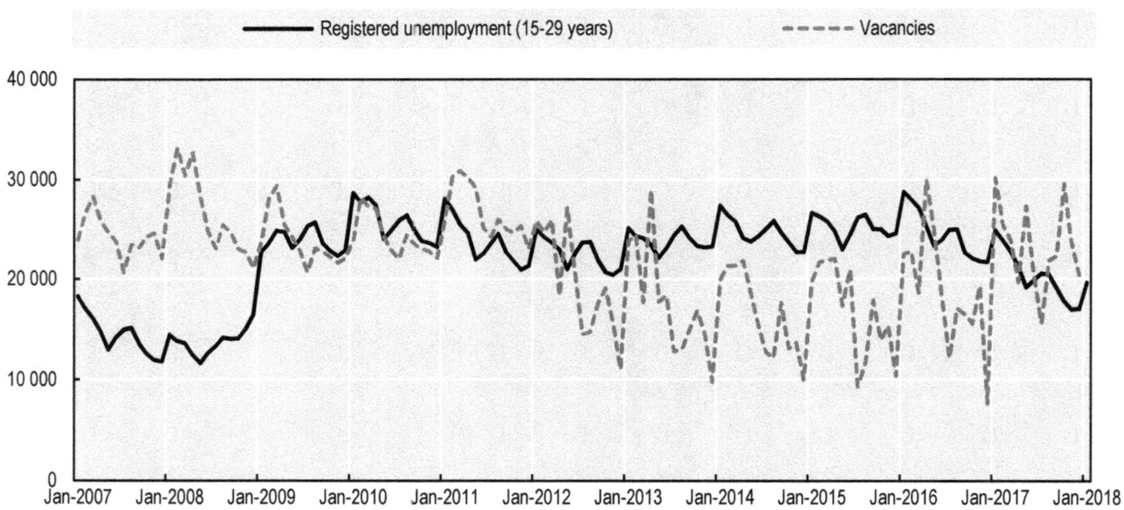

Note: Data on registered jobseekers include below-15 year-olds in 2015-17.
Source: NAV (2018[1]), OECD (2018[2]) and Statistics Norway (2018[3]).

This chapter provides an analysis of policies and programmes to support NEETs in Norway, outlining recent developments and assessing coverage and adequacy. Section 5.1 describes the architecture of employment and social service provision for NEETs, and discusses co-ordination and governance issues. Section 5.2 presents the main options for reaching out to NEETs. Section 5.3 assesses strategies to re-engage young jobseekers in employment, education or training. Section 5.4 discusses the evaluation of employment and social programmes for young people in Norway.

5.1. The architecture of the employment and social service provision for NEETs

National and municipal authorities in Norway share the policy responsibility for employment and social services for NEETs. At the national level, the Ministry of Labour and Social Affairs is in charge of labour market and welfare policy, the Ministry for Children, Equality and Social Inclusion is responsible for child welfare services and the Ministry of Local Government and Modernisation manages (social) housing. The municipalities provide social policies and administer means-tested Social Assistance.

5.1.1. Employment and social service provision

Employment services and most social services for young people are delivered jointly by the Norwegian Labour and Welfare Administration (NAV).[1] Established through a 2006 reform (see Box 5.1), the NAV consists of a "state arm" (the Labour and Welfare Service) that pays social insurance benefits and provides employment services to registered jobseekers and a "municipal arm" that pays means-tested Social Assistance and provides social support. Social support includes general advice and guidance, temporary emergency accommodation for households who cannot find housing independently and labour market integration for persons with reduced work capacity through the so-called Qualification Programme (*Kvalifiseringsprogrammet*).[2]

NAV offices can outsource the provision of certain social or employment services to non-governmental providers, most of whom operate on a not-for-profit basis. Private providers currently also deliver support to jobseekers with high assistance needs through a labour market measure called "follow-up" (*Oppfølgingstiltak*), though this service is increasingly delivered through NAV directly.[3] Standard procurement rules apply for the selection and contracting of these providers. Unfortunately, no country-wide data exist on the frequency of provider-based service delivery.

NAV offices are generally very well equipped to serve young users: most offices have specific contact points for young people. Larger offices usually employ youth teams that offer specialised services and adopted means of communication, for instance through the use of social media and text messaging. They also stay in touch with relevant stakeholders to co-ordinate outreach and service delivery to upper-secondary drop-outs. Many smaller offices, which lack the capacity for a youth team, select specific caseworkers to be the contact person for young users. A recent government-commissioned research report into the support provided by NAV to young people documents that out of 200 NAV offices surveyed, only 17% indicated having neither a youth team nor a special contact person for young people. Managers in NAV offices with a specialised youth team were much more likely to express themselves satisfied with the quality of the follow-up provided for young users than those of offices that only had a specified youth contact person, or not even such a contact person (Strand, Bråthen and Grønningsæter, 2015[4]).

Box 5.1. The integration of employment and social services at NAV

NAV delivers both employment and social services jointly since the so-called *NAV Reform* implemented between 2006 and 2011. The reform aimed primarily to increase the efficiency of service delivery, facilitate access to services especially for users with complex problems, promote employment and reduce passive benefit dependence. It merged the national public employment service and the national insurance administration with the municipal social welfare services, and formalised the collaboration between state and municipal authorities.

NAV users receive employment services, income support, social and housing support and in many cases also other municipal services through a countrywide network of 457 one-stop offices. The responsibility for delivering and funding services remains formally separated between the state (employment services) and the municipalities (social services), and the two NAV arms use separate IT data systems for administration. NAV users will in most cases not be aware, however, whether they are dealing with a municipal or state employee, and most NAV offices are headed by a single manager.[1]

The implementation of the reform has been challenging: As Christensen, Fimreite and Lægreid (2014[5]) lay out, the different agencies each came with their own history and organisational and professional culture that needed to be aligned during the merger. Establishing a partnership between state and municipal services was difficult as local governments perceived the relationship as being too one-sided with the central government having the stronger role. The specialised NAV experts had to adapt to providing a more comprehensive range of services. All 20 000 employees of the merged institutions initially received a job guarantee. The total cost of the reform was substantial at around EUR 700 million (Christensen, Fimreite and Lægreid, 2014[5]).

After major efforts to comprehensively review the effects of the reform, the verdict on its success remains mixed: the reform succeeded at creating a fully-integrated and co-ordinated network of front-line services, which eased service access especially for the most disadvantaged users. Evidence suggests that among long-term NAV users, those with more complex problems and requiring different types of services are relatively satisfied with the local one-stop shops (Laegreid and Rykkja, 2013[6]). And while a smooth co-operation between central and local authorities remains challenging, and problems with the ICT structures persist, effective organisational structures and a joint "NAV culture" seem to have developed (Christensen, Fimreite and Lægreid, 2014[5]; Fossestøl, Breit and Borg, 2014[7]).

By contrast, there is little evidence until now that the reform had the intended effects on employment or benefit dependence. At least in the initial post-reform years, the reform appears not to have raised NAV users' employment probability or reduced benefit receipt, including for early school leavers (Aakvik, Monstad and Holmås, 2014[8]). Some studies even find negative effects on the transitions into employment or education (Schreiner and Markussen, 2012[9]; Fevang, Markussen and Røed, 2014[10]). These may, however, simply reflect difficulties during the transition process.

Norway's annual citizens' survey continues to list NAV among the country's public institutions with the lowest user satisfaction ratings, though scores have improved in recent years.[2] A government-appointed expert group presented a proposal for comprehensive further reforms in 2015 (NAV Expert Group, 2015[11]).

1. 42 NAV offices have two heads for the separate parts.
2. See www.difi.no/rapporter-og-statistikk/undersokelser/innbyggerundersokelsen-2017/hva-mener-brukerne

NAV's youth specialists moreover work with moderate caseloads. A recent survey conducted among NAV managers indicates that youth caseworkers are on average responsible for 68 young persons at a time, a reasonable number considering that not all young users require intensive support. In some counties, caseloads reach 80 persons or more, however, and NAV managers in offices with higher caseload numbers were much more likely to report having too little time to follow up on young jobseekers (Strand, Bråthen and Grønningsæter, 2015[4]).[4] NAV specialists perceive low caseload numbers to be one of the key factors for a successful support for young jobseekers and have expressed concerns about having insufficient time to systematically follow-up on young people with greater labour market difficulties (Myklebø, 2012[12]; NAV Expert Group, 2015[11]). While caseload numbers vary greatly across OECD countries, some achieve lower caseload numbers for their youth support staff: in Japan, for instance, specialists at Regional Youth Support Stations who provide social support and career orientation to NEETs who are not job-ready work with only 40 to 70 users at a time (OECD, 2017[13]).

5.1.2. Income support

NEETs have to register with NAV to claim most types of income support, including contribution-based Unemployment Benefits, mean-tested Social Assistance, the Transitional Benefit for low-income single parents, Sickness Benefits, the Work Assessment Allowance or Disability Benefits (see Chapter 3).[5]

Employable jobseekers have to comply with activity requirements under a mutual obligations approach to remain entitled to benefits (see Section 5.3). Social Assistance recipients are automatically registered as jobseekers unless they are obviously unfit for work and face in principle the same requirements as Unemployment Benefit recipients. For single parents on Transitional Benefit, an activity requirement applies once the youngest child is at least one year old.

Jobseekers who participate in labour market programmes continue receiving their standard benefits. Those not eligible for Unemployment Benefits may receive an Activity Allowance (*Tiltakspenger*), and young people are an important recipient group of this benefit.

5.1.3. Governance and co-ordination

Support services for NEETs are highly integrated. In many municipalities, NAV offices provide not only employment and social services, but function more broadly as "one-stop shops" for a range of other municipal services including support for migrants, housing services, health care or support for the elderly. User information tends to be exchanged routinely between the different agencies that provide youth services even though the two NAV arms continue to operate separate data processing systems and other municipal services may have yet other data structures.

NAV increasingly relies on non-governmental providers – both for profit and not-for-profit – for the delivery of labour market programmes for jobseekers. This includes training courses and rehabilitation programmes organised by private training companies, work experience programmes and sheltered employment programmes offered by firms and sheltered co-operatives, and subsidised employment in the standard labour market. NAV purchases these services through tendering procedures at the national, regional or local level with tendering contract durations ranging from somewhere between one-half to three years. The overall budget for provider-based services was a substantial

NOK 7.65 billion (EUR 790 million) in 2015. The role of non-governmental actors in the provision of social services is weak, by contrast.

There appears to be scope for improving the quality and efficiency of employment and social service provision by strengthening performance-based components in the tendering procedures. A detailed analysis of NAV tendering practices is difficult because the Ministry of Labour and Social Affairs does not systematically collect information on local practices, such as on the share of private vs. public providers, provider turnover between contracts or contract design. Providers carrying out follow-up and the work capacity assessment for jobseekers are however compensated on an hourly/per-participant basis, i.e. irrespective of the quality of their services. The low incidence of outside contracting in social service provision moreover appears to be partly the result of an insufficiently flexible legal framework. Where NAV offices purchase such services from outside contractors on a small scale, tender contracts are only weakly performance-related: they can specify explicit performance targets, for instance a share of users who should be in education, employment or social programmes 16 weeks after programme completion. NAV however usually compensates providers fully up-front. This leaves only weak leverage to encourage strong performance except by threatening to select different providers in the next tendering round.

Granting NAV greater flexibility to design tender contracts with effective incentive structures could encourage local offices to trial the provider-based provision of services that are most difficult to deliver in-house. A systematic reporting of tendering practices and outcomes could moreover permit geographic comparisons of results and the sharing of best-practices. In some cases, the perceived hurdles for disengaged young people to seek support may moreover be lower if the services were delivered through an NGO or a private provider instead of a government agency. An interesting experience in this respect can be the one of Australia, where all employment services are delivered by private providers. Tight follow-up and performance-based compensation ensure that providers have a strong incentive to service the most disadvantaged users (see Box 5.2).

In a 2013 trial funded by the Ministry of Labour and Social Affairs, three counties (Vest-Agder, Sogn og Fjordane and Olso) tested delivering job search assistance through private providers with payments depending on the clients' job-finding rates. This trial however focused on operational questions, such as the procedures for provider and participant selection, rather than on the participants' employment outcomes (Proba, 2014[14]). A later survey by the Ministry of Labour and Social Affairs moreover concluded that the trial had been too small to allow for a meaningful impact assessment. The Ministry intends to re-visit the issue in 2018, possibly by launching a randomised controlled trial (RCT) (Ministry of Labour and Social Affairs, 2016[15]). An evaluation of the effects of introducing tendering for the provision of follow-up and work capacity assessments on supplier diversity and the measured offered is forthcoming in 2018 (Proba, 2017[16]).

Box 5.2. Provider-based employment service delivery in Australia

The Australian Department of Employment purchases all employment services for jobseekers from non-governmental providers, including private companies and community-based organisations, in five-yearly tender rounds carried out since 1997. Providers are selected based on 1) past performance, 2) the organisation's ability and capacity to achieve outcomes for jobseekers, 3) the organisation's strategy to meet the needs of employers, and 4) governance, i.e. the organisation's structure, capacity and skills for delivering services. Selected providers are required to offer case management, job search assistance and placement, as well as to monitor jobseekers' compliance with their activity requirements.

Providers are funded through a combination of lump-sum per-client *administration fees* and *outcome payments* made 4, 12 and 26 weeks after a jobseeker has found employment. Payment levels depend strongly on a jobseeker's expected barriers to re-integration such that providers have clear incentives to serve more disadvantaged groups. Providers can allocate these funds to clients as they see fit as long as the jobseekers meet their obligations and servicing is commensurate to the jobseekers' needs. An Employment Fund is available to help providers pay for services and interventions aimed at improving clients' employability.

Providers' relative performance is continuously measured through *Star Ratings* published online on quarterly basis. Ratings are a function of employment retention outcomes and jobseeker activation achieved by the provider adjusted through an econometric model for client characteristics and the state of the local labour market. They serve as an important reference for jobseekers when choosing a provider, and the Department of Employment uses them for allocating funding and selecting providers in the following tender round.

Source: OECD (2016), *Investing in Youth: Australia,* OECD Publishing, Paris. http://dx.doi.org/10.1787/9789264257498-en

5.2. Reaching out to NEETs

Norway devotes substantial resources to active outreach to ensure that young people out of school and work are quickly connected with NAV or an education provider rather than to slip into long-term inactivity.

The county-level Follow-up Services (*Oppfølgingstjenesten*) are the central actor for NEET outreach, as described in more detail in Chapter 4. They track and contact all young people up to the age of 21 years who leave school without an option in upper-secondary education or employment to ensure that they are offered an education or training option. To this end, they closely co-operate with educational institutions and NAV, and in some counties even have counsellors located directly in NAV offices. The discussion presented in Chapter 4 suggests that the Follow-up Services are highly effective at reaching out to young NEETs and at putting them in touch with NAV or county or municipal authorities. Indeed, referrals from the follow-up or child welfare services account for the majority of NEETs who newly register with NAV. Norway is looking to further strengthen the co-operation between NAV, the Follow-up Services and educational institutions through the *NyGIV* initiative (see Box 4.1 and NAV Expert Group (2015[11])).

A few recent trial projects have moreover looked into possibilities of further promoting a direct collaboration of NAV with schools and other youth policy actors to ensure that at-risk students are identified and receive support quickly. In the framework of the ongoing "NAV counsellors in upper-secondary schools" pilot, for instance, 33 NAV offices have placed youth specialists directly into upper-secondary schools to provide career guidance and support the transition to work (Box 5.3).

The municipal arm of NAV moreover uses street outreach and social work to connect vulnerable young people; no comprehensive data exist however on the extent of these efforts, or their effectiveness.

Box 5.3. The "NAV counsellors at upper-secondary schools" pilot

The Norwegian "NAV counsellors at upper-secondary schools" pilot (*NAV-veiledere i videregående skoler*) tests a promising model for a closer collaboration between employment and social services and schools. NAV youth specialists are placed into upper-secondary schools for four days per week to provide information and counselling, notably by offering career guidance, helping students find opportunities for work practice and supporting transition into work.[1] The project aims to help NAV identify and support young people with multiple barriers, collect information training needs and improve cross-sectoral collaboration.

The pilot project was launched in 2013 in initially four municipalities, but has since been extended to at least one municipality in each of the 19 Norwegian counties – covering 33 NAV offices and 28 schools participated in autumn 2017. Schools and NAV offices had to apply jointly to participate in the project and could secure funding for up to three years. The main pre-conditions for participation were that NAV had to have a specialised youth team and that the school had to be in an area affected by poverty and social problems. NOK 14.5 million (EUR 1.5 million) have been allocated to the project.

First results from an independent evaluation of the pilot at nine sites suggest that the intervention indeed strengthened the co-operation between the schools and NAV and raised awareness of available NAV services (Schafft and Mamelund, 2016$_{[17]}$).[2] The authors did not detect any statistically significant programme impact on non-completion rates, students' transition into work, the stock or inflow of new jobseekers or NAV users with reduced work capacity, or benefit receipt. This may however simply reflect the very small sample size. The final evaluation will be released in 2019.

1. The pilot is a follow-up of the 2008-14 *Development Work for Youth at Risk* project (*Utviklingsarbeid rettet mot unge i risikosoner*) which aimed to lower young people's barriers to NAV access. Local NAV offices could apply for funding for 15 so-called "development projects" targeted at 14-25 year-old NEETs at-risk of developing drug or behavioural problems. That project's objective was to trial models of cross-sectorial cooperation and coordination between social and employment services, schools, the county Follow-up Services, the CWS and health services (Frøyland, Maximova-Mentzoni and Fossestøl, 2016$_{[18]}$).

2. The authors estimate the quantitative programme impact by comparing year-on-year changes in outcomes at the nine pilot schools with those in nine "control" schools, which were selected based on school characteristics.

The effectiveness of outreach in Norway is difficult to assess, because the number of NAV users and that of all NEETs cannot easily be put into perspective without a comprehensive analysis of administrative microdata:

- Estimates of the NEET count vary substantially by data source: calculations using the European Labour Force Survey (EU-LFS) suggest that there were around 87 000 NEETs between 15 and 29 years in 2014, one-third of whom were actively looking for work. This number is likely an underestimate, however, as the EU-LFS is known to suffer from high non-response among non-working migrants (see Chapter 2, endnote 2). Statistics Norway produces a higher estimate of around 130 000 NEETs in 2014 on the basis of administrative data, but may misclassify certain groups of self-employed.
- Not all registered young NAV users are NEETs: of the 77 000 monthly NAV users in 2014, around 10% were only part-time unemployed and may hence have been working or studying at reduced hours; another 29% were participating in labour market measures, including subsidised or sheltered employment, and therefore also not NEETs. Some persons with reduced work capacity moreover combine receipt of the Work Assessment Allowance with standard employment or studies.[6]

Irrespective of the precise numbers, Norway appears to be very successful at ensuring that young people out of education and work who require income support or help with the transition to education or work are connected with NAV. Not all NEETs are moreover vulnerable and need support.

5.3. Re-engaging NEETs in employment, education or training

Various types of interventions aim at bringing NEETs into employment, including job search assistance and counselling, work experience programmes or hiring subsidies for private-sector employers. The impact of such measures often depends heavily on how well they are designed and targeted, however. Sustainable improvements in labour market and social outcomes are difficult to achieve, especially for highly disadvantaged young people. And even as programme participation may have positive employment and earnings effects, these effects must be weighed against longer unemployment spell durations as programme participants reduce their job search effort during programme participation ("lock in", Røed and Raaum (2006[19]); Gaure, Røed and Westlie (2012[20])). Given limited financial resources and capacity constraints weighing on public employment and welfare services it is vital that existing programmes target those most likely to benefit.

5.3.1. Early profiling and activity requirements

Norway systematically profiles all jobseekers upon initial registration with NAV, irrespective of whether or not they qualify for income support, to channel resources to users with the greatest level of disadvantage. This profiling process consists of two steps:

- A "needs assessment", done jointly by the caseworker and the jobseeker, determines the jobseeker's educational attainment, competencies, work experience and job preferences and evaluates job prospects and the type and intensity of support needed.

- A "work capacity assessment" is then carried for persons who face substantial barriers to employment – often health issues, but potentially also social problems, or a lack of transport or adequate housing. It serves to map jobseekers' capabilities and obstacles in order to determine their work readiness. All jobseekers who apply for the Work Assessment Allowance, Disability Benefits or participation in on-the-job training through the Qualification Programme (see Chapter 3 and the discussion below) need to undergo a work capacity assessment.

On the basis of this profiling, NAV classifies jobseekers into four categories that determine support intensity and benefit entitlements:

1. *Standard support*: persons with the required qualifications to quickly find work with only basic NAV support. These jobseekers usually receive Unemployment Benefits or Social Assistance.
2. *Situation-specific support*: persons who need some NAV support to find and keep employment, often because they lack the qualifications demanded in the labour market. This group includes early school leavers, persons with language difficulties, jobseekers who lack work experience, senior jobseekers and those with a previous unemployment history. Jobseekers in this category will typically have undergone a work capacity assessment and also receive Unemployment Benefits or Social Assistance.
3. *Specially adapted support*: persons with reduced work capacity, as confirmed by the work capacity assessment and often a doctor's recommendation. Jobseekers in this category may require medical treatment, rehabilitation, training or work practice to get ready for entering or returning into the labour market. They mostly receive the Work Assessment Allowance or Social Assistance or participate in the Qualification Programme.
4. *Permanently adapted support*: persons who have been assessed as permanently unfit for work based on the work capacity assessment and often a doctor's recommendation. They typically receive Disability Benefits.

All employable income support recipients, i.e. those in user categories 1 to 3, face relatively strict activity requirements: recipients of Unemployment Benefits or the Work Assessment Allowance have to complete a fortnightly reporting card listing job search activities, programme participation and absences (due to holidays, sickness, etc.) and potential periods of employment.[7] The required intensity of active job search, for instance in terms of a minimum number of job applications per fortnight, depends on the user's profile. Failures to complete a reporting card, to accept an adequately paid job offer or to attend an agreed labour market measure can lead to benefit reductions on a day-per-day *pro rata* basis. Few such sanctions, however, are imposed in practice.[8] Activity requirements for employable Social Assistance recipients are generally a local responsibility, and approaches hence vary across municipalities. Norway strengthened activity requirements for young benefit recipients in 2017, however, introducing a national activation requirement for below-30 year-olds. Critics have questioned the usefulness of such a requirement in light of already existing requirements as part of the Youth Guarantee (Grødem, 2016[21]). Stricter conditionality of Social Assistance has however been shown to reduce benefit receipt and raise high school completion rates among young people in Norway, and hence to positively affect education levels, employment chances and earnings in the long run (Hernæs, Markussen and Røed, 2017[22]).

Young people with reduced work capacity account for a substantial share of young NAV users. While most new registrees require little support, 13% of new newly registered young NAV users in 2017 were classified as needing *specially adapted support* and another 4% required *permanently adapted support* (categories 3 and 4, Figure 5.2, Panel A). Users with reduced work capacity moreover make up the majority of the current user caseload: 56% of registered young NAV users, or 4% of all 15-29 year-olds, receive *specially adapted* or *permanently adapted support* from NAV (Figure 5.2, Panel B). The reason for this is that young people with ill health often remain registered with NAV for long periods (see the discussion of benefit spell durations in Chapter 3), partly also because they are much more likely than other users to participate in labour market programmes.

Figure 5.2. Most new NAV users require only standard support, but persons with reduced work capacity account for the majority of all young NAV users

Panel A: Inflow of young NAV users by support category, absolute number and percentage of all inflows, 2017

Panel B: Stock of registered young NAV users by support category, as a percentage of all 15-29 year-olds, 2010-17

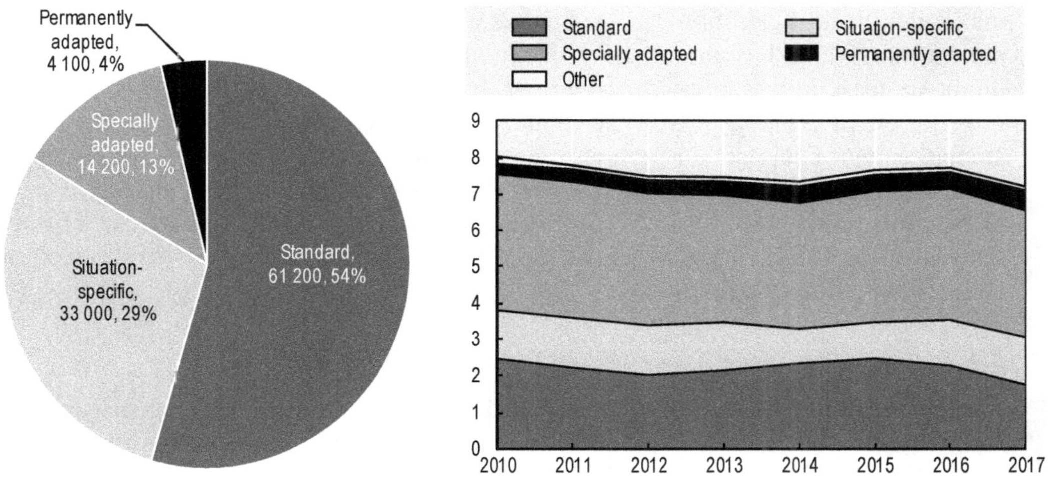

Note: Panel B: The number of jobseekers is measured in the month of August of each year. The main text defines the four user support categories.

Source: OECD calculations using NAV data and Statistics Norway (2017), Norwegian population statistics Table: 07459: Population, by sex and one-year age groups. 1 January (M) https://www.ssb.no/statistikkbanken/.

NAV users should meet their caseworker at least once every quarter to discuss their changing support needs, for instance as they encounter unexpected difficulties in finding work or participating in an activity or after successful programme completion. Such re-assessments should also take place whenever users apply for participation in the Qualification Programme or for receipt of the Work Assessment Allowance or Disability Benefits. Users requiring *specially adapted support* (category 3) should have their work capacity re-assessed every six months.

In practice, caseworkers often find it difficult, however, to rigorously determine users' work capacity, and they hence struggle with the competing demands of having to activate highly disadvantaged users while ensuring that they remain entitled to the income support they need (OECD, 2013[23]; Gjersøe, 2016[24]). There are too few effective support options for users with more complex health issues and a lack of recent work experience; as a result, these users often remain "locked into" the Work Assessment Allowance for years unless if they find work or are moved to Disability Benefits. Of all young users who started receiving the Work Assessment Allowance upon its introduction in spring 2010, around 33% remained in the scheme for the full permitted four-year period, a larger share than for other age groups. Half of all young users who completed the four-year benefit receipt period moreover saw their time limit waived and continued receiving the benefit, while only 5% moved into employment (Sørbø and Ytteborg, 2015[25]).[9] For users whose work capacity is not permanently reduced but who do not find work, Social Assistance is often the only viable "exit option"; as NAV has fewer resources available to support these users once they stop receiving the Work Assessment Allowance, many re-apply after having reached their time limit.

In an effort to promote employment of those highly disadvantaged jobseekers, Norway tightened access to the Work Assessment Allowance in early 2018 and strengthened support for benefit recipients notably by: clarifying the conditions for access to the scheme; increasing work incentives and follow-up entitlements; reducing the maximum benefit duration from four to three years; tightening the conditions for an exception from this time limit; and extending the minimum period after which users who have reached the maximum benefit duration can re-apply. While these steps should further lower the receipt rate, which has already been declining for young people over the last years, they might at least initially lead to a further increase in disability benefit receipt (NAV, 2017[26]; OECD, 2018[27]). Norway should consider complementing these steps through a strengthening of support for highly disadvantaged young jobseekers on Social Assistance as an alternative to the Work Assessment Allowance. The most recent *Economic Survey* of Norway moreover called for a tighter gatekeeping in the Disability Benefit scheme through clearer guidelines to general practitioners who carry out disability assessments and a better compliance monitoring (OECD, 2018[27])

5.3.2. From the Youth Guarantee to the New Youth Effort

As one of the pioneers of the so-called youth guarantees (YG), Norway has had comprehensive provisions in place for the last three decades that entitle young jobseekers to additional, targeted support.[10] First introduced in the early 1980s in response to rising youth unemployment, the Norwegian Youth Guarantee (*Ungdomsgaranti*) initially targeted workless under-20 year-olds, focusing primarily on re-engaging those with no more than compulsory education in education or training. Its implementation went hand-in-hand with capacity extensions of upper-secondary schools and financial subsidies to employers who provided training opportunities to young people. Norway extended its YG to 20-to-24 year-olds in 1995 and then further to 25-29 year-olds with reduced work capacity in 2009 (Hummeluhr, 1997[28]; Hardoy et al., 2016[29]). In 2017, Norway carried out a substantial reform of its YG to strengthen and individualise support for young jobseekers, remarkably dropping the well-known "Youth Guarantee" label in favour of a new name – "New Youth Effort".

The old Youth Guarantee and its implementation

The YG in its previous form came with a three-tiered approach:

- *All under-20 year-olds* outside of education or work – the YG's main target group – should be offered a place in a labour market programme, though no maximum time limit before enrolment was specified. In practice, NAV focused primarily on re-integrating these young people into education, because they typically had not completed upper-secondary education.[11]

- *All 20-24 year-olds* requiring *situation-specific support* (category 2) were entitled to an activity plan within one month of registration.
- *Of all 20-29 year-olds with reduced work capacity* (categories 3 and 4), 90% should have an activity plan at any time.

While the YG was always understood primarily an expression of policy priorities, rather than to equip young people with any *legal entitlements*, its effectiveness at shaping youth employment policy appears to have been limited. A study commissioned by the Ministry of Labour, which looked into the follow-up guarantee for 20-24 year-olds, found that NAV indeed prioritised young people in providing employment support.[12] Caseworkers were often not aware of the precise contents of the YG, however, and took little account in their daily work of whether or not a young jobseeker was part of the YG's target groups (Rambøll, 2011[30]).

The absence of any outcome monitoring system was an additional shortcoming. NAV offices were not required to regularly report on a set of indicators that would have served to measure the implementation of the YG's main elements. Some of the types of data that would be required for such an evaluation were not even collected: notably, NAV does not have access to educational statistics that would permit measuring what share of young jobseekers move back into education or training, and into what types of programmes. This makes it difficult to assess a systematic implementation of the YG, or to track and compare results across offices or over time.

Available data moreover suggest that the YG's specific targets have not been met:

- Of registered under-20 year-olds, only 24% attended a labour market programme in August 2015. NAV does not collect "flow data" that would permit analysing how long it typically takes until a young person in this group is offered a place in a labour market measure. Similarly, NAV does not collect data on the share of young people who are successfully re-integrated into education.
- Of 20-24 year-olds who require *situation-specific support*, only 35% had an activity plan in August 2016. Users in this group moreover received their activity plan on average only around three months after registration; less than half of all users who had an activity plan got theirs within the specified one-month period (NAV Expert Group, 2015[11]).
- Among 20-29 year-olds, the share of users with an activity plan was 65% for those requiring *specially adapted support* (category 3) and around 25% for those requiring *permanently adapted support* (category 4) in August 2016 – much below the target rate of 90%.

Another more comprehensive research report cast further doubts on the YG's effectiveness at shaping NAV's support to workless young people, hence triggering the 2017 YG reform (Strand, Bråthen and Grønningsæter, 2015[4]).[13] It emphasised the YG's symbolic importance for making youth unemployment a policy priority, but confirmed that NAV caseworkers were insufficiently aware of the YG's actual contents. The report called for a closer and more tailored follow-up to all young NAV users, including for those with lower employment barriers such as to prevent the building up over time of additional hurdles, notably mental health issues. It also recommended creating additional opportunities for workless young people to participate in educational and labour market programmes.

The New Youth Effort

The 2017 reform, which replaced the old YG through the New Youth Effort (NYE, *Ny ungdomsinnsats*), addressed many of those issues. Under the NYE, Norway commits to providing all under-30 year-olds in the top three user categories with personalised employment-oriented follow-up within eight weeks of registration with NAV. This may include counselling and job search assistance, but also participation in labour market programmes. The Government hopes that replacing the YG's three-tiered approach with a single eight-week follow-up commitment will permit NAV to move away from a rules-based approach to a more user-centred one. If systematically implemented, the new rules should shorten the time until young users benefit from support through NAV and strengthen support in particular to users in their 20s and those with lower support needs. The Norwegian Government made available an additional NOK 100 million (EUR 10.2 million) in funding for the implementation of the NYE in 2018 – of those, NOK 70 million (EUR 7.3 million) go directly to NAV to finance the foreseen intensified follow-up, hence permitting an increase in staff levels for youth teams.

The NYE's impact on employment support for young jobseekers will crucially depend on how the new policy framework translates into day-to-day practice, and unfortunately, no data are available yet that would permit an assessment of the NYE's initial impact. An encouraging sign, however, is that the Ministry of Social Affairs and Labour has begun developing a set of indicators to measure the NYE's implementation. The first two such indicators, on which NAV will have report to the Ministry once per quarter, are the share of young jobseekers requiring *standard support* whose follow-up needs have been reassessed within eight weeks of their registration; and the share of users requiring *situation-specific* or *specially adapted support* who participate in various labour market measures eight weeks after registration. The regular reporting on such indicators should contribute to caseworkers' awareness of the NYE's key elements and permit evaluating and improving on the implementation of the policy.

5.3.3. Participation in labour market programmes

NAV successfully targets labour market programmes to users who face the greatest difficulties in finding employment, and under-24 year-olds, young people without an upper-secondary diploma and persons with reduced work capacity are among the priority groups. Already during the initial profiling process, caseworkers sometimes use the quick engagement of a user in a labour market measure as a way of testing the person's suitability for education or work: as a young person's social or health problems may not become immediately apparent during the initial interview, the quick placement of a user into work or training can provide an indication of whether or not the person is ready for work or needs further support first – at least in cases were no major hurdles are apparent. The frequency with which young people participate in labour market programmes, as well as the types of measures they participate in, are hence closely associated with the user support category, with most resources flowing to the users in the higher categories. This is remarkable, as there is often a concern that caseworkers tend to sign up the most *motivated* jobseekers for labour market measures, rather than those who likely benefit the most ("cream-skimming").

Labour market programme participants receive an Activity Allowance (*Tiltakspenger*) for the duration of the activity. As this payment is more generous than Social Assistance, it makes programme participation particularly attractive to young people without Unemployment Benefit entitlements (see Chapter 3). Norway raised the minimum age threshold for receipt of an Activity Allowance from 16 to 18 years in 2016 to avoid encouraging young people to quit school and register as jobseekers. A recent study suggests, however, that at least for 18- and 19-year-olds, receipt of an Activity Allowance by itself does not have any effect on school drop-out, the completion of the labour market measure, employment and jobseekers status or Social Assistance receipt (Drange, Frøyland and Mamelund, 2015[31]).

Overall, however, Norway devotes fewer resources to labour market programme participation than comparable countries. Programme participation rates among jobseekers of any age have trended downwards over the last decade, and were only about half as high as in Denmark or Sweden in 2015 (Figure 5.3, Panel A). Norway also spends significantly less than these two countries and less than it did a decade ago (Panel B).

Figure 5.3. Few Norwegian jobseekers participate in labour market programmes

Panel A: Labour market programme participants per 100 persons wanting to work, 2006-15

Panel B: Expenditures on labour market programmes per person wanting to work (in EUR*), 2006-15

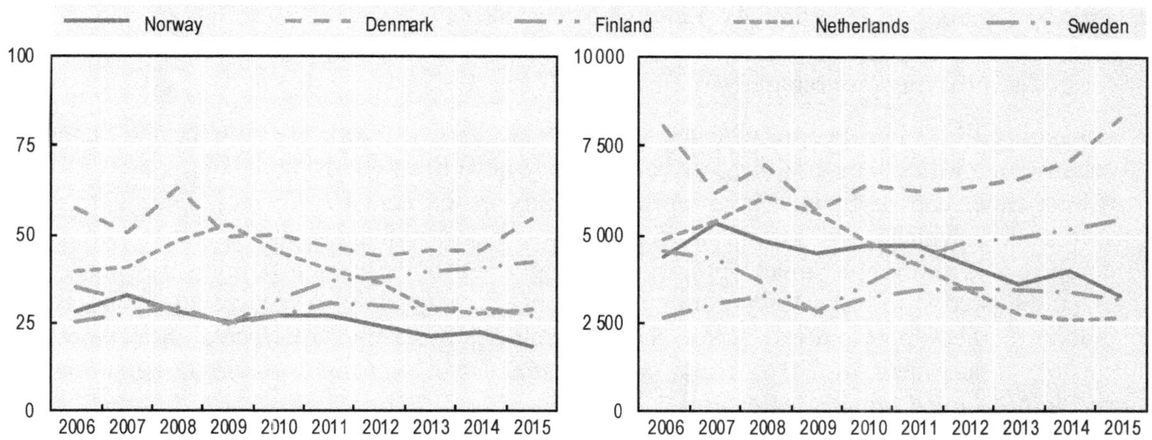

Note: * Expenditures are adjusted for purchasing power in the EU-25, and expressed in terms of the Purchasing Power Standard (PPS).

Participant and expenditure figures refer to LMP measures of categories 2 to 7, i.e. training, employment incentives, supported employment and rehabilitation, direct job creation and start-up incentives.

There is a break in the time series for programme participant numbers in Norway in 2009.

Source: Eurostat (2017), "Activation-Support - LMP participants per 100 persons wanting to work" (http://appsso.eurostat.ec.europa.eu/nui/show.do?dataset=lmp_ind_actsup&lang=en) and Eurostat (2017), "LMP expenditure" (http://appsso.eurostat.ec.europa.eu/nui/show.do?dataset=lmp_ind_exp&lang=en).

It is unfortunately difficult to tell based on these numbers alone to what extent lower participation rates can be explained – at least in part – through a tighter targeting on those jobseekers who are mostly likely to benefit. Internationally comparable numbers specifically for young people are unfortunately not available for Norway, but NAV user statistics show that the share of young users who participate labour market measures has declined from 40 to 29% in the decade up to 2016 (Table 5.1).

Job search assistance and counselling

The type and intensity of job search assistance that young NAV users receive varies by user category and the perceived need for support. Users with Unemployment Benefit entitlements who have been profiled as requiring *standard support* (category 1) typically have to participate in "Jobseekers' Club" counselling sessions of about 1.5 hours per day for over two to four weeks. Thereafter, they are left to independent job search for a period of three months, before NAV gets back in touch with them to provide closer assistance in case of continued joblessness. Social Assistance recipients and users who have been profiled as requiring *situation-specific support* (category 2) receive much closer attention from the point of initial registration, and are obliged to immediately participate in a labour market measure. In the city of Kristiansand, where the OECD review team visited a NAV office, all young Social Assistance claimants were automatically enrolled in some type of measure – typically a training course – in the week after their initial registration.

Users who require more intensive assistance can participate in a labour market measure called "follow-up" (*Oppfølgingstiltak*), delivered mostly through private providers. As part of this measure, they may benefit of intensive assistance or guidance and motivation programmes during the job search process; the support can however also continue after the young person has taken up an activity, for instance in the form of mentoring at the place of work or training.[14] On average around 5% of all young NAV users participated in a follow-up measure in a given month in 2016, or about 17% of all young programme participants (see Table 5.1). The largest user group were those requiring *specially adapted support* (category 3, Figure 5.4). Follow-up was also the most frequent labour market measure for users requiring *standard support* (category 1), who however accounted only for 2% of all young programme participants in 2016.

Unemployed[15] young people who are unsure what types of work are suitable for them because of an illness or disability, or because they have been out of the labour market for a long time, can participate in a work capability assessment (*Avklaring*). During this assessment, which can last up to four weeks, NAV evaluates the persons' skills, competences and employment options, including whether the person requires assistance or an adjusted workplace to take up employment. Participants also receive guidance on labour market opportunities. About 1% of young jobseekers participated in a work capacity assessment in 2016, nearly all of them users requiring *situation-specific or specially adapted support* (categories 2 and 3).

Table 5.1. Work experience measures and training account for the bulk of labour market programme participation among young jobseekers

Young labour market programme participants as a percentage of registered jobseekers, monthly average for below-30 year-olds

	2007	2010	2014	2015	2016
Job search assistance and counselling					
Follow-up	3	4	5	5	5
Work capability assessment	1	1	1	1	1
Training					
Training	16	11	6	6	7
Work experience					
Work practice	13	10	11	11	12
Subsidised employment					
Wage subsidies	2	2	2	2	2
Adapted employment in a sheltered work place	3	2	3	3	3
All measures	41	30	27	28	29
Number of registered jobseekers	43 521	76 235	77 198	80 326	82 172

Note: The table excludes measures with a participant number below 1% of registered jobseekers. The following programmes are shown in the table: *Oppfølging*; *Avklaring*; *Opplæring*; *Arbeidspraksis*; *Lønnstilskudd*; *Tilrettelagt arbeid*.
Source: OECD calculations based on NAV data.

Figure 5.4. NAV strongly targets labour market programme participation to jobseekers with special support needs

Breakdown of young labour market programme participants by jobseeker category and type of measure, 2016

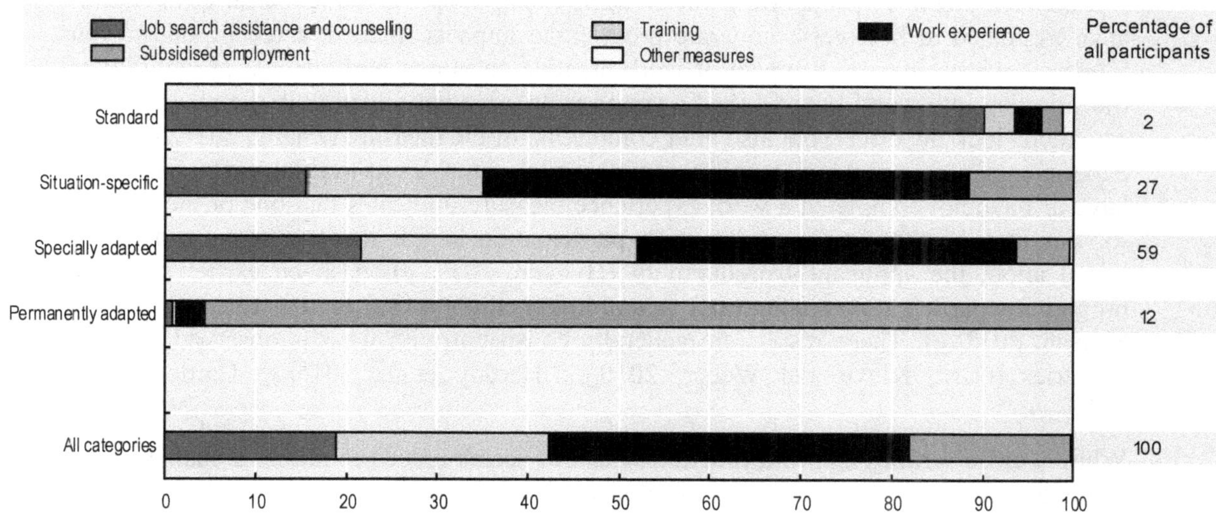

Note: See Table 5.1 for a breakdown of the labour market programme categories.
Source: OECD calculations based on NAV data.

Unfortunately, no formal impact evaluations exist that could provide insights into the effectiveness of the follow-up measure or the work capacity assessment at bringing young people back into education or sustainable employment. A recent trial carried out in Nordland County, the "Project 300", however illustrates the possible benefits of providing disadvantaged young jobseekers with counselling and career guidance (Nieuwejaar and Hagen, 2011[32]). Over a three-year period until 2013, nearly 600 unemployed young people without upper-secondary qualification received a six-week programme in career guidance, motivational courses and validation of completed training and work experience. The goal of the programme was to work with the young people towards a realistic career plan that would help them resume education or training or to start working. While NAV did not carry out a formal impact evaluation, nearly two-thirds of programme participants resumed education at upper-secondary level after programme completion.

Work experience

Work practice (*Arbeidspraksis*) with private or public employers is the most important labour market measure for young people in Norway, with participants accounting for 12% of all jobseekers or 40% of total programme participants in 2016 (Table 5.1). It provides participants with simple on-the-job training for a period of up to one year, or 1.5 years for those with reduced work experience. The measure aims to help jobseekers gain work experience, get a better impression of an occupation of interest and develop their labour market skills. Participants do not earn a wage but can receive an Activity Allowance, and NAV continues to closely follow up on them for the duration of the programme. NAV targets this measure on users with little to no previous work experience and those with reduced work capacity, i.e. mainly users requiring *situation-specific* and *specially adapted support* (categories 2 and 3). Often, NAV moreover co-operates with the county-level Follow-up Service to combine work practice with elements of education or training through standard educational institutions. In such cases, young people may be registered as part-time unemployed and part-time student.

The Ministry of Labour and Social Affairs is however currently re-considering the central role of work practice in supporting out-of-work young people given that a series of studies have estimated at best very moderate programme impacts. Indeed, a recent study even found significant *negative* impact of work practice on young participants' probability of transitioning into work, both while the young people are participating in the measure (the so-called "lock in" effect) but also after completion of the measure (Zhang, 2016[33]).[16] An experimental study, in which employers are asked to rate CVs of fictitious applicants who have or have not completed a work experience measure, indicates that one of the reasons for this may be that employers perceive participation in this measure to be a negative signal about the applicant's productivity (Hyggen, 2017[34]). Also an earlier study of programme participation among early school leavers did not find any positive effects (von Simson, 2012[35]). These results are generally consistent with what is observed in other countries (Card, Kluve and Weber, 2010[36]; Hardoy et al., 2016[29]; Hardoy et al., 2017[37]).

While a close scrutiny of work practice measures seems indeed required, a challenge for evaluating the programme is a lack of information on the scheme's local implementation. Indeed, the Ministry currently does not possess data on such key issues as the shares of young programme participants who get their work practice in the private vs. public sector, the most important occupations and the nature of the training provided or the typical durations of these programmes. Judging from international evidence, the programme's effectiveness could probably be raised by limiting it to the private sector while formalising and potentially strengthening the training component.

Training

Jobseekers who require simple training can acquire the skills they need for job search or in the labour market via courses offered by NAV through private providers. These can last up to ten months and focus on providing job search methods, boosting motivation or developing simple practical skills, for instance in nursing. Training accounted for 23% of labour market programme participation of young jobseekers in 2016 (Table 5.1), and is nearly exclusively targeted on users requiring *situation-specific* or *specially adapted support* (categories 2 and 3, Figure 5.4).

The municipal NAV arm moreover provides much more intensive training to jobseekers with severely reduced earnings capacity (typically those requiring *specially adapted support*, i.e. category 3) without entitlements to insurance-based out-of-work benefits via the so-called Qualification Programme (*Kvalifiseringsprogrammet*). The Qualification Programme offers a full-time schedule of life skills and simple training – often with a significant on-the job component – for up to two years. It can contain components similar to those of standard simple training programmes, participants are however followed up much more tightly by their caseworkers. Participants often have a long sickness history, have been cycling into and out of unemployment, or are long-term Social Assistance recipients. Also migrants with a lack of Norwegian language skills form an important participant group. Participants are paid the Qualification Benefit (*Kvalifiseringsstønaden*), which is higher than Social Assistance and provides participants with a stable income over a longer period. Qualification Programme participants do not, however, have the chance to earn a formal diploma.

The results of the Qualification Programme are encouraging: about 42% of the 3 100 persons who completed the programme in 2015 succeeded in making a transition to work – a considerable number given the participant's high level of disadvantage.[17] A recent evaluation concluded that the Qualification Programme indeed substantially raises participants' employment prospects (Markussen and Røed, 2016[38]). Since former Qualification Programme participants tend to work only part-time and at low wages, however, the positive employment effects are generally not large enough to permit self-sufficiency. The positive evaluation of the Qualification Programme is in line with similar results from other countries showing that he combination of simple one-the-job training with intensive support and close follow-up has proven highly effective for highly disadvantaged jobseekers (Carcillo and Königs, 2018[39]; OECD, 2016[40]).[18]

In light of these positive results, Norway may want to consider devoting greater resources to this programme, which is quite expensive to operate. Caseloads of NAV staff responsible for the Qualification Programme in the offices visited by the OECD review team were much lower than usual, at around 15 to 30 users. Companies who employ Qualification Programme participants moreover often instructed selected staff members to act as mentors. Because of these high resource requirements, NAV offices in smaller municipalities or those with limited capacities appear not to make systematic use of the programme.

Norway recently filled an important gap in upper-secondary training options for jobseekers in their early 20s. NAV traditionally does not provide such more comprehensive training as upper-secondary, vocational and professional education is a county responsibility (see Chapter 4). According to the Norwegian Education Act, only 16-19 year-olds were legally entitled to enrol in public upper-secondary education free of charge,[19] however, while upper-secondary programmes in adult education are available only from the age of 25. Consequently, 20-24 year-olds who aimed to obtain an upper-secondary degree generally had to rely on costly private schools, though some counties with sufficient capacities opened their schools for young people in their early twenties.[20] This gap was closed from August 2017 through a reform of the Education Act, which extended access to regular upper-secondary programmes to young people up to the age of 25. This removed pressure from NAV to offer training at upper-secondary level to young jobseekers. It also lowered incentives for caseworkers to move young people onto the Work Assessment Allowance, where they had greater access to training programmes at upper-secondary level.

Still before this legislative change, NAV has moreover been trialling two-year upper-secondary vocational training programmes (*To-årig opplæringstiltak*) for low-skilled jobseekers since the beginning of 2016. The programmes, which are offered together with county-level educational authorities, are targeted at young people in their 20s but open also to older jobseekers. They come with a strong practical training component, often provided on-the-job by local employers, and focus on sought-after professions such as nursing and health care or crafts. Participants continue to receive their income support, typically Social Assistance, while employers qualify for receipt of apprenticeship grants from the educational authorities. At 300 students, the programme is however still very small, and no data are available yet that would permit evaluating its effectiveness.

An apparent shortage in simple training concerns language classes for migrants who lack Norwegian language skills. For humanitarian migrants and their families, the two- to three-year Introduction Programme provides language training and an introduction to Norwegian (work) culture (OECD, 2012[41]).[21] Upon programme completion, a large share of participants then move on to the Qualification Programme: in the city of Kristiansand, for instance, close to 80% of Qualification Programme participants had previously completed the Introduction Programme. By contrast, non-refugee migrants who lack Norwegian skills only qualify for standard employment support and cannot directly benefit from language courses offered through NAV.[22] This can be a hurdle in particular for the labour market integration of unemployed persons from Eastern European countries, for example, who came to Norway to work in the construction sector, and do not necessarily return to their sending countries after losing their job.

Subsidised and supported employment

Wage subsidies are an important instrument for NAV to improve the employment opportunities of jobseekers who have difficulties finding work or keeping their job at standard wages because of a lack of skills, long unemployment or reduced work capacity. There are two major types of wage subsidies schemes in Norway:

- Wage subsidies (*Lønnstilskudd*) for those in ordinary employment can replace, for a period of up to one year, up to 50% of the salary of a person working full-time or part-time in the private or non-governmental sector; employers who hire persons with reduced work capacity can benefit of a subsidy of up to 75% of the salary for up to three years. Wage subsidies can be paid for an unlimited duration to employers who hire a person with substantially and permanently reduced work capacity; in this case, the subsidy equals 75% during the first year and 67% thereafter. About 2% of all young jobseekers received a wage subsidy in 2016 (Table 5.1), in particular those requiring *situation-specific* or *specially adapted support* (categories 2 and 3).
- NAV uses adapted employment in a sheltered workplace (*Tilrettelagt arbeid*) to support jobseekers with severe reductions in work capacity. This measure accounts for a slightly larger share of jobseekers – 3%, or 10% of all programme participants in 2016 (Table 5.1). It is by far the most important measure for users who require *permanently adapted support* (category 4, see Figure 5.4).

In neither of the two schemes, employers are formally required to retain participants after the subsidy has expired, though NAV would exclude employers who are perceived as trying to trick the system.

In an ongoing trial, NAV is moreover testing using the Work Assessment Allowance as a wage subsidy for persons with reduced work capacity who take up employment. Users in the five participating Norwegian counties are permitted to keep some of their benefit payments while working either full-time or part-time for a period of up to three years; participating employers receive a wage subsidy.[23] Both employees and employers moreover benefit from follow-up through NAV. Initial results from a qualitative evaluation suggest a high degree of satisfaction with the programme among jobseekers and employers alike (Spjelkavik and Terjesen, 2016[42]) – results from an impact evaluation will be published in late 2018.

Existing evaluations of the Norwegian wage subsidy schemes generally suggest that they are effective and promoting employment (see von Simson (2012[35]) or a discussion of a series of earlier evaluations by Hardoy et al. (2016[29])). Again, this is consistent with the international literature on the topic. The relatively tight targeting of wage subsidies in Norway to more disadvantaged jobseekers moreover limits the risk that employers pocket the subsidy to recruit jobseekers whom they would have hired anyhow (i.e. of so-called "deadweight effects").

5.4. Systematically evaluating programme impacts

Policies and programmes to support NEETs should be regularly assessed with regards to their impact on young people's employment, educational and social outcomes to ascertain their effectiveness and an efficient use of public resources. Norway devotes considerable funding to evaluating its policies and programmes – whether through local-level pilot schemes or comprehensive national-level evaluation reports – often drawing on its excellent administrative microdata for empirical analyses. Authorities moreover systematically rely on the insights gained from such studies to develop and adjust their policies or even to replace them if they have been shown to be insufficiently effective – with the recent Youth Guarantee reform being a case in point.

Norway has scope, however, to further improve on its use of evaluations to inform policy design:

- *Data collection and sharing:* Labour market challenges and opportunities for young people vary across Norway, and NAV offices enjoy a healthy level of discretion to adapt programmes to local needs. While this provides ample scope for innovation and mutual learning, the identification of best-practices is hindered by a lack of systematic reporting on the details of local-level programme implementation. As highlighted in this chapter, neither the NAV Directorate nor the Ministry of Labour and Social Affairs possess data, for instance, on the extent to which NAV offices use pay-for-performance when purchasing employment services from external providers, on the type of employers – public or private – that offer work practice to young jobseekers or on the retention rates of jobseekers who participate in the wage subsidy scheme once subsidies run out. The municipal NAV arm moreover does not directly provide any data on user characteristics or social support interventions to the NAV Directorate or the Ministry at all. Norway could much better exploit the diversity in local programme implementation for identifying and sharing best practices if NAV offices were required to report more systematically on the employment and social support they provide, and if such statistical results were more routinely transmitted to the Ministry.
- *Measuring programme impacts:* The bulk of policy evaluations commissioned by the Norwegian authorities are qualitative or descriptive in nature. These studies provide valuable insights, see again Strand, Bråthen and Grønningsæter's comprehensive report on the YG (2015[4]); yet, robust evidence is lacking on how effective Norway's labour market programmes are at bringing young people into education or work or at promoting better social outcomes. When commissioning research, the Ministry and NAV should more systematically require the use of randomised controlled trials (RCTs)[24] or quasi-experimental techniques for evaluating youth programmes, and implement new programmes in ways that facilitate rigorous impact evaluations. In light of relatively low jobseeker numbers and limited capacity in smaller municipalities, this may require expanding pilots across several municipalities to secure a smooth implementation and sufficient sample sizes.

Round-up and recommendations

The labour market situation of young people in Norway is very favourable by OECD standards, which implies that young people who find themselves out of education or work for longer periods are often highly disadvantaged. Norway devotes considerable resources to helping those NEETs overcome barriers to educational and labour market participation and find work. Through its Follow-up Services, Norway provides exemplary outreach efforts to school leavers who do not have an immediate option in education or work; also the integrated delivery of social and employment services through NAV – often by specialised youth teams with moderate to low caseload numbers – can be considered a best practice. NAV moreover appears to make good use of its resources by carefully profiling all users upon registration and targeting labour market support to those who need it most. High receipt rates of incapacity-related benefits – the Work Assessment Allowance and Disability Benefits – are a major concern, however.

Norway could further strengthen the support for NEETs along the following dimensions:

Further promote labour market integration of young people with reduced work capacity

- *Ensure rigorous work capacity assessments:* Receipt rates of incapacity benefits remain very high in spite of significant reform efforts. Norway should monitor the effects of the recent Work Assessment Allowance reform on the receipt of incapacity benefits, and ensure notably that NAV caseworkers receive clear guidance on how to carry out work capacity assessments. Gatekeeping for Disability Benefits should be improved by providing clearer guidelines to general practitioners who carry out disability assessments and by better monitoring their compliance with these guidelines.
- *Strengthen support for young Social Assistance recipients:* As a result of the tightened access to the Work Assessment Allowance, Social Assistance receipt will likely surge, in particular for jobseekers with (mental) health problems and little work experience. Norway should devote additional resources to supporting these users. This may include expanding the Qualification Programme, which has proven effective for highly disadvantaged jobseekers. The currently low Social Assistance benefit levels could be raised to tackle youth poverty.

Improve the effectiveness of labour market measures

- *Permit tendering of social services and strengthen pay-for-performance for service providers:* Labour market measures for jobseekers are largely delivered by non-governmental providers, who are compensated per hour or per user irrespective of their performance. The tendering of social support services remains rare. Norway should grant NAV offices greater freedom in contracting out social service delivery, and strengthen the link between the compensation of employment and social service providers and the results they achieve.
- *Re-assess the strong reliance on work experience measures:* Work practice in the public or private sector is the most widely used labour market measure for young people, but a series of studies have suggested that it is ineffective at moving young people into stable employment. Norway should re-consider the widespread use of this measure, possibly with a view to restricting it to private-sector employers and strengthening and formalising its training component.
- *Expand the use of training programmes:* NAV currently provides training to jobseekers mostly through very short programmes in basic skills. After the recent opening of the public upper-secondary education system to young people in their early 20s, NAV and educational authorities should consider jointly expanding vocational training programmes for low-skilled jobseekers. NAV should moreover introduce Norwegian-language classes for the growing share of young migrants.

- *Increase the use of rigorous impact evaluations:* The Ministry of Labour and Social Affairs and NAV regularly commission evaluations of their policies and programmes to support NEETs. Most of these studies are qualitative in nature, however, providing little insights on programmes' actual impacts. To ensure an efficient use of resources, Norway should expand the use of randomised controlled trials and quasi-experimental techniques for evaluating employment and social support programmes for young people, and implement new programmes in ways that facilitate rigorous impact evaluations.

Ensure a systematic application of the New Youth Effort

- *Create awareness of the New Youth Effort and systematically report on its implementation:* The discontinued Youth Guarantee failed to effectively shape youth employment support because NAV caseworkers were often insufficiently aware of – and bound by – its contents. For the New Youth Effort to bring substantial improvements, Norway should clearly communicate to NAV specialists the entitlements that the New Youth Effort grants to young people. It should also establish an effective monitoring system that permits comparing jobseeker outcomes across NAV offices against clear benchmarks.

- *Make sure that resources match the increased requirements:* NAV caseworkers have pointed to the importance of low caseload numbers and intensive follow-up as perceived success factors for an effective support of NEETs. In light of the higher follow-up entitlements under the New Youth Effort, Norway should commit additional resources to strengthening NAV's youth teams and permit raising participation in labour market measures, which is lower than in other Nordic countries.

Expand data collection and exchange

- *Intensify reporting of local-level implementation of employment and social support:* NAV offices enjoy considerable discretion in implementing employment support and developing their own social support policies. To promote the identification and sharing of best practices and facilitate cross-regional learning, Norway should require local offices to collect data on the implementation of labour market measures and social service delivery and transmit these to national authorities.

- *Facilitate data exchange between the educational authorities and NAV*: In the context of relatively high early school leaving rates, NAV rightly focuses primarily on moving young jobseekers back into education or training. NAV caseworkers currently do not have access to administrative information on the educational attainment of their users, however, and they have no reliable way of telling whether and when their users move into education or training. Norway should improve data exchange between the educational authorities and NAV to facilitate a better follow-up of users through their caseworkers, and to permit NAV to observe and analyse movements into education and training.

Notes

1. Young persons qualify for NAV employment services if they are above the age of 16 years. The Social Welfare Act foresees no age threshold, but young people below the age of 18 years typically do not individually qualify for Social Assistance or NAV-provided social services but are supported through the municipal child welfare services (CWS). CWS support can be extended to the age of 23 for children in foster care ("after-care measures"). Outside of NAV, municipal health and care services provide general health support, including psychological services funded through the Directorate of Health.

2. Persons are generally required to independently find housing in the private market, except where this in not possible for instance in cases of substance abuse problems. There is only very little social housing in Norway, but NAV can provide financial support to help households cover the initial deposit or parts of the rent.

3. The trial project "Core Tasks in NAV" tried to assess the effect of delivering this service directly through NAV instead of through private providers. A quasi-experimental evaluation that compared results in five "treated" and five "control" municipalities did not yield any significant results, however (Grimsmo, Mamelund and Spjelkavik, 2015[30]).

4. Caseload numbers are lowest in Finnmark (40) and highest in Buskerud and Vestfold (85 users). The survey was conducted among the managers of the 200 largest NAV offices in the country, who were asked to pass it on to four staff members working with young people. 346 caseworkers from 172 NAV offices responded to the survey (86% response rate). Norwegian authorities do not collect caseload numbers.

5. Low-income households can moreover receive a means-tested housing allowance through the State Housing Bank, which is not administered through NAV.

6. Meanwhile, in the EU-LFS, the variable indicating whether a respondee is registered with the public employment service is not filled for Norway.

7. The reporting card can be completed online. Activity requirements do not apply to NAV users who do not receive any income support.

8. NAV temporarily suspended benefits to 2 640 users below the age of 30 years in 2016; while there were nearly 40 000 employable young NAV users on benefits at any single point in time. Sanctioned jobseekers who have troubles covering their costs of living can apply for a lower emergency benefit.

9. More generally, transitions between the different user categories – and in particular movements into a better category – are rare: only about 1 000 young people move out of a different category into user category 2 every month, less than 8% of the caseload in that category – only around 50 of these users move "up" from category 3 (Calculations based on NAV data comparing users' status in August and September of 2016.

10. The European Union (EU) countries recently followed suit by introducing their own national youth guarantees in the framework of the 2013 EU Youth Guarantee scheme. Under the EU Youth Guarantee, all young people below the age of 25 years should receive an offer of employment, continued education, or training within four months of leaving formal education or becoming unemployed.

11. Approximately two-thirds of under-20 year-olds registered with NAV in 2016 did not have an upper-secondary degree.

12. A later study confirmed that young users generally receive more intensive support than others; over 90% of registered users under the age of 25 in late 2014 had received work-related follow-up through NAV within the last three months (NAV Expert Group, 2015[7]).

13. Unfortunately, no comprehensive empirical assessment exists of the YG's impact on participants' educational or labour market outcomes. A quasi-experimental evaluation of an "enhanced youth guarantee" trial carried out in the late 1990s, which provided intensified support to long-term unemployed 20-24 year-olds, demonstrated positive effects on the employment transition of long-term unemployed youth and a reduction in benefit receipt. The trial did not raise young people's likelihood of taking up education. (Hardoy et al., 2006[29])

14. This measure should not be confused with the standard "employment-related follow-up" provided by NAV (see Section 5.3.2) or the county-level "Follow-Up Services" for school leavers (*Oppfølgingstjenesten*, see Chapter 4).

15. The measure is also available for employed users who are on sick leave.

16. Having participated in work practice was however associated with a stronger positive employment effect of subsequent training programme participation.

17. Specific numbers for young people and programme non-completion rates are not available.

18. Specifically, the authors estimate that the programme raises participants' employment rate by 18 percentage points four years after programme start, though the size of this effect is estimated quite imprecisely. Earlier evaluations provided descriptive and qualitative results (Schafft and Spjelkavik, 2011[32]; Lima and Naper, 2013[33]).

19. This training entitlement has to be claimed over a maximum period of five consecutive years, or six years in case vocational education that is at least partly company-based.

20. The same applies to students below the age of 25 years who have completed vocational training and would like to enrol in a "third stage" programme to obtain a university admission certificate.

21. The Introduction Programme is run by the municipalities under the responsibility of the Ministry of Children, Equality and Social Inclusion, and offered through NAV in many municipalities.

22. These jobseekers have the option of enrolling in language classes offered for a fee by the municipalities, albeit at their own cost.

23. The trial was initially launched in 2013 in the counties of Østfold, Vest-Agder, Hordaland and Oslo; Troms participates since 2014. The trial is supposed to be budget-neutral in the sense that the costs of continuing to pay partial WAA and wages subsidies to employers should not surpass the amount of WAA that would have been paid to the users had they not started working.

24. The Ministry of Labour and Social Affairs commissioned a research institute with the implementation of two RCTs on policies for person with reduced work capacity in 2011 – one examining the impact of reducing the time until these jobseekers are given access to a labour market measure, the second one comparing the effects of supported employment and standard follow-up. Neither of the two studies has been completed yet.

References

Aakvik, A., K. Monstad and T. Holmås (2014), "Evaluating the Effect of a National Labour and Welfare Administration Reform (Nav-reform) on Employment, Social Insurance and Social Assistance", *Stein Rokkan Centre for Social Studies Working Paper*, No. 4-2014, http://bora.uib.no/handle/1956/9375. [8]

Carcillo, S. and S. Königs (2018), "Skills for at-risk youth -- lessons from the United States", *OECD Social, Employment and Migration Working Papers (forthcoming).* [39]

Card, D., J. Kluve and A. Weber (2010), "Active labour market policy evaluations: A meta-analysis", *Economic Journal*, Vol. 120/November, pp. F452–F477, http://dx.doi.org/10.1111/j.1468-0297.2010.02387.x. [36]

Christensen, T., A. Fimreite and P. Lægreid (2014), "Joined-Up Government for Welfare Administration Reform in Norway", *Public Organization Review*, Vol. 14/4, pp. 439-456, http://dx.doi.org/10.1007/s11115-013-0237-8. [5]

Drange, I., K. Frøyland and S. Mamelund (2015), *Unge mottakere av tiltakspenger - Om betydningen av tiltakspenger for gjennomføring av utdanning og overgang til arbeid [Young recipients of Activity Allowance - On the importance of the Activity Allowance for the completion of education and the transition into work]*, Arbeidsforskningsinstituttet AFI, Oslo, http://www.hioa.no/Om-HiOA/Senter-for-velferds-og-arbeidslivsforskning/AFI/Publikasjoner-AFI/Unge-mottakere-av-tiltakspenger. [31]

Fevang, E., S. Markussen and K. Røed (2014), "NAV-reformen: Støvet legger seg etter en turbulent omstilling [NAV reform: The dust settles after a turbulent restructuring]", *Søkelys på arbeidslivet*, Vol. 31/01-02, https://www.idunn.no/spa/2014/01-02/nav-reformen_stoevet_legger_seg_etter_en_turbulent_omstill?mode=abstract_no&skipDecorating=true (accessed on 11 October 2017), pp. 83-99. [10]

Fossestøl, K., E. Breit and E. Borg (2014), *NAV-reformen 2014 - En oppfølgingsstudie av lokalkontorenes organisering etter innholdsreformen [The 2014 NAV reform - A follow-up study into the organisation of local offices after the content reform]*, Arbeidsforskningsinstituttet AFI, Oslo, http://www.hioa.no/content/download/67792/1702255/file/r2014-13.pdf (accessed on 14 February 2018). [7]

Frøyland, K., T. Maximova-Mentzoni and K. Fossestøl (2016), *Sosialt arbeid og oppfølging av utsatt ungdom i NAV [Social work and follow-up for vulnerable youth through NAV]*, Arbeidsforskningsinstituttet (AFI), Oslo, http://www.hioa.no/content/download/121317/2806871/file/r2016_01%20Sluttrapport%20utsatt%20ungdom%20AFI.pdf. [18]

Gaure, S., K. Røed and L. Westlie (2012), "Job search incentives and job match quality", http://dx.doi.org/10.1016/j.labeco.2012.04.001. [20]

Gjersøe, H. (2016), "Getting Sick and Disabled People off Temporary Benefit Receipt: Strategies and Dilemmas in the Welfare State's Frontline", *Nordic Journal of Working Life Studies*, Vol. 6/S1, https://tidsskrift.dk/njwls/article/view/26656/23428?acceptCookies=1, pp. 129-145. [24]

Grimsmo, A., S. Mamelund and Ø. Spjelkavik (2015), *Evaluering av forsøket Kjerneoppgaver i NAV. Delrapport 2 [Evaluation of the experiment Core Tasks in NAV. Volume 2]*, Arbeidsforskningsinstituttet (AFI), Høgskolen i Oslo og Akershu, http://www.hioa.no/Aktuelle-saker/Evaluering-av-forsoeket-Kjerneoppgaver-i-NAV. [44]

Grødem, A. (2016), "Mandatory activation for recipients of social assistance in Norway", *ESPN Flash Report*, No. 2016/6, European Social Policy Network, http://ec.europa.eu/social/BlobServlet?docId=15052&langId=en. [21]

Hardoy, I. et al. (2006), "Virker ungdomsgarantien? [Does the Youth Guarantee work?]", *Søkelys på arbeidsmarkedet*, Vol. 23, pp. 21-30. [43]

Hardoy, I. et al. (2016), *En komparativ analyse av effekter av innsats for å inkludere utsatte unge i arbeid i Norden [A comparative analysis of the effect of policies to improve the labour market prospects of at-risk youth in North European countries]*, Institutt for samfunnsforskning, Oslo, https://brage.bibsys.no/xmlui/handle/11250/2442577. [29]

Hardoy, I. et al. (2017), "Effekter av arbeidsmarkedspolitikk rettet mot ungdom i Nord-Europa – en metaanalyse [The effects of youth labour market policies in Northern Europe – a meta-analysis]", *Søkelys på arbeidslivet*, Vol. 34/03, pp. 167-181, http://dx.doi.org/10.18261/issn.1504-7989-2017-03-02. [37]

Hernæs, Ø., S. Markussen and K. Røed (2017), "Can welfare conditionality combat high school dropout?", *Labour Economics*, Vol. 48, pp. 144-156, http://dx.doi.org/10.1016/J.LABECO.2017.08.003. [22]

Hummeluhr, N. (1997), *Youth Guarantees in The Nordic Countries*, Background paper commissioned by the OECD, https://www.oecd.org/norway/1925599.pdf. [28]

Hyggen, C. (2017), "Etterlater arbeidstrening arr hos unge ledige? Et vignett-eksperiment av arbeidsgiveres beslutninger ved ansettelser av unge i Norge [Does work training leave scars on the young unemployed? A vignette experiment of employers' decision in hiring youth in Norway]", *Søkelys på arbeidslivet*, Vol. 34/04, pp. 236-251, http://dx.doi.org/10.18261/issn.1504-7989-2017-04-01. [34]

Laegreid, P. and L. Rykkja (2013), *Coordinating Norwegian welfare: the NAV reform*, Coordinating for Cohesion in the Public Sector of the Future (COCOPS), http://www.cocops.eu/wp-content/uploads/2013/06/Norway_Employment_NAV-reform.pdf (accessed on 11 October 2017). [6]

Lima, I. and S. Naper (2013), "Do the participants in the Qualification Programme find work? [Kommer deltakerne i kvalifiseringsprogrammet i jobb?]", *Arbeid og velferd*, Vol. 2, https://www.nav.no/no/NAV+og+samfunn/Kunnskap/Analyser+fra+NAV/Arbeid+og+velferd/Arbeid+og+velferd/kommer-deltakerne-i-kvalifiseringsprogrammet-i-jobb, pp. 43-59. [46]

Markussen, S. and K. Røed (2016), "Leaving Poverty Behind? The Effects of Generous Income Support Paired with Activation", *American Economic Journal: Economic Policy*, Vol. 8/1, pp. 180-211, http://dx.doi.org/10.1257/pol.20140334. [38]

Ministry of Labour and Social Affairs (2016), *NAV i en ny tid – for arbeid og aktivitet [NAV in a new era - for work and activity]*, Melding til Stortinget 33, https://www.regjeringen.no/contentassets/8f9e56528fb340eb9f6515cc21ab5119/no/pdfs/stm201520160033000dddpdfs.pdf. [15]

Myklebø, S. (2012), "Unge arbeidssøkere - hvem de er og oppfølging fra NAV [Young jobseekers - who are they and what follow-up do they need from NAV?]", *Arbeid og velferd*, Vol. 1, https://www.nav.no/no/NAV+og+samfunn/Kunnskap/Analyser+fra+NAV/Arbeid+og+velferd/Arbeid+og+velferd/_attachment/305693?_download=true&_ts=1361b9e6090, pp. 50-61. [12]

NAV Expert Group (2015), *Et NAV med muligheter - Bedre brukermøter, større handlingsrom og tettere på arbeidsmarkedet [A NAV with possibilities – Better user meetings, more leeway and closer to the labour market]*, Final Report of the NAV Expert Group, April 2015, https://www.regjeringen.no/globalassets/departementene/asd/dokumenter/2015/sluttrapport-ekspertgruppen-nav_9.4.15.pdf. [11]

NAV (2017), *Mottakere av uføretrygd etter kjønn og alder [Beneficiaries of disability benefits, by sex and age]*, https://www.nav.no/536879/mottakere-av-uf%C3%B8retrygd-etter-kj%C3%B8nn-og-alder.pr.31.12.2008-2017.antall. [26]

NAV (2018), *Arkiv - Helt ledige [Archive - fully unemployed]*, https://www.nav.no/no/NAV+og+samfunn/Statistikk/Arbeidssokere+og+stillinger+-+statistikk/Helt+ledige/Arkiv+Helt+ledige (accessed on 16 March 2018). [1]

Nieuwejaar, K. and I. Hagen (2011), *Peer country paper Youth Guarantees*, The European Commission Mutual Learning Programme for Public Employment Services, http://ec.europa.eu/social/BlobServlet?docId=7594&langId=en. [32]

OECD (2012), *Jobs for Immigrants (Vol. 3): Labour Market Integration in Austria, Norway and Switzerland*, OECD Publishing, Paris, http://dx.doi.org/10.1787/9789264167537-en. [41]

OECD (2013), *Mental Health and Work: Norway*, Mental Health and Work, OECD Publishing, Paris, http://dx.doi.org/10.1787/9789264178984-en. [23]

OECD (2016), *Society at a Glance 2016: OECD Social Indicators*, OECD Publishing, Paris, http://dx.doi.org/10.1787/9789264261488-en. [40]

OECD (2017), *Investing in Youth: Japan*, Investing in Youth, OECD Publishing, Paris, http://dx.doi.org/10.1787/9789264275898-en. [13]

OECD (2018), *OECD Economic Surveys: Norway 2018*, OECD Publishing, Paris, http://dx.doi.org/10.1787/eco_surveys-nor-2018-en. [27]

OECD (2018), *Registered Unemployed and Job Vacancies*, http://stats.oecd.org/Index.aspx?DataSetCode=LAB_REG_VAC# (accessed on 16 March 2018). [2]

Proba (2014), "Forsøk med resultatbasert finansiering av formidlingsbistand [A trial of performance-based funding of job search assistance – Mapping the starting phase]", *Proba-rapport*, No. 2014-12, http://proba.no/app/uploads/sites/4/rapport-2014-12-forsok-med-resultatbasert-finansiering-av-formidlingsbistand1.pdf (accessed on 19 October 2017). [14]

Proba (2017), *Evaluering av offentlig anskaffelse: Nytt avklarings-og oppfølgingstiltak Delrapport 1 [Public procurement evaluation: New work capacity assessment and follow-up measures - Interim Report 1]*, http://proba.no/app/uploads/sites/4/proba-rapport-2017-01-evaluering-av-offentlig-anskaffelse-delrapport-1.pdf. [16]

Rambøll (2011), *Forprosjekt - Oppfølgingsgarantien for ungdom 20 - 24 år [Research project - the follow-up guarantee for 20-24 year-old youth - final report]*, Report commissioned by the Ministry of Labour, Oslo, http://www.ramboll.no/-/media/images/rm/rm-no/pdf/forprosjekt_oppfolgingsgaranti.pdf?la=no. [30]

Røed, K. and O. Raaum (2006), "Do Labour Market Programmes Speed up the Return to Work?", *Oxford Bulletin of Economics and Statistics*, Vol. 68/5, pp. 541-568, http://dx.doi.org/10.1111/j.1468-0084.2006.00177.x. [19]

Schafft, A. and Ø. Spjelkavik (2011), *Evaluation of the Qualification Programme - final report [Evaluering av Kvalifiseringsprogrammet - Sluttrapport]*, Arbeidsforskningsinstituttet AFI, Oslo, http://www.hioa.no/content/download/53876/812279/file/r2011-4.pdf. [45]

Schafft, A. and S. Mamelund (2016), *Forsøk med NAV-veileder i videregående skole - En underveisevaluering [The NAV counsellors at upper-secondary school pilot - an ongoing evaluation]*, Arbeidsforskningsinstituttet (AFI), Oslo, http://www.hioa.no/content/download/123729/3198472/file/r2016_04_NAV-veiledereIVidereg%C3%A5endeSkole.pdf. [17]

Schreiner, R. and S. Markussen (2012), "NAV-reformen: "Færre i arbeid og lenger på trygd" [The NAV reform: "Fewer in work and longer in social security"]", *Søkelys på arbeidslivet*, Vol. 29/01-02, https://www.idunn.no/spa/2012/01-02/nav-reformen_faerre_i_arbeid_og_lenger_paa_trygd, pp. 151-162. [9]

Sørbø, J. and H. Ytteborg (2015), "Arbeidsavklaringspenger: Hva har skjedd med de som har passert fire år? [Work Assessment Allowance: What happened to those who passed four years?]", *Arbeid og velferd*, No. 3-2015, NAV, https://www.nav.no/no/NAV+og+samfunn/Kunnskap/Analyser+fra+NAV/Arbeid+og+velferd/Arbeid+og+velferd/_attachment/425417?_download=true&_ts=150adc3ecf0. [25]

Spjelkavik, Ø. and H. Terjesen (2016), *Evaluering av forsøket "Arbeidsavklarings- penger (AAP) som lønnstilskudd" - Sluttrapport fra følgeforskningen [Evaluation of the trial "Work Assessment Allowance (WAA) as a wage subsidy - Final report of the follow-up research"]*, Arbeidsforskningsinstituttet AFI, Oslo, http://www.hioa.no/content/download/130092/3422387/file/r2016-08_ArbeidsavklaringspengerSomL%C3%B8nnstilskudd.pdf. [42]

Statistics Norway (2018), *10539: Unemployed persons registered at the Employment Offices 15-74 years, by age (M) 1990M01 - 2017M11. Statbank Norway*, https://www.ssb.no/en/statbank/table/10539/?rxid=7278b0f6-520c-460f-8b97-082346e9de29 (accessed on 16 March 2018). [3]

Strand, A., M. Bråthen and A. Grønningsæter (2015), *NAV-kontorenes oppfølging av unge brukere [NAV offices' follow-up of young users]*, Fafo-rapport 2015:41, Oslo, http://www.fafo.no/images/pub/2015/20446.pdf. [4]

von Simson, K. (2012), "Veier til jobb for ungdom uten fullført videregående opplæring: Kan vikarbyråer og arbeidsmarkedstiltak lette overgangen fra utdanning til arbeidsliv? [Pathways to work for young people without completed upper-secondary education: Can temporary employment agencies and labour market measures facilitate the transition from education to work]", *Søkelys på arbeidslivet*, Vol. 29/01-02, https://www.idunn.no/spa/2012/01-02/veier_til_jobb_for_ungdom_uten_fullfoert_videregaaende_opplaer, pp. 76-97. [35]

Zhang, T. (2016), "Virker arbeidspraksis i ordinær virksomhet etter sitt formål? [Is work practice an effective labour market measure?]", *Søkelys på arbeidslivet*, Vol. 32/01-02, pp. 45-65, http://dx.doi.org/10.18261/issn.1504-7989-2016-01-02-03. [33]

ORGANISATION FOR ECONOMIC CO-OPERATION AND DEVELOPMENT

The OECD is a unique forum where governments work together to address the economic, social and environmental challenges of globalisation. The OECD is also at the forefront of efforts to understand and to help governments respond to new developments and concerns, such as corporate governance, the information economy and the challenges of an ageing population. The Organisation provides a setting where governments can compare policy experiences, seek answers to common problems, identify good practice and work to co-ordinate domestic and international policies.

The OECD member countries are: Australia, Austria, Belgium, Canada, Chile, the Czech Republic, Denmark, Estonia, Finland, France, Germany, Greece, Hungary, Iceland, Ireland, Israel, Italy, Japan, Korea, Latvia, Luxembourg, Mexico, the Netherlands, New Zealand, Norway, Poland, Portugal, the Slovak Republic, Slovenia, Spain, Sweden, Switzerland, Turkey, the United Kingdom and the United States. The European Union takes part in the work of the OECD.

OECD Publishing disseminates widely the results of the Organisation's statistics gathering and research on economic, social and environmental issues, as well as the conventions, guidelines and standards agreed by its members.

OECD PUBLISHING, 2, rue André-Pascal, 75775 PARIS CEDEX 16
(81 2017 66 1 P) ISBN 978-92-64-28362-6 – 2018

www.ingramcontent.com/pod-product-compliance
Lightning Source LLC
Chambersburg PA
CBHW061217240926
51846CB00006B/1257